"He was choking me, and my gun out and shot him. thought he was going to kill me."

"You emptied the gun into him, didn't you?" asked her attorney.

"I emptied the gun in him, yes, I did. I am so sorry!"

Rhonda Glover sobbed on the witness stand, but a moment later, when Assistant District Attorney Bryan Case cross-examined her, she was suddenly a different person altogether. The tears were gone; her tone brittle. Her eyes were ice.

"Ms. Glover," asked Bryan Case, "your earlier testimony on direct was that you and he basically met at the threshold of the door?"

"Yes, and he began choking me."

"He began choking you. And you are going towards him pointing a gun at him, right?"

"Yes."

"Going towards him, yes?"

"Yes," Glover replied coldly.

"And is that the way they taught you in the defensive use of firearms to deal with a dangerous situation?"

"Yes."

"To go at it with a gun?"

"Yes."

"And he begins choking you, and you have shot this gun a number of times, correct?"

Glover was getting progressively irked.

"Yes."

"And if you shot it a number of times, you know how to shoot the gun, and how is it that your testimony now, I assume, is that you started pulling the trigger and just never stopped, right?"

"Yes, I shot him. It just," Glover paused, and then napped, "I shot him. The gun just went off."

Also by Burl Barer

Mom Said Kill

Broken Doll

Body Count

Head Shot

Murder in the Family

FATAL BEAUTY

BURL BARER

PINNACLE BOOKS
Kensington Publishing Corp.

http://www.kensingtonbooks.com

Some names have been changed to protect the privacy of individuals connected to this story.

PINNACLE BOOKS are published by

Kensington Publishing Corp.
119 West 40th Street
New York, NY 10018

All Kensington Titles, Imprints, and Distributed Lines are available at special quantity discounts for bulk purchases for sales promotions, premiums, fund-raising, and educational or institutional use. Special book excerpts or customized printings can also be created to fit specific needs. For details, write or phone the office of the Kensington special sales manager: Kensington Publishing Corp., 119 West 40th Street, New York, NY 10018, attn: Special Sales Department, Phone: 1-800-221-2647.

Pinnacle and the P logo Reg. U.S. Pat. & TM Off.

ISBN-13: 978-0-7860-1910-6
ISBN-10: 0-7860-1910-7

First Printing: January 2011

10 9 8 7 6 5 4 3 2 1

Printed in the United States of America

For Jordan Barer, my beloved son ·

Make your home a haven of rest and peace.
                                                    —Abdu'l-Bahá

This is about the right of a woman to defend herself in her own home.
                                                    —Rhonda Glover

This is about a mentally ill woman murdering the father of her child.
                                                    —Travis Webb

This is about the strangest story of madness and murder I've ever encountered.
                                                    —Fred Wolfson

The government is not allowed to take it upon itself to kill someone first and declare him or her an abuser later—only a woman can do that to a man.
                                                    —Warren Farrell

Prologue

The story of James "Jimmy" Joste and Rhonda Glover has all the ingredients of a Shakespearean tragedy: the rich prince, the beautiful ingénue, true love, hot sex, backstabbing, intrigue, conspiracy, intoxicants and the contemporary equivalent of witches and ghosts.

For fifteen turbulent years, Glover and Joste had all the trappings of marriage—except the certificate. He purchased her a $350,000 engagement ring and numerous extravagant residences; he fathered her son. The storybook romance of the wealthy Prince Charming and the all-American princess is heavily footnoted with episodes of irrational violence, illegal drugs, delusional mental states and frequent visits to their residences by law enforcement.

Any story that combines vast wealth, exotic locales and beautiful women, with mind-altering drugs, Devil worshipers, demons and a Glock 9mm handgun, is, as the saying goes, "all good fun until someone gets hurt."

We're talking death here. Rhonda shot Jimmy at least ten times. "I emptied the gun into him," she told police. "I just kept shooting until he fell, but I honestly didn't think I mortally wounded him. I wasn't that good a shot."

She didn't have to be a good shot. This was close range, rapid-fire. One expert insisted that six of the shots were fired into Joste after he was on the ground, including two well below the waistband of his shorts.

To Rhonda Glover, the entire issue is the right of a woman to protect herself in her own home. "I am," she proudly asserted, "the self-defense poster child.

"On July 21, 2004, just five days before my birthday, I was brutally attacked, choked, and my life threatened by my ex-boyfriend, in my home in Austin, Texas," said Glover. In her version of events, she was separated from her longtime millionaire boyfriend, Jimmy Joste, because she feared his violent and abusive nature.

"I lived in fear of Jimmy Joste," insisted Rhonda Glover, and her personal recollection of their fifteen-year relationship could very well be something along these lines:

"When I met him, he was warm, kind, clever and crazy about me. We moved in together, but it wasn't long before his drunken rage and violent outbursts had me shaking in terror. I couldn't live with him, and he said he couldn't live without me. He wouldn't let me go. He stalked me, he scared me, he bought me and he forced himself on me. I bore him a son and placated him by allowing him to do what he wanted—to play the part of the generous lover. He could buy me gifts and houses, but he couldn't claim my heart or my soul. No one except me knows what Jimmy Joste was like behind closed doors. He had one face to his friends, but it was a mask. The dollars he flashed blinded people, including me, to his dark side. He was sick, perverted, evil and dangerous. He wasn't alone in his duplicity and deceit. I can give you names—important names of important people who use their wealth and prestige to obscure their true nature."

Rhonda claimed that she broke free from Joste, as best she could, living in a different city, and avoiding him at all costs. "I was terrified that I would be a missing person," said Glover. "I would be one of those skeletons in a remote area where hikers go, or that I would be a mother searching for her child on an AMBER Alert. Life was very weird for me. Jimmy had lost his mind. He had a secret life, and after he got comfortable doing drugs in my house, he decided to let me in on his alternative lifestyle. I am not crazy. I was with a crazy man. He was out of his mind. He threatened me, called me a bitch, said he was going to kill me, and then grabbed me by the throat. He was choking me. I shot him because I thought he was going to kill me. It was self-defense. I feared for my life."

The story of a battered beauty who, in final desperation, ends the cycle of violence sounds like a made-for-television movie. "It is more a made-up excuse for murder," insisted a Travis County assistant district attorney (ADA). "She was waiting for him in the upstairs bedroom wearing a lovely flower-print sundress with no pockets. In her hand was a Glock nine-millimeter handgun. This was cold, calculated murder."

1

You never forget your first car, first kiss or first corpse. That new car smell only lasts so long, and the olfactory sensation instigated by your best girl's perfume, or lover's cologne, lingers as treasured nostalgia. The stench of death clings to you like a parasite, fouling your mind and haunting your memories. No homicide detective forgets that first dead body.

When you're a homicide detective in Texas, snuffed lives litter your career's landscape like so many scattered leaves. Each victim's dignity must be preserved, and each crime scene must be kept pure. When you discover a corpse, investigate, don't contaminate.

The bullet-riddled body of Texas millionaire/oil entrepreneur James "Jimmy" Joste was discovered July 25, 2004, in the upscale Austin Mission Oaks residence technically owned by his estranged girlfriend, Rhonda Lee Glover. This event triggered a multistate investigation requiring involvement by the Bureau of Alcohol, Tobacco, Firearms and Explosives (ATF), the United States Secret Service, the Kansas State

Police and the homicide division of the Austin Police Department (APD).

Prior to arresting the person responsible for Joste's death, Austin homicide detectives Keith Walker and Richard Faithful uncovered allegations of conspiracy, financial fraud, manipulation of oil markets, kidnapping, child murder, drug dealing, satanic rituals and perverse sexual behavior by respected members of Texas's social elite. The investigation began with a phone call from Janice Van Every on Sunday, July 25, 2004.

"I came up to Austin to visit my son, Paul Owen," explained Van Every. "At approximately nine-thirty P.M., Saturday night, July twenty-fourth, we went to the residence of my niece [Rhonda Glover] at Mission Oaks. I observed that the garage door was open, and a car parked inside. No lights were on, and we decided not to go in. We came back the next morning. The garage was still open, and a navy blue Volkswagen was still parked inside. I could see that the utility door was open. I tried knocking on the door and ringing the doorbell several times, with no luck. I also tried calling on the phone, but received no answer. I tried the front door, and it was unlocked. I opened it a crack, and then closed it. I yelled for whoever was inside to answer, but no one came. We became concerned and called police."

The first respondents on the scene were Officers Martinez and Paez. Knocking on the front door, they repeatedly made loud announcements of their presence, but no one responded. "We entered the house," said Officer Richard Paez, "and immediately noticed the foul smell of something rotting. There were also large insects throughout the house—

a possible indication that there was a dead body inside the home." As the two Austin police officers moved up the stairs, the offensive odor increased in intensity.

"Almost as we reached the top of the stairwell," said Paez, "I saw what appeared to be a deceased person lying on the hallway floor. We decided not to go farther, walked out the way we came in, and then called our supervisor, and advised dispatch to summon all necessary units to the crime scene."

Homicide detectives Keith Walker, Eric De Los Santos and Richard Faithful were soon on their way to the Mission Oaks residence, along with Austin's crime scene analysis team. "I'd been with the Austin Police Department about eleven years when that call came in," recalled Keith Walker, "and I'd been a detective for about five and a half years. Homicide detectives investigate any unnatural death or any death that is not known to be natural. That includes accidental, overdoses, homicides, anything of that nature that doesn't involve traffic."

It was Walker's turn to take the role of lead detective under Austin's rotation system. "Once you are assigned to a case," explained Walker, "you then start again at the bottom and work your way up. Detective De Los Santos was there to assist me. Detective Faithful was number two, my backup detective, so to speak, and we also use other members to take statements and assist in the investigation, as needed."

When Walker arrived, the crime scene specialists had not yet entered the house: "That's because we didn't know at that time who owned the house, and we didn't know for sure the identity of the victim. Once it was determined that the death was suspicious, the house was left alone, pending entry into the house in a legal manner. In this case a search warrant was required. We needed to know who owned the house, whose name was on the utility bills and who was paying the property taxes. Our Detective Fortune got right on that, Eric De Los Santos was already canvassing the neighborhood, and Ms. Van Every told Detective Faithful that the victim in the house was most likely Mr. James Joste, father of her niece's nine-year-old son."

"Okay, here's the story," Faithful told his fellow detectives. "She says that her niece, Rhonda Glover, and Joste had split up, and that Glover had their son. There was supposed to be some sort of custody problem over their son, and neither of them was supposed to have custody of the boy. The aunt came looking for Glover because no one had heard or seen her for several months. She says that she was concerned for the boy and Glover, and she hoped that maybe Glover and the boy came back to Joste, or at least talked to him, and that he might know where they were. That's why she came to the house."

The only thing detectives knew for sure was that there was a dead body, not yet identified, in the upstairs hall. The fact that the individuals who called the police were looking for Rhonda Glover and a nine-year-old child weighed heavily on Walker's mind.

"We didn't know what had happened in that house," affirmed Walker. "We didn't know if there were other crimes involved as well. We had two major concerns. One was that Ms. Glover might be a suspect, and that her son could be in danger from her. The other concern was just as disturbing. It was equally possible that Glover and her son had been abducted, and both of them were in danger for their lives. We issued a broadcast nationwide to be on the lookout for them based on what little information we had at the time."

By the time everyone dispatched to the scene arrived, and Faithful had elicited basic information from Janice Van Every, Detective De Los Santos had spoken to most of the neighbors, including Andy and Judy Granger.

"Andy Granger began to tell me how he only saw an older white male at the unit," recalled De Los Santos, "but Judy Granger interrupted. She said that they would give us information, but did not want to be called into court. I tried to explain to her that if the information they provided was considered significant by the district attorney, then there was a possibility they could be called in. Judy stated that if that were the case, they have nothing to say. I left it at that and continued canvassing."

At 11:43 A.M., De Los Santos spoke with April Lord, Shannon Hopkins and Allison Atchley. "The three women could only recall that an older white male lived in the unit. They recalled that he seemed nice, waving, and he had a black motorcycle."

"The last time I saw the guy who lives there," Paul Mathews told De Los Santos, "was on Tuesday. I saw him come in through the gate, and backing the VW into the garage. I didn't pay a lot of attention because I was simply getting my mail."

Neighbor Nellie Byrne walked the neighborhood frequently, but did not notice anything out of the ordinary. She did recall seeing Joste's garage door open on Thursday. Kathleen Dunegan also recalled seeing the garage door open on either Monday or Tuesday.

"I had never seen him leave it open before," she said. "In fact, I walked over and knocked on the door to check on him. I didn't get any answer, so I left."

Jack Young told De Los Santos that he knew an older man lived in that unit, but didn't know him personally. "I think he may have had a girlfriend," said Young, "but that was some months ago."

"I know my neighbors slightly," said Patricia Reichle. "I haven't seen Rhonda Glover in about a year, or her son. Mr. Joste told me that Rhonda was living in their house in Houston. He's had different people house-sitting from time to time," Reichle explained, "but I think the last time anyone house-sat was several months ago. As for the garage door, I think I noticed it open since about Wednesday, the twenty-first."

Sara Buss also spoke freely. "I haven't seen anyone around the house other than the man who lives there," she said. "The overhead garage door has been open for several days. I don't recall if he left the garage door open all the time, but I definitely remembered that it has been open several days, and that there was that car backed into the garage. I haven't seen anyone at the house for a few days."

Detective Faithful was standing in front of the residence when Wanda Stevens, a member of the home owners' board for the community, pulled up to him. She kindly offered assistance. "Stevens informed me that the access codes to get into the gate are personalized, but that they have no way of tracking them," said Faithful. "Stevens also informed me that there are no cameras in the community to monitor entry and exit."

* * *

Forty-five minutes after his final interview with Jimmy Joste's neighbors, De Los Santos left the scene and drove to the station to draft a search warrant. Detective Fortune completed the required research, passing it on to De Los Santos.

"According to Travis County Appraisal District information," Fortune told him, "the home on Mission Oaks is owned by Rhonda Glover. City of Austin utility records also show an active account in Glover's name for that same residence. The Texas Department of Public Safety has records confirming that Rhonda Glover is a white female born July 26, 1966, and she has a Texas driver's license."

In addition to the information acquired by Fortune, De Los Santos also checked Austin Police Department records for any previous police response to the address on Mission Oaks Boulevard.

"Austin PD was very familiar with Rhonda Glover," confirmed De Los Santos. "I found plenty of activity for both Rhonda Glover and James Joste."

"Activity" is a polite way of saying that there were numerous calls to 911, all placed by Rhonda Glover, and all contained the notation of *EDP,* the abbreviation for emotionally disturbed person.

A review of the records pulled by De Los Santos provides a chilling glimpse into the terrified mind of Rhonda Glover, a woman so beset with fear and panic that she called 911 to report a burglary in progress almost every other day. When Officers Funderburgh and Fiske arrived at the Mission Oaks home on March 3, 2003, they found Rhonda Glover still on the phone, updating 911 on the demons in her walls and the disembodied life-forms threatening her.

"This was the third time in the space of a week or

two that Ms. Glover called 911 to report a burglary in progress," confirmed Officer Fiske. "Rhonda was sure that there was someone in her house. Even while I talked with Rhonda, she kept looking around the house for the intruder."

There never was an intruder. "This wasn't the first time that week that police had been called to her house," revealed Fiske, and there were no intruders the other nights either. Unlike the other responding officers, Fiske wasn't responding to the burglary. "I am a mental-health officer, so one of the officers on the scene called me. I am really just a regular police officer who has had training in mental illness and the procedures that police use when dealing with the mentally ill."

The officers on the scene had searched Glover's residence up and down and didn't find any intruders inside. "I talked to her for some time, but she didn't believe that there was not a person or persons in the house, and she kept repeatedly asking me, 'Did you hear that?' and stuff like that. It was difficult to talk to her because she was so paranoid. I remember one time while I was talking to her, she got up and went into the kitchen and was searching the kitchen and just left me sitting in the other room. She was acting in a very bizarre fashion.

"She never calmed down the entire time I was with her," said Fiske. "She was fearful, distraught and paranoid.

"My main job," said Fiske, "is to assist with mentally ill people that become involved with law enforcement. One of my responsibilities is if I get called to a scene, or am at a scene, and there is a mentally ill person actively dangerous to either themselves or others, I have the authority to have them committed to the hospital to be evaluated." Her job description was seemingly custom crafted for her encounter with Rhonda Glover.

The threshold by which dangerousness is measured is quite high, and they have to be so out of touch with reality that it is feared that if this person is left alone, they may hurt themselves or others. "The institutions I take them to," explained Fiske, "public or private, have some very high standards of what they will and will not accept for immediately dangerous. That is a determination that they make independent of my own concern. I have had several rejected by the hospitals.

"Rhonda Glover told me that she was seeing Dr. Jones at MMHR," said Fiske. "Well, I determined that she wasn't an immediate danger to herself or others, but since she was under so much stress and fearful, and she told me that she was bipolar, I asked her if she would like to go to Psychiatric Emergency Services to talk to somebody. She agreed, and she followed me to Psychiatric Emergency Services.

"What I do," explained Fiske, "is when it is on a volunteer basis like that, when she wants to speak with somebody, she wants the help, I will go in, and I will help them fill out the forms. It just gives [the staff] a small synopsis of why we are even there, and what that does a lot of times is it will expedite them talking to her as opposed to having her wait in a line that is generally very long." Once there, Fiske did not stay with Rhonda Glover. "I don't stay there," she said, "because it could be hours before they see her."

* * *

As De Los Santos flipped the pages of the APD reports, a definite pattern became evident—Rhonda Glover calls 911 in a state of panic. Officers arrive, find nothing, and leave. Rhonda was not always alone, discovered De Los Santos. Most often, the one calming influence was Mr. James Joste.

At 6:25 P.M., November 15, 2003, Rhonda Glover called 911, out of breath, asking for police. "I arrived a short time later," recalled Officer Kelly Moore, "and noticed that there were a few items lying in the driveway, including a disposable camera, travel map and various papers. I rang the doorbell and a male answered the door. His name, James Joste."

Moore interviewed Jimmy Joste, and it didn't take long to get to the bottom line. Basically, Joste advised him that Rhonda Glover had been diagnosed with two different forms of mental illness, but he couldn't tell which condition was responsible for her current symptoms. "His wife, Rhonda, had been prescribed medication to control her condition," said Moore, "but she hadn't taken them in about a month."

Joste informed Moore that Rhonda had been able to self-medicate by consuming no fluids other than Austin tap water. Moore had good reason to doubt the power of the tap water, due to the fact that Rhonda, according to Joste, was becoming increasingly irritable and irrational. "She had thrown a fit, called various people saying Joste was holding her hostage, wouldn't let her leave the house, et cetera. Joste, however, had let her take their son in their Suburban and leave."

Rhonda called Joste twice while Officer Moore was at the Mission Oaks home. "Joste was very calm with her, and seemed to fully be aware of the subtleties of her condition, and how to handle her. The second time she called, she told him that she wanted to stay in a hotel in Austin, and he agreed quite easily to this. Joste told Rhonda to call him back, and he would book her a room at a downtown hotel. He later told me," said Officer Moore, "that he believed that she would simply come home, and that she sounded like she has returned to normal during the second conversation."

Several times during his conversation with Joste, Officer Moore asked him if Rhonda Glover was a danger to him, herself or anyone else. "No," said Joste. Again he was asked if he was in any danger from Rhonda Glover. "No, absolutely not," replied Jimmy Joste. "I am not in any danger from Rhonda, none at all."

Ten days later, on November 25, 2003, Officer George Burbank was dispatched to the Mission Oaks house in reference to a family disturbance. "Upon arrival," stated Burbank, "I met with Rhonda Glover. She told me that she has been staying in Houston, and that her husband, James M. Joste, has been staying at the residence with their son. Rhonda said that she and James had been staying at the Omni Hotel, where she was now staying, when James told her that their son was in a crawl space in the attic. Rhonda stated that she was sure that her husband, James Joste, had killed their son and hidden his body somewhere in the attic."

Officer Burbank dutifully searched the attic and any other part of the house where Rhonda Glover feared Jimmy Joste had stuffed the dead body of their son. "She also told me that Joste was not only a murderer, but worked for the CIA, and was connected to John Wayne Gacy and the John Lennon murder."

There was no body in the attic, and Rhonda's son was safe and sound. Glover, according to the multiple incident reports in the files of the Austin Police Department, was an EDP, but she did not seem to pose an immediate threat to anyone.

"Obviously there were some mental issues involved," confirmed Burbank, "and I titled my report in such a manner that it clearly said 'Emotionally Disturbed Person.' At that time I didn't think she was a danger to herself or anyone else at that immediate time, so I didn't call a mental-health officer."

Burbank later acknowledged that everything Glover said—the body in the attic, something dead in the trash and something weird on a fork—were all connected. "It was all related," he said. "I mean, it all seemed to be one linked episode of things that she was concerned about. While she was going through all this talk about John Wayne Gacy, John Lennon, bodies in the wall, she also mentioned that Joste had struck her on the back, and chased her around the house with a beer bottle. She didn't have any pain, or indications of injuries of any kind. Her husband, Jimmy Joste, wasn't home at the time. That may have been the time he and the kid went to the movies together. Anyway, as she wasn't dangerous, I left and filed my report."

There was one call to 911 that did not originate with Rhonda Glover, or with James Joste. The call was placed by contractor Larry Colt. The responding officer was Richard Cross. "Colt called 911 and told the operator that Glover had been behaving very strangely. Namely, she destroyed the bathroom with a sledgehammer, and said people were hiding in her sink."

Cross spoke directly with Glover, and she admitted that she tore up the tub, but wouldn't say why she did it. "My toilet is hooked up wrong," said Glover, who told Cross that she had been diagnosed with bipolar disorder, and was taking Risperdal for it.

"Glover certainly seemed EDP, but did not pose a threat to herself or others. Glover insisted that everything was okay, and we were not needed. I stood by and typed this report while the contractor worked on the plumbing."

The most troubling incident of those retrieved by De Los Santos was the one where Glover called 911 to report a homicide: There were dead bodies buried in her backyard; there was "something dead in the trash"; there was "someone in her attic." When a complaint involved trash, the appropriate agency was the City of Austin Solid Waste Services.

Mrs. Eagleston, from Solid Waste Services, went to the residence. Rhonda Glover told her that Jimmy Joste had murdered someone and put the body in the trash.

"Why do you think he did that?" asked Eagleston.

"Because," explained Glover, "I was reading some type of crime book, and one of the suspects in the book looked like Jimmy."

It was on the basis of that—and that alone—that

Rhonda Glover concluded that Jimmy Joste was a
murderer, and that there was a dead body in the
trash. Employees of Solid Waste conducted a thorough search of Glover's trash container.

"What we found," states Mrs. Eagleston, "was trash."

Rhonda, however, was not convinced. She continued insisting that there was something weird going
on, and that there were people buried in her backyard. At this point it was obvious to Eagleston that she
was dealing with an EDP, but Rhonda posed no direct
threat to herself or others.

"Austin police show exemplary sensitivity to dealing with the emotionally disturbed," commented investigative journalist Jeff Reynolds. "The very fact
that Fiske received such training shows how responsive the Austin Police Department had become to
this very real and challenging issue facing police departments nationwide. New York City, for example,
didn't have the type of training for officers that Fiske
received until at least a year [after] the (1984) shooting of Eleanor Bumpurs, a sixty-six-year-old emotionally disturbed woman.

"Bumpurs freaked out during a failed eviction
from her apartment," recalled Reynolds, "and lunged
at someone with a kitchen knife. Cops shot her dead,
and the public outcry was deafening."

Detective Rafaella Valdez, a hostage negotiator,
said Bumpurs's death was a wake-up call for the department. The incident gave rise to a new form of
training to respond to people in psychiatric crisis who
fell through the cracks of the system.

"We realized that you had to respond to these jobs

with more than just a bulletproof vest, more than just the weapons that we carried. We had to respond with the knowledge of how to deal with mentally ill people," she said.

The emergency psychological technician–training course, which has been altered little since its rollout in 1985, is a one-week, thirty-five-hour session taught by trainers from John Jay College of Criminal Justice and the New York Police Department (NYPD). Classes are held about six times a year.

Officers, such as Fiske, in other police departments in various cities addressing this issue attend special courses that focus on a variety of topics, including basic negotiation issues, types of mental illness, assessing behavior and dangerousness, substance abuse, officer suicide and domestic violence. Participants are led through role-playing exercises by actors and trainers to explore the various situations officers and negotiators may face.

"With the advent of this type of responsive sensitivity by police departments," says crime researcher Travis Webb, "when a 911 call indicates the involvement of an emotionally disturbed person, a first-responding officer, a supervisor and an Emergency Medical Service Unit are often dispatched to the scene. In a barricade situation hostage negotiators are also sent in."

Police and hostage negotiators often deal with barricade situations, which are much different than a "body in the trash" phone call from Rhonda Glover. "When an emotionally disturbed person is out on the street, dealing with that individual becomes a patrol function, unless a knife or some other weapon is involved," said Dr. Raymond Pitt, an emeritus professor of sociology at John Jay who runs a training course for police officers.

"Patrol officers do not receive any additional training in handling the mentally ill beyond what is taught at the police academy. I have been a firm and long-standing advocate of patrol officers and sergeants knowing more about this," said Pitt. "They are the ones who are the first responders, at least the officers are."

Every time police responded to one of Glover's calls, they all ended with the all-important question: "Does she pose a danger to herself or others?"

The definition of dangerousness has been broadened over time by state courts, noted Mary Zdanowicz, executive director of the Treatment Advocacy Center, a group working on behalf of the seriously mentally ill. After the standard for involuntary commitment was changed in the early 1970s, police using the narrowest interpretation would have to wait until a crime was committed before they could intervene.

One of the biggest problems with police response to someone such as Rhonda Glover has been giving officers enough training so they could recognize psychiatric problems and then access the proper resources. Another issue is outpatient commitment, in which those with mental illness are ordered by a judge to take medication that would control their behavior.

Jimmy Joste would tell responding officers that Rhonda was off her medications, but that he could "calm her down." Unless refusing to take medication is a criminal offense, there isn't much a police officer can do.

· "Jimmy always told the police I was mentally ill," said Rhonda Glover. "He would say that I was off my medication. This is how I could be discounted, and ignored. He made sure people thought I was crazy when I wasn't. He was the one who was out of his mind, deluded, dangerous and doing all sorts of sick things. But who do you think the police believed— me or Jimmy? I would call the police, but they treated me as if there was something wrong with me."

"I come to deal with this person," stated an Austin patrol officer, "they're clearly mentally ill and they're making themselves mentally ill because they've chosen not to take their meds. What am I supposed to do? How am I to determine if they are dangerous or not? If her husband says that she doesn't pose a danger, and he keeps insisting that things will be okay, I pretty much have to take his word for it."

Laws that make dangerousness to oneself and others the standard for taking a mentally ill individual into custody are not always clearly defined from one community to another. In the mid-1970s, the pendulum began swinging back when a man who could not be hospitalized committed a double homicide in Washington State. It was the first state to add to its law a standard that looked at the progression of the illness, or the person's mental deterioration.

Since that time, about half the states have adopted standards in addition to dangerousness that include the person's history of noncompliance and the lack of awareness of an illness that could lead to the inability to make good decisions.

The whole issue of dangerousness is troubling for another reason. Mental-health workers, concerned with health and communication, may not realize the degree of danger to themselves in some situations. Police officers, concerned with safety first, realize how dangerous situations can become. "A person threatening suicide can decide to take you with them," remarked Fred Wolfson, an investigator who had former police department experience. "There is a dimension of unpredictability when dealing with the emotionally disturbed. If their thinking is fragmented, subject to sudden changes, and if they are prone to violence, they can go from weeping and asking for help, to pumping you full of lead or slashing your throat with a razor. They may see you as an angel from God one minute, and a demon from hell the next."

When Austin police responded to Rhonda Glover's numerous calls, she would point out areas of the house in which she believed Jimmy Joste had removed parts of the wall or brick and had replaced them. Officers found nothing to support these claims. Rhonda then showed police a plastic fork with what appeared to be the residue of some sort of cake on it. "I want this fork analyzed," she said. "There is something strange about it."

There was something strange about Rhonda Glover, but she did not seem to pose a threat to herself or others, and James Joste continually assured them that he was in no danger from Rhonda Glover. He could handle her. He could calm her down.

2

Armed with the history of the police department's previous interaction with Rhonda Glover and the all-important search warrant obtained from Judge Landers, of the Austin Municipal Court, Detectives Fortune and De Los Santos notified Walker, and then headed to the crime scene. "Once they knew there was a search warrant," said De Los Santos, "they didn't waste another moment. When we arrived to assist, Walker and Faithful were already conducting the search. The crime scene specialists were there too."

Anyone who watches such television programs as *CSI* or *Forensic Files* knows the importance of crime scene investigators in solving a homicide. In this case the specialists were Victor Ceballos, William Welch and James Bush.

"Being a crime scene investigator," explained Welch, "means an individual that responds to crime scenes within the city limits of Austin. Basically, we document crime scenes through notes and photographs and sketches, collect evidence, secure that evidence for presentation in the trial, and that is basically the gist of it." Welch had been with the Austin Police Department in that capacity for five years at the time of Joste's death. "I have over four hundred hours of classroom training," Welch said. "I am also a certified crime scene specialist through the International Association for Identification."

"Ceballos was assigned to photograph," recalled Detective Faithful. "Welch was assigned to collect evidence. Bush was assigned to video. All of us put on shoe covers and gloves and proceeded into the residence."

In homicide there is a general procedure that is followed in how evidence is seized, and how the crime scene is photographed. "When we respond to the scene, after doing our initial assessment or walk-through, the first thing that will happen is that the entire crime scene will be videotaped, every room, every item of evidence, basically an overall video. Then after that," said Welch, "Victor Ceballos will enter the scene, and he will do his photography, same thing as the video, basically overall photography, every room, every area of the crime scene.

"After that is done," Welch explained, "usually a lead detective or a detective involved in the case and the other crime scene specialists will enter the scene and mark items of evidence with tent numbers. Basically, any item of evidence that we see that we believe pertinent to the crime will be marked with a number throughout the crime scene."

After the items are marked, they will go through and do video again; this time, with more detail on the items of evidence that are marked, but also doing an overall video again, just to give an idea of where the items of evidence are within the crime scene.

"There was the unmistakable smell of decomposition emitting from within the residence," said Detective Fortune. "The front door was unlocked. Ceballos took photographs as we proceeded through the scene to get an idea of what needed to be done. We were careful not to disturb any impressions in dust that were on the tile floor around the stairs because we could see a faint foot/shoe impression in dust at the foot of the stairs. I noticed that the back door was also unlocked."

Faithful proceeded upstairs where the decomposition smell grew stronger. "The stairs opened on the second floor into a loft or living area, where there was a large desk and a couch," he recalled. "The desk was very messy and covered with piles of mail opened and unopened. There was a coffee table in front of the couch that also had a lot of opened and unopened mail along with other papers. There was a TV on a table next to the desk that faced the couch. There were pillows and a blanket on the couch, as if Joste might have been sleeping there. There was also a floor fan that was at the end of the couch, near the TV, that was on and pointing toward the couch."

The loft had a hallway that led off to two bedrooms and a bathroom. Joste's body was in the hallway. "There was a lot of blood and bodily fluids on his clothing and in the carpet around his body," Faithful stated. "Joste was in the advanced stages of decomposition, and there were flies everywhere. Some of the flies were already dead. Joste was fully clothed, lying on his back, blackened and swollen. There were nine-millimeter shell casings in the hallway, and two bullet holes in the wall in the hallway."

One bullet hole was in the wall, and the other was in the door on the same wall. Both were in close proximity to each other. Familiar with bullet holes, Faithful could easily discern that both holes were fired from within the master bedroom. "There were another 4 nine-millimeter shell casings in the bedroom on the floor in close proximity to the bedroom door." The bedroom itself, Faithful noted, "was very tidy."

The French criminalist Edmond Locard stated his belief that anytime someone enters a crime scene, they take something away, and leave something behind. Essentially, whenever two items come into contact with one another, there is an exchange of material from one to the other. This is known as Locard's principle of exchange, or exchange principle.

When you walk across a floor, or any surface, there is an exchange of material from your shoes to the floor, or vice versa. This type of evidence is perishable and delicate. It is of utmost importance that crime scene technicians make every effort to preserve, document and collect any evidence that might be "under their feet."

This evidence is ignored only when there is a lack of training in how to search a crime scene, and how to properly collect and preserve the evidence. "Sometimes," commented investigative journalist Jeff Reynolds, "there is a deficient understanding of footwear impression evidence and its value to a case. Of course you can't often see footprints—even when they are there. For example, a dust impression on a light-colored hardwood floor, tile or linoleum can be difficult, if not impossible, to see."

The best way to search for such an impression is to place a bright flashlight on the floor and allow the light to simply skim across the floor. Even if no impression is visible where the suspect is known to have stepped, there still may be latent impressions that can be detected and collected.

The APD crime scene investigators are exceptionally thorough, and took two "static lifts" of the tile floor at the foot of the stairs. The static lift was created by three identification experts with the Metropolitan Police Department of Japan. They developed a new method to detect and collect dust impressions at crime scenes.

"They rubbed the surface of a black celluloid sheet with a woolen cloth to generate static electricity," explains crime scene expert William Bodziak. "They then placed the celluloid over a dust impression on the floor and rubbed it again with the same woolen cloth. The static electricity caused the dust impression to cling to the celluloid sheet, lift off of the floor, and appear distinctly on the sheet."

Recently electrostatic dust lifters have evolved into powerful yet simple tools used to search for, detect and collect impressions in dust at crime scenes. The power packs of some units are small enough to fit in a pocket and take just minutes to set up and use.

"While we were working the scene," Faithful recalled, "another neighbor drove up and I talked to her. She was Susan West. She told me that she noticed the garage door to Joste's residence had been open for the past few days, but she was not sure if the interior door was open. She also told me that there should be two small dogs inside the residence, and that she used to see a woman walking the dogs all the time. West didn't remember the name of the woman walking the dogs."

Following the static lifts, Detective Faithful located personal papers for both Joste and Glover in the kitchen drawers; De Los Santos located a business card from Red's Indoor Range lying on the bar counter that separated the kitchen from the living room.

"There was a backpack in the laundry room, just off the kitchen," said Faithful. "Inside were some of Joste's personal papers, and his driver's license. Also in the backpack was an apple that wasn't rotten yet, and Jimmy Joste's cell phone."

While Faithful checked out Joste's cell phone, De Los Santos called the gun store. "I called," said De Los Santos, "and spoke with Red, one of the owners. I asked him if it were possible to search for gun sales if I provided two names."

"Sure," said Red. "I can search paper records if the sale occurred within two years. After two years a computer search would have to be done."

The names of James or Jimmy Joste and Rhonda Glover were provided, and thirty minutes later, Red called back. "Okay," said Red, "a month ago, almost exactly, June 24, 2004. . . ." The weapon was a Glock 9mm handgun. The purchaser was Rhonda Glover.

"I'm on my way," said De Los Santos.

"Hold on," said Red. "I can only release the ATF form to an ATF agent." ATF special agent San Marcos was contacted, and he met De Los Santos at Red's office. Red handed the ATF form over to San Marcos who, in turn, handed it to De Los Santos. "We have to do things according to the law," Red told De Los Santos, "as a police officer, I'm sure you understand."

Before returning to the crime scene, the two detectives made arrangements to interview Red's employees who interacted with Rhonda Glover. Back at the crime scene, they reviewed the incoming and outgoing calls on Jimmy Joste's cell phone. "There were between twenty and thirty missed phone calls, and all from the same number," recalls Faithful. "Obviously, there was some reason why the same person would call twenty times in a row. The person placing those calls was a Mr. Rocky Navarro. We decided to return the call."

"My first thought when the police called," recalled Navarro, "was that one of my girlfriends got drunk and got in a car accident or something. I wasn't ready for what I heard next."

"Jimmy Joste has been found murdered," said the officer on the other end of the line. "He had his cell phone on him, and it looks like you called him about twenty times. We think you may have been the last person to see him alive."

Stunned, Rocky Navarro yelled his reply. "I promise you one fucking thing—I'm not the last person to see him alive. The fucking killer was the last person to see him alive!"

"Mr. Navarro," pleaded the police officer, "please calm down. We need to talk with you. . . ."

Navarro was in no mood to talk. He'd just been informed that his best friend was murdered. "While I wasn't the last person to see Jimmy alive, I was the last person who meant him no harm to see him alive. Jimmy was my closest friend for over twenty years."

Rocky Navarro, a gregarious Austin bachelor with

an appreciative eye for exceptionally attractive females, remembered the first time he saw Jimmy Joste. "I was on an evening dinner date several years ago with a leggy fashion model," Navarro recalled. The entranced ingénue couldn't take her gaze from the most handsome man she'd ever seen. Sadly, it wasn't Rocky Navarro.

"She was my date, and we're having dinner together," related Navarro, "but she kept staring at this white-haired guy at the next table, and it pissed me off. I said to her, 'Hey, you're with me. You're not supposed to be looking at him.'"

She blushingly apologized, saying, "I'm sorry, but I can't help it."

The next day Navarro returned to the same restaurant for an organized civic/social event. Seated next to him was the white-haired man from the night before.

"Hey, buddy," said Rocky, "I've got a story to tell you. . . ."

Navarro told the story, and both men had a good laugh. "We hit it off immediately," said Navarro. "That was the day I met Jimmy Joste, the man who became my best friend."

For more than two decades, Joste and Navarro were close pals, despite differences in age and income. "Jimmy was eight to ten years older, and he had white hair ever since the day we met. Maybe it was always white. I look like a *Sopranos* reject. Jimmy looked like a movie star. He was handsome as hell, and had more money than I'll have in my lifetime. I made a good living in real estate," said Navarro, "but Jimmy was heir to an oil and gas fortune. He wasn't one of those guys who live off an inheritance or a trust fund. He rode the oil and gas world up and down. When the crash came, he crashed with everybody. When it came back, he came back. He wasn't just a trust fund guy. Jimmy was anything but lazy. He was a hardworking man, a risk taker, innovator, and one hell of a great guy. He started off inheriting it. Then he invested it and lost it and got it back, and most of what he did was in the Texas oil and gas industry, mostly on shore Texas."

All his friends agreed that Jimmy Joste was incredibly generous, gregarious and friendly. "He saw no social divisions," insisted Navarro. "He would tip the valet twenty dollars for a five-dollar parking fee, and then invite the guy to have a drink with us. He could talk to a king or a yardman. To Jimmy, people were people."

Another trait Joste manifested was uncompromising honesty. "Sometimes Jimmy was so damn honest, you just had to shake your head," said Navarro, eager to share a specific example.

"Jimmy was not really much of a drinker. One night we were celebrating a birthday party for a friend of mine. Well, we were all drinking champagne and tequila. Jimmy tried to keep up with the drinking and really got sloshed. I saw him doing this, and I said, 'Jimmy, you're not a drinker. Why are you doing this?' He said he just wanted to participate and be one of the guys. Well, his house was right down the street from where we were. I told him that he was too drunk to drive, and that I should give him a ride. There was no way to convince him. Well, he pulled out of the parking lot and immediately got a DUI."

Joste and Navarro met with Joste's attorney. The lawyer read the arrest report, then shook his head in dismay. Jimmy Joste asked his attorney, "What's the problem?"

"When the cops pulled you over and asked if you'd been drinking, you told them that you had spent the evening drinking champagne and tequila. Why on earth would you tell a bunch of cops that?"

"Because," replied Joste, "I am incapable of lying."

Navarro and the lawyer rolled their eyes. "I'm sorry, guys," said Joste. "I don't know any other way."

Even with his affability and honesty, Joste wasn't perfect. He had a fatal addiction. "If Jimmy met a certain type of woman," explained Navarro, "he was her slave. She owned him. He was powerless, and would do anything for her, give her anything she wanted, and he knew it. Maybe the reason Jimmy and I got along so well is that I'm the same way."

For the femme-addicted duo of Navarro and Joste, it wasn't about conquest or variety. "It was never an ego trip of how many women. It was more of a victim identity. If we were in love, or thought we were, they had complete control over us. It was like we were high-school girls who—the minute they get laid— think they are in true love. That was us. When we had great sex, we fell madly in love. Oh, I'm sure they could see us coming a mile away."

The primary control tool was sexual virtuosity. "Our brains were below our belts," admitted Navarro. "If they were absolutely sexually incredible, we were done for. When he met Rhonda Glover in about 1990, well, that was it. According to Jimmy, she was beyond the beyond."

Rhonda, Jimmy and Rocky were all living in the Houston area at that time, and Navarro moved to Austin in 1994. Joste and Glover also established a residence in Austin. It was there, following Navarro's divorce, that he and Joste became closer friends.

"We would go to Kenichi's sushi bar every Thursday, or every other Thursday, to have sushi," recalled Navarro. "Ron was the sushi man, the chef there, and we met there two or three times a month. Rhonda and I and Jimmy and a bunch of people would go to the sushi bar and hang around the warehouse district, and we did that frequently, probably two or three times a month.

"Jimmy was madly in love with Rhonda," insisted Navarro. "He worshiped her. He loved her more than I could describe. Although they were not married, he treated her as if she were his wife. He provided for her—he bought her homes and cars and supported her as if she were his wife.

"It didn't much matter whose name was on the property," said Navarro, "the one who paid for it, the one who put up the money, was Jimmy Joste. He bought her plenty of houses. You know, Rhonda Glover wasn't Jimmy's first Rhonda. Jimmy and I called Rhonda Glover, 'Rhonda Two,' because Jimmy had been dating another woman, Rhonda Brown, for ten to twelve years before he took up with Rhonda Glover.

"Rhonda Two was the sequel," explained Navarro. "She was younger than Rhonda Brown, and Glover did stuff sexually that blew Jimmy's mind. When he fell in love with Rhonda Glover, she owned him. It wasn't that Rhonda Glover could do no wrong. She could do all the wrong she wanted."

While Jimmy wasn't a party animal, Rhonda was a one-woman zoo. This "girl gone wild" partied as heavy as she petted, and any pleasure-providing person or product didn't escape her ingestion, inhalation or absorption. She could leave Jimmy and run off with a younger man; then, exhausted in resources, she would make one phone call and have Jimmy back.

"One day she calls him," described Navarro, "and tells him she's pregnant. Well, all of his friends were worried that maybe the kid wasn't his. He hoped it was, and we wanted it to be his too. None of us ever questioned if the baby was his or not—we never broached the subject. We never said anything, because he really wanted it to be his kid. He thought that if she had the baby, that might tie her down and keep her from running off all the time.

"The general consensus amongst Jimmy's pals," admitted Navarro, "was that Rhonda was with Jimmy for what he had in his wallet more than what was in his pants, if you understand what I mean. If size matters, for Rhonda it was the size of a bank balance. Oh, that isn't to say that Rhonda wasn't fun to be around a lot of the time, and because Jimmy was crazy about her, I figured she must have something spectacular going for her. But, bottom line, we all pretty much agreed that Rhonda was after Jimmy for his money. She believed that having a baby with Jimmy was her way into having access to his money."

"Any woman, at any time, can file for child support from any man, including a man whom she has never met," Charles E. Corry, Ph.D., of the Equal Justice Foundation, has noted. "In some cases she simply picked the wealthiest candidate from the list of her paramours, often a considerable list."

According to Corry, the notice of the paternity hearing will be sent to the address the woman has provided. "The court does not check on whether that address is accurate, or [if the woman] has, or ever had, any relationship to the putative father." When the man, who probably never received the notice, doesn't appear, the court will make a default judgment. "At a minimum," Corry said, "this is happening to thousands of men a month in the United States."

Rhonda Glover had a baby boy, and named him Ronnie. "Jimmy was thrilled," Navarro said. "They still didn't get married, and the baby didn't tie her down. It didn't work that way. She used the baby as an excuse to double and triple up on the money."

Rhonda wanted a new home in Houston; Jimmy bought her a home in Houston. Becoming bored, she then wanted a new home in Lakeway; Jimmy bought her a home in Lakeway. Bored again, she wanted a boat. Stan Wiener, a good friend of Jimmy Joste's, took her out to buy a boat with Joste's money. After she concluded the transaction, Rhonda said, "I want to name my boat."

When Wiener asked her what name she wanted inscribed on the craft, she readily replied, "P.O.P."

"Stan asked her what P.O.P. stood for," recalled Navarro, "and she told him, 'You boys still don't get it. Power of the Pussy.' That pretty much says it all. And yes, she named the boat P.O.P."

Rhonda, twenty years younger, was bigger and stronger than Jimmy Joste. "This girl was extremely physical. She was a thousand times more aggressive than Jimmy. He was the ultimate pacifist. In fact, he was a noncombatant in the war, and worked in the medical corps."

Joste's reputation as a peacemaker was so well-established that his pals gave him the nickname "Preacher." The reason for the religious appellative, according to Navarro, was because anytime an argument broke out, it was Jimmy Joste who intervened, calling for cool heads to prevail, and for the abandonment of anger and fisticuffs. "He was," insisted Rocky Navarro, "the most loving, caring guy in the world."

There was, sadly, one period of extended silence in the Joste/Navarro friendship. "One day I had a party for my children's birthday," Navarro explained. "I invited both Jimmy and Rhonda to the party, and I had just put in a swimming pool at my home here in Lake Travis. The party was breaking up, Rhonda was floating in the water, and Jimmy was here with his son, and I was dating a girl at the time, and my mother and sister are all here. Anyway, it was about midnight, and folks are kind of moving back into the house, getting ready to go. Well, Rhonda calls me over to the pool and says, 'Rocky, come in the pool and fuck me.' I was pretty stunned. I said, 'I beg your pardon,' and she kept at it. 'C'mon, get in the water and fuck me!'

"'Are you crazy?'" responded Rocky. "'My kids are here, your son is here, my mom and sister and girlfriend are all here, and Jimmy is here, and you're asking me to fuck you? You must be out of your mind.'"

"'Oh, don't be scared,'" said Rhonda. "'You can fuck me. All his friends have.'"

"'No way,'" said Navarro. "'You need to get out of the pool and go home. You gotta leave.'"

The following week Navarro received troubling

telephone calls. "My mom called me from Houston, and my sister did too, and the message was that at the next kids' party, which was coming up in a couple weeks, they didn't want me to invite anyone other than immediate family. They didn't want to have to deal with people drinking and stuff like that. What they meant is that they didn't want to have to deal with Rhonda Glover."

Navarro had already invited Jimmy, Rhonda and little Ronnie to the upcoming pool party in honor of his other child's birthday. "Both my kids were born in August," Navarro said, "and I already extended invitations that I had to take back."

Rocky arranged to visit Jimmy and Rhonda at a local restaurant. "We are so excited about coming to your house again," said Rhonda.

"Guys," Rocky told them, "we decided not to have a party this time. We're just going to have a family deal. We are not having a party this time."

Rhonda broke out screaming and crying. "You just don't want me there, Rocky, I can tell. You just don't want to have me."

"Jimmy was looking down at the table," Rocky remembered, "because he's embarrassed. He's my good friend, and here he is caught in the middle."

Rhonda continued crying, insisting it was all about her. "I told both of them that really the party was canceled, it was a family thing, and nothing personal against her, her son or Jimmy. Now that wasn't one hundred percent true, but because it was going to be all family, I wouldn't be having other people there either."

Jimmy Joste, ever the peacemaker, looked at Rocky Navarro with compassionate understanding. "Don't

worry about it, Rocky," he said, "I'll calm her down.
Everything will be okay." It wasn't. Rocky Navarro
didn't hear from Jimmy Joste for an entire year. "Not
a word. Nothing. No returned calls. It was as if he vanished off the planet."

It was a full year later that Rocky Navarro got a
phone call from a landscape company, the Big Red
Sun. "Mr. Navarro, we have a delivery to make for
you from a Mr. Jimmy Joste. It's a gift. He gave us
your phone number, but we need your address for
delivery."

"A gift? What is it?"

"It's a plant," he was told, "in a planter."

Navarro provided the address, and the next day
the "plant" was delivered. "They brought this great
big huge five-foot-wide metal saucer. It's a fabulous
self-contained cactus garden with rocks and cactus
and succulents. It took five of us to move it out by the
back pool. I mean, this thing must have cost between
two and three thousand dollars. I was stunned. I
asked them to tell me about Jimmy buying it for me,
and they said that Mr. Joste came into their store, saw
this thing and said that it would be perfect in one of
his friend's houses. He paid them for it and told
them to deliver it to me."

Not having heard a word from his friend in many
months, Rocky immediately began calling Jimmy. "I
called and called, and finally he answered. I said,
'Jimmy, what are you doing spending that kind of
money on me?'"

True to his character, Jimmy Joste had an honest
answer. "Rocky, I haven't been a good friend. I
haven't spoken to you in a year. I haven't been

around, and I just felt bad about it, and I wanted to send you a gift."

"Listen, Jimmy," said Navarro, "let me take you to dinner. Let me take you for drinks. Let me take you for lunch."

"No, no," said Joste. "That's okay. You don't have to do that."

Rocky, however, wanted a renewed relationship with his best friend, and finally caught up with him in person, offering Joste a free lunch or a round of drinks. "I'm not drinking at all," replied Joste, "no drinks."

This was in the early afternoon, around two o'clock on July 20. "I believe it was a Tuesday," said Navarro. "I was trying to quit smoking, and I wanted to have my last cigarette where it was cool, because it was hot outside. So we went to the Bellagio on Ben White Boulevard. I ordered beer, he ordered water. I had my last cigarette, and then we left."

The Bellagio was not a place previously frequented by Navarro and Joste. "In fact, we had never been there together before. We went there because I was looking to have a cigarette in the air-conditioning, and in Austin that is pretty hard to find. Anyway, we left, drove around and talked for a bit, and then we decided on lunch, but nothing fancy."

"Let's just go to Central Market for lunch," suggested Joste. "You know, we can check out all the divorced mothers with their kids, and you can tell me about all your girlfriends."

Rocky asked Jimmy about Rhonda. "For the first time," said Rocky, "Jimmy didn't want to say a word about her. Not a word. He flat out told me that he didn't want to talk about Rhonda Glover."

Joste and Glover hadn't lived together for several months. Rhonda moved out of Jimmy's house in the Park at Travis County, a gated subdivision, and had taken off first to Houston, and then to Kansas.

"Jimmy said that he didn't want to talk about himself or his life at all—he only wanted to hear about my adventures. By that, he meant my adventures with women. As I said before, that was the common bond of our friendship—our addiction to sexually incredible yet highly controlling women."

3

Rocky Navarro and Jimmy Joste were again the best of friends, sharing the sunny summer day of Austin, Texas, strolling Central Market, sampling the food, admiring the pleasant view of diverse femininity. Rocky bought Jimmy a salad for $5, and felt guilty for spending so little on a man who gave him a $2,000 gift. "I told him," Navarro remembers, "'A five-dollar salad isn't enough. C'mon, let me take you out to dinner.'"

"Tell you what," said Joste, "take me home, let me shower and change my clothes. You do the same, and then give me a call when you're ready to leave the house. You pick me up, and we'll go out to dinner." Rocky dropped him off, went home, got ready and placed the first of numerous calls to Jimmy's cell phone.

"I couldn't figure out what the hell was going on," said Navarro. "We made plans, and I was expecting Jimmy to answer on the first ring, or at least the second call, if he were in the shower or something. Well, I kept calling and calling, and never got an answer. I mean, what the hell? So I must have called Jimmy twenty to thirty times over the next three days, trying to take him out to dinner. I didn't get a phone call back until Sunday, and that was the cops telling me that Jimmy was dead."

That was the last Rocky Navarro heard from the Austin Police Department. "I guess they didn't need me to tell them anything. They must have had plenty of evidence or information. I mean, if they needed to know more about Jimmy, the guy to ask is Danny Davis. Jimmy and Danny have been buddies since grade school."

Davis was going into sixth grade at Spring Branch Elementary School in Houston, Texas, when he met Jimmy Joste. "He was going into eighth grade for the second time," explained Davis, "and driving to school in a yellow Corvette. We could drive to school when we were fourteen. He was older than the rest of us. Well, we have been friends ever since we met."

Best buddies through school, the two boys matured into men with common interests and shared business ventures. "We formed two companies together," confirmed Davis. "The first one was in 1980—Texas Ranger Oil and Gas. The second one we formed in 1990—Energy Discovery Group." When the oil and gas industry fell on hard times in the mid-1980s, Davis and Joste went broke almost immediately.

"It was a rough time," said Davis, "but we recovered. As for Jimmy, it was the late 1980s and early 1990s when he pioneered horizontal drilling, which is now used worldwide. Jimmy started drilling wells again, and making a decent amount of money."

Joste's horizontal-drilling efforts were both financially lucrative and of lasting impact on the industry. He and his partner, Ted Garner, came up with the original idea in 1985, and they had the rights to this technology for all of Texas. The partners sold their rights for a substantial profit about five years later.

"When Jimmy told me that Ted Garner and he came up with the technique of horizontal drilling, I didn't believe him," recalled Rhonda Glover. "I contacted Tom Johnston with BecField in Houston. He confirmed that Jimmy was telling me the truth, and that horizontal drilling was really a major breakthrough."

"As you can imagine, Jimmy rebounded quite well," recalled Davis. "When Joste had money, Rhonda had money—Jimmy's money. Jimmy was always buying her cars. She owned a Cadillac. Jimmy bought Rhonda a Cadillac Allanté. He took the money out of the Energy Discovery account, the company we had together."

Rhonda enjoyed the Cadillac, and when Davis met the couple at the Houstonian Hotel, she was behind the wheel. "They were checking into the Houstonian for the weekend," said Davis. "He would stay there, and he would stay at other places. Even though he had a place to live, Jimmy would check into a hotel for a few days."

Stepping out of the Cadillac, Rhonda proudly said to Davis, "Look what Jimmy bought me."

* * *

Glover had often said that Jimmy Joste was broke when they started dating, but Joste's business associates placed the years of Joste's financial difficulties at a much earlier date. "Off and on through the '80s and '90s," said businessman Robert Dillon, "Jimmy had dealings that put him back on track to recovery. In fact, Jimmy was doing okay in the early 1990s, plus he had the Joste family resources.

"Jimmy's family owned property just down the street from where I lived," recalled Dillon. Jimmy Joste's father was Martin William Joste, and his mother was Barbara Kelly Joste. His grandfather was Forrest Kelly, of Wichita, Kansas, a successful wildcatter, and the CEO of the Tret-O-Lite, Petrolite Corporation.

"They had a beautiful home up front and three residences in the back, with a swimming pool in the middle," recalled Dillon. "I think Jimmy was living in one of those residences at the time, as was Danny Davis. I lived just down the block, about a half block away, but I never lived on those premises."

Dillon met Rhonda Glover while she was vacationing in Acapulco at the Via Verde Hotel. "She was out by the swimming pool," he recalled. "I had no idea she was there until she walked up to me and said hello." Glover wasn't with Joste. She was with bodybuilder and personal trainer Sean Kelly, who, for a time, was her live-in boyfriend. "Rhonda recommended that I hire him," said Dillon, "and I did, and the three of us trained together for a brief time."

Rhonda's regimen of weight lifting and bodybuilding made her exceptionally strong—much stronger than her nonathletic and older boyfriend, Jimmy Joste. "She is an exceptionally strong woman," said

Dillon. "She could lift three hundred fifty pounds with no problem. That was more than I could do. Now, you must understand that anyone who says that Jimmy abused her, or beat her up, is out of their mind. Rhonda could whip his ass in a heartbeat. In fact, my wife, Christy, and I saw Rhonda Glover beat up Jimmy Joste. He defended himself by blocking a few blows, and they were wrestling together and fell on the floor because he was holding on to her as she was trying to pummel him. I jumped over a chair that Rhonda had knocked over, jumped in and physically separated the two of them."

Robert Dillon, Danny Davis and Rocky Navarro all agree that Rhonda was a high-strung hellcat with a marked propensity for irrational outbursts and episodes of physical violence. Joste, they insist, was docile and passive, despite a publicized episode known as the "Barton Creek Incident."

Rhonda Glover represented the situation as one in which Jimmy Joste tried to choke her at Barton Creek Country Club. He was arrested for domestic violence and got put in jail. Jimmy's friends, however, believed that Glover went down to the bar and got drunk. Then, reeking of booze and ready to rumble, she returned to their room and instigated the fight with him.

According to court records, "Glover stated that Joste hit her with his fist on her stomach, kicked her on her left leg and slammed her head into the floor of their hotel room." Joste admitted to pushing Glover, but he said he did not assault her in any other way.

The couple's son, who was six years old at the time, witnessed the assault and told investigators that he yelled, "Don't hurt my mother." At one point the boy got out of bed *and attempted to assist her when Joste picked him up by his neck and threw him on the bed,* court records said. The child suffered no obvious injury.

Joste was charged with assault of family violence, but Glover later asked that the charge be dismissed. Prosecutors refused to dismiss the charges, and Joste eventually pleaded no contest to that charge and was placed on deferred adjudication.

In deferred adjudication, explained investigator Fred Wolfson, a defendant is required to meet certain criteria for a period of time. At the end of that time, if the defendant has met a set of court-set requirements, no conviction will appear on his record. In Joste's case, he was released from deferred adjudication on March 24, 2003.

Rhonda Glover called Anthony "Tony" and Duanna Barder, close friends of Jimmy's, twice the night of the Barton Creek Incident. The first time was to beg them not to get Jimmy out of jail. A few minutes later, Glover called back. She changed her mind and entreated Tony Barder to go rescue her beloved Jimmy.

"That was in 2000," said Ruben Garcia, of the Travis County Sheriff's Office (TCSO). "I was sent out in response to a family disturbance. I encountered Rhonda Glover, and she was very distraught, and had bruises and other marks on her. I observed redness and slight swelling on Glover's right cheek, just beneath her right eye, and the beginnings of a black eye. Gina Hill, a female officer, conducted a physical inspection and found injuries also in her groin area. There was a large oval-shaped knot on her left leg on the shin area. Rhonda Glover," added the deputy, "was intoxicated. I detected the odor of alcohol on her immediately."

This deputy was the same man who was instrumental in securing an emergency protective order in this incident against the arrested Jimmy Joste. "I have a lot of training in spousal abuse, and the sheriff's office takes this issue very seriously," he said. "Most of the cases are prosecuted by the county attorney's office, and they take this issue very seriously also."

If Rhonda Glover pressed charges against Jimmy Joste, the county attorney would not necessarily allow her to drop the charges. "If Glover were to drop charges," stated the deputy, "they could still pick them up and file them. In such a situation the county attorney takes it to trial. If the trial were to take place, Rhonda Glover would have had to testify against Jimmy Joste."

According to Garcia, women in these cases often withdraw or recant their story, but the county attorney may go to trial whether the victim wants to or not. The alleged victim, Rhonda Glover, would then have to attend classes on battered spouses. Joste pleaded no contest.

"Jimmy went along with that," said Rocky Navarro, "even though it was Rhonda who was the violent one. He never raised a hand to her except to defend himself, I'm sure of that. He was not a violent man at all. Rhonda admitted that she probably did take back her statement that Jimmy had been the aggressor. She was perfectly clear in her recollection that she tried to drop the charges."

"I had a conversation with Rhonda in Houston," recalled Robert Dillon, "and she told me the same thing, that things didn't happen the way she initially said they did. That is the full extent of any known official claim—later retracted—that Jimmy Joste ever lifted a finger to Rhonda Glover."

"Jimmy was a great guy with a lot of class," said Danny Davis. "Everyone liked him and enjoyed being with him, until he started getting into drugs with her. I didn't see him at that time, as he was up in Austin, and was pretty much isolating himself from his old friends. He would get away from her, pull himself together, and be the old Jimmy."

"Why would someone like Jimmy be head over heels in love with a whirlwind like Rhonda Glover?" asked Rocky Navarro rhetorically. "Well, if you knew Jimmy Joste, you would understand completely. According to Jimmy, she was incredible in bed. She had other qualities, I'm sure. She always was a real go-getter."

4

"Rhonda came from an excellent family," said Danny Davis, a friend of Jimmy Joste's since childhood. "Both her mother and father are good people. Both of them cared deeply for her, and even though she was always a handful, they really did their best by her."

As a young girl, Rhonda Glover was adventurous and athletic. She played baseball and other sports, and placed fourteenth in the state of Texas for barrel racing, a rodeo event.

"I grew up in rodeo," said Rhonda Glover. "I was only fourteen years old when I won about twenty thousand dollars from competing in rodeo events. I also had a colt that I was planning to take to the World Quarter Horse Show, as well as the Arkansas Futurity. She had wobblers disease and was crippled. I was devastated by this. I never dreamed that I would be anything but a rodeo world champion cowgirl."

"Rodeo is the state sport of Texas," confirmed journalist Steven Long, owner and editor of *Horseback Magazine,* "but rodeo is more than a sport here. It is an integral aspect of Texas identity and culture, and it is also a multimillion-dollar enterprise."

Texas gave birth to cowboy legend. For Rhonda Glover, and innumerable other Texans, that legend lives in rodeo. Houston's rodeo culture is a unique cross between agricultural heritage and high society, where the social climax of the rodeo season is the Junior Market Steer Auction.

"Take one look at the folks bidding on those steers," remarked Steven Long, "and you'll get an eyeful of people with a wallet full. You see men wearing cowboy boots crafted from ostrich and alligator, women bedecked in diamond-studded Western wear, and they are bidding big bucks for well-bred livestock. These folks aren't just buying a steer. They are funding an educational scholarship, and they know it."

Glover's $20,000 income from a rodeo event is easily trumped by the monetary rewards of even younger participants at the Junior Market Steer Auction. A champion steer recently fetched a handsome $300,000. The twelve-year-old owner received $85,000.

"Texas rodeo culture embraces events that combine publicity, philanthropy and status," said Rhonda Glover, proud of her past association and competition. "This is the stuff that Houston is famous for," she said, "rodeo, high society, charity, fashion, and BBQ. I grew up in that world, and I loved it."

Rhonda Glover was born in the Heights Hospital on July 26, 1966. "That's the same birthday as Mick Jagger and Sandra Bullock," explained Rhonda Glover. "I was born to twenty-year-old parents. My mom worked as a secretary at SW life insurance, and my dad was a parts man at Osmond Apple Ford in Pasadena. My dad raced motorcycles, and did demolition derbies. My parents met at a drive-in movie. My dad was saved from going to Vietnam due to my mom being pregnant with me. I always told him he owed me big-time. I guess now that I am in this mess, he has the opportunity for paybacks."

Friend and foe alike have always regarded Rhonda Glover as highly erratic. Even former high-school classmates recalled her as being both friend and enemy, depending upon nonspecific variables. "Yes, that's the way she was," confirmed a former classmate. "She was my friend. She would sleep over and stuff, but then she could just turn on you and not be a friend, and then back to being a friend again, depending on her mood. Sometimes it would throw you really off-guard because you didn't know where you stood with her."

The pattern of Glover shifting alliances was one she readily acknowledged, and offered the example of her forming a temporary friendship with a girl with whom she had long-standing problems. "She was mean as a rattlesnake," said Glover. "She and her friends tormented me at school. I thought maybe if I became her friend, things would be different. I don't know what in the world I was thinking. At one point she tried to implicate me in the theft of a guy's rodeo jacket, and later jumped me in a parking lot. We had quite a falling-out, that's for sure. My daddy always said that success was the best revenge. So I forgave her and concentrated on myself. Years later, when we were adults, I ran into her. I was driving a

Cadillac and waved at her as I drove by. Those old
school days were over, and [I] didn't hold a grudge."

Rhonda Glover grew up near a town called the
Woodlands, and went to McCullough High School. "I
was on the track team in junior high, and played first-
chair clarinet until high school. After that, I had to
quit the marching band, because I rodeoed every
single weekend and could not make the games."

Glover's life experiences as a teenager were those
of accomplishment, adventure and reward. For her
sixteenth birthday Rhonda's mother gave her an all-
expense-paid trip to London, England. "While I was
there, I fell madly in love with a young Iraqi named
Faris Al Sadi," recalled Glover. "I wanted to marry
him, and told Mom of our plans. She encouraged me
to come home so she could help me plan the wedding." On the way home from the airport, Rhonda's
mother asked to see her daughter's passport. "She
said she wanted to look at it because she had never
taken a good look at one before. She grabbed and
then stuck it between the driver's seat and the door,
refusing to give it back. She had no intention of planning my wedding. Instead, she took my passport and
gave me a lecture about how much I would miss if I
moved away and got married at such a young age."

Glover's mother was certainly acting in her daughter's best interest, but young Rhonda perceived the
passport snatching as a dishonest act of interference
and control. This episode seemingly set a template
for the future relationship of Rhonda Glover and her
mother.

"Rhonda always blamed her mother for things that
didn't work out," confirmed Patti Swenson, a longtime Austin acquaintance. According to Swenson,

Rhonda Glover regarded her mother's actions as unsympathetic, controlling and ill-intentioned. "In retrospect, her mother was always trying to protect her, look out for her and help her. Rhonda never saw things that way."

Glover also attended Klein High School, located in Klein, a community in unincorporated Harris County, Texas, about a thirty-minute drive from downtown Houston. "I won grand champion in 1981 at Klein High School," she stated proudly. "I grew up with friends whose fathers were in the oil business. My grandfather ran Scurlock Oil Trucking for twenty-five years."

Glover credited founder Eddy C. Scurlock with giving her a piece of life-changing advice. "He caught me red-handed riding one of his horses without permission. Instead of reading me the riot act, he told me that I wouldn't get anywhere in life unless I was willing to take risks. I never forgot that, and I've always been willing to take risks." Rhonda was friends with the most popular boys in school, and the most beautiful girls. "I had the best of both worlds, as I knew just about everyone. Having been beat up a lot, I got a bad attitude a few times, and stood up for myself. In reality I was never a person who enjoyed arguing," she insisted, "or especially being hit in the face."

When she was eighteen, Rhonda Glover's parents divorced. Refusing to play favorites, she spent time with both of them. She went on to compete on the Texas beauty circuit in pageants, such as Miss Houston. "I did well as Miss Houston, and was invited to compete at Miss Texas USA in San Antonio," recalled Glover.

Texas beauties often have show business aspirations, and Rhonda Glover was no exception. She and her friend LeeAnne Locken were featured as eye candy in the 1989 Adam Sandler film, *Going Overboard: The Unsinkable Shekky Moskowitz*. The two attractive women made many contacts in Hollywood, but only Locken pursued a film career.

"LeeAnne did very well for herself," said Glover, "but I was homesick and wanted to go back to my boyfriend in Texas. He was the jealous and controlling type, and there was pressure to return.

"I went back to Houston, and one day I was working out at the gym, and met a great-looking guy on the StairMaster next to me. His line was, 'Don't I know you from somewhere?' I had a lot of guys say that, because I had done the Miss Rockwear competition, and they sold the video to cable TV. They played it over and over, and I wore a silver leather bikini. The guy turns out to be a dentist who had just graduated dental school. He was so handsome and was so sweet to me."

The dentist who had just graduated from dental school was Dr. John Krell, D.D.S., a native Houstonian. He came from a family of four members who became dentists, so it was only natural that he pursued a degree in dentistry.

According to Glover, her friendship with the dentist drove her boyfriend over the edge. "My so-called boyfriend was a jerk in all senses of the word," said Rhonda of the jealous beau. "He went out of his way to stand me up, go on vacations with his friends and never tell me where he was going, hang out at a place where the girls served food in lingerie and, basically, was a loser. Dr. John Krell, D.D.S., proved what true

love was to me. He and I were at the pool one day
lounging around in the sun, and we were talking
about how much it would cost me to start my own
business. I was so confident that I could make money
for myself. I figured that it would cost me thirteen
hundred dollars to get started. Krell showed up one
morning at my apartment with thirteen roses and
thirteen 100-dollar bills. He gave me a card that I
have kept all these years. It said, *I believe in you and love
you. Go make it happen.*"

Overcome with emotion, Rhonda Glover broke
into tears. "I couldn't believe it was coming true.
What a great man he is. I don't think either one of us
was over our previous relationships enough to be
committed. I saw John, Dr. Krell, D.D.S., about eight
months before my 'incident.' He has the most presti-
gious office and the best staff. I am very proud of him
and his accomplishments. He saw me and my son as
patients. I think back and realize that he was one of
those that I let get away. I am glad he is happy and
married."

Shortly after John Krell and Rhonda Glover
"broke up" was when she met James Joste. "Beverly
Bogle Sanders and I were invited to a black-tie event
for the Cancer Society," Glover remembered. "Dr.
Michael Ecklund, D.D.S., was one of the hosts. It was
held at Houston City Club, next to Maxim's in Green-
way Plaza. We had champagne and caviar and a wonderful buffet. We were stuffed and just relaxing and
talking with a few friends, and here comes Jimmy. He
introduced himself to me and said, 'Someone just
told me that you were Miss River Oaks USA, and I

think I saw you on TV that year.' I said, 'Oh, really? Do you make it a habit to watch young girls in beauty pageants? What are you, some talent scout or agent?' He says, 'Well, I just scouted you out, didn't I?' I was not impressed much, especially when his friends told me that he already had a Rhonda at home, but that she was in Europe. I asked Jimmy why she was there for such a long time. Was she a flight attendant or something? He said, 'No, I get sick of her asking for money, so I send her away with her friends for a while.' Then his friends chimed in and said, 'You can be the Rhonda in Texas, and she can be the one out there in Europe.' I asked Jimmy how long he had been with this other Rhonda, and he said it was eight long years, and he was sick of it.

"I always did like smart guys," said Rhonda, "especially smart and funny guys. Jimmy was both smart and funny."

Jimmy Joste kept asking Rhonda Glover and her friend if they wanted to join him for dinner, but they declined his offer. "I wasn't about to go off with a man who lived with another woman for eight years," said Glover. "After all, that is what happened to so many of my friends, where they had caught their boyfriends cheating, and it just made no sense to me.

"After that, I ended up seeing Jimmy Joste everywhere. I was out with Kay and Daniel Drohr. He drove a Bentley, and the three of us went to dinner at Tony's Restaurant that evening. It was Lucho Florez' birthday and he was having a party at his house on San Felipe and invited us over. I was wearing summer wool, and so was Jimmy Joste when we happened to run into each other at Lucho's party." Lucho Florez now retired to Peru, remembered those days with fondness, and confirmed Rhonda's story.

According to Glover, Kay and Daniel "Danny" Drohr got into a fight and left her there. "Jimmy drove me home," she recalled. "We ended up at a home in River Oaks owned by John Howenstein, the man who invented Teddy Ruxpin, the talking bear."

In Rhonda Glover's life narrative, names drop faster than quarters in a Las Vegas slot machine. Howenstein did not invent Teddy Ruxpin. He was, however, a director of Worlds of Wonder (WoW), a company formed in 1985 by Donald Kingsborough to manufacture and distribute the Teddy Ruxpin product line of animated toy bears.

Rhonda was impressed by success, and she wanted others to be impressed by her success, and that of her friends. When she began dating Jimmy Joste, she knew he was a high roller, although his fortunes often shifted wildly.

Fred Wolfson mused on Joste's financial situation. "Sometimes he was on top of the market. Other times he was behind the eight ball. Eventually, according to Rhonda, he was spending money on eight-balls. Not everything that glitters is gold. Sometimes what glitters is cocaine. Sometimes gold diggers get the two confused."

While some portray Rhonda Glover as a gold digger, her attorney, Joe James Sawyer, often called James or Jim, and her young son say that she had money in her own right. Her 1998 income tax return showed an adjusted gross income of $60,448. According to Glover, that was a bad year. "Take a look at my other income tax statements and you will see that I was bringing in over four hundred thousand a year."

"Nonsense," insisted Danny Davis. "She never made that kind of money on her own, not in a million years."

Travis County ADA Bryan Case also found Glover's assertion absurd. "If there were any other tax returns validating that claim, they would exist. And the reason you don't see those tax returns is because there are none. They don't exist."

Glover, Case insisted, didn't make enough profit to have taxable income. Rhonda, of course, insisted that simply wasn't true. "I didn't need Jimmy's money," she said. "I didn't need it at all. There was no reason for me to need it. I have always paid my way. I have always worked and made money."

The business Rhonda Glover ran in 1998 and 1999 was Insurance Resource Group (IRG), a recruiting company for insurance companies. Kimberlee "Kim" Waters was Glover's employee at IRG for two months.

"I hardly ever saw her," said Waters. "She didn't come in a lot. She just wouldn't show up. Not only did I not see a lot of cash or money come into the business during the time I worked there, I had problems getting paid myself by Ms. Glover."

In December, as the happy holiday season approached, Waters's little girl was taken ill. "I called Rhonda and told her that I couldn't come to work that day because of a sick child. To my surprise, she became very angry with me."

"You fucking bitch!" screamed Rhonda. "I'm going to kill both you and your daughter!"

Threatening the life of a four-year-old, even in hyperbole, is disconcerting to any caring parent. "I was even more scared when Rhonda drove over to my house and began banging on the door," recalled Waters. "She banged on the front, and then she ran around and banged on the back. Both the front and the back are glass, with the exception of the door. She banged on the door, and she banged on the glass."

Calling the police, Waters and her little girl huddled inside, while Glover huffed and puffed, banging on the house and yelling obscenities. "The police showed up, and they talked to Rhonda in the driveway. Then they came and talked to me. I wanted them to file a report on the incident, but they didn't. I wasn't happy at all about it. Later, Rhonda tried to get me to come back to work for her, but I refused. She even called my husband, and I didn't feel good about that either."

If Rhonda Glover's interpersonal and business skills were exemplified by that particular incident, lack of financial success would not be surprising. Glover, however, maintained the assertion—and the belief—that she always made money from rodeo in her childhood, and a variety of jobs in adulthood.

"For reasons unexplained," said her attorney, Joe James Sawyer, "she was always drawn back to Jimmy Joste."

"I can explain what drew her back to Jimmy," said Rocky Navarro. "Money. Jimmy was spending at least ten thousand dollars a month on her. That kind of money would draw almost anyone. Sure, they argued almost all the time, but Jimmy's money and extreme generosity, plus his calm and centered attitude, was something she never wanted to lose."

"They argued constantly," confirmed Charles Glover, Rhonda's father. "I liked Jimmy, and I sat down and had a heart-to-heart talk with him back in 1995. He and Rhonda had just had another one of their arguments. I actually asked him and Rhonda both to take some time and get away from each other because they were not good for each other. They were always arguing and fighting. I asked him at that time, 'Please take your checkbook and leave.' I told him that I believed that leaving was the best thing he could do for both of them."

"Jimmy just couldn't stay away from Rhonda," said Rocky Navarro. "He was addicted to her, I guess you could say. It was as if Rhonda was a drug, and he was an addict."

"It is difficult to understand," offered Bryan Case, Travis County assistant district attorney, "how Jimmy Joste could have such an attraction and love for Rhonda Glover. But if you think about how people describe Jimmy Joste as the most generous person, how he would give anybody anything, then you have to realize how Jimmy really was. It wasn't just for show.

"Perhaps an important aspect of love for Jimmy Joste was taking care of someone," said Case. "Obviously, Rhonda Glover was an attractive woman, but attraction alone just doesn't do it. There has to be something more, and there was just something good in his heart."

"Rhonda would never stay away from Jimmy for long," said Danny Davis. "Oh, she maybe had her own business, but I think maybe it was more that she had her own business cards. Her primary source of money was always Jimmy. Sure, they did argue most of the time, but Jimmy always felt he could calm her down, cool her off, and that everything would be okay. I'm sure he never imagined that she would purchase a Glock nine-millimeter [handgun] and do target practice at Red's with him as a future target."

Austin detectives interviewed employee Jeremy Lynn Bohac, of Red's Indoor Range, the day following the discovery of Joste's body. "I met Rhonda Glover twice. The first time I met Rhonda Glover was when she came in to purchase a pistol. She told me that she'd been training with another gun range in Houston, Top Gun, and that they recommended that she purchase a Kimber forty-five caliber."

Detective Walker was taken aback when he received a telephone call from Kelly Joste, Jimmy's brother, alerting him to Rhonda Glover's activities at Houston's Top Gun Range. "We knew about Rhonda Glover's association with Top Gun in Houston," recalled Walker, "because an employee at Red's told us about it. I was surprised, however, that Mr. Joste called me with that same information. Amazingly, Top Gun is owned by Grace Ann Saragusa, an acquaintance of Jimmy Joste for almost a decade."

Saragusa was also familiar with the Joste/Glover relationship. "I never knew Jimmy to be violent at all," she said. "He was always a laid-back and happy person. Rhonda, however, was known to be volatile and violent. Rhonda was absolutely crazy, and would do things to Jimmy to get him mad and angry, like sleep with other men. I never observed Rhonda Glover at the store, but knew that she was target practicing at Top Gun of Texas. I would see invoices with her names on it in my office. On July 26, 2004, I received a phone call that Jimmy had been murdered in Austin, Texas. I was told to call Jimmy's brother, Kelly Joste, and give him the information that Rhonda had been shooting at the range, and I believed that she had murdered Jimmy."

William Johnston, employed at Top Gun Range in Houston, Texas, remembered when Rhonda Glover bought a Kimber Custom .45. "I met Rhonda when she came in to buy a gun. She wanted a Kimber Custom forty-five. We completed all the paperwork on it, but she changed her mind. Rico Mastroianni was in the shop too. That was in 2004, possibly at the beginning of the summer. She said she wanted the gun to protect herself and her son. She said something about people living in her house off and on. She called up here once a week or every two weeks. She wanted to talk directly to Rico or Mr. Saragusa. I don't know what she was calling about. She was always trying to find out when Rico was here, but he didn't want to deal with her. She seemed like she might have been crazy. She wanted to know different scenarios about how to use a gun. The only one I know about was one where she asked, if she were to enter her house, and someone was sitting right there, how to draw her weapon and go from there. I told her the first thing to do was to call the police. Twice, Rhonda had her son with her. He went back and shot a twenty-two. I know Rhonda only by her first name. That's the name she gave me."

Americo Mastroianni, the range instructor at Top Gun in Houston, had been there several years when he first met Rhonda Glover.

"I first met Rhonda Glover when she inquired about taking a basic handgun lesson for herself and her son. That was prior to May 1, 2004, when she signed a waiver and release for both her and her son. She signed for him because he was only about nine years old—and being [that he was] under twenty-one, she signed for him. She made it clear that she wanted him to participate in this training."

There were two basic handgun lessons. "They come to the counter," he explained, "fill out the waivers, and then choose a weapon to use for that particular lesson. Ms. Glover chose a Glock nine millimeter, and her son chose a twenty-two semiautomatic handgun. Once the weapon is chosen, they proceed to the classroom.

"At that point we go over the safety, first and foremost, features of the particular guns that they will be using, proper stance, grip, sight alignment, sight picture, trigger pull, what to do after they pull the trigger, and understand the mistakes that they may be making, all at that time, and all that is rehearsed prior to going out on the range."

Before going to the range, Glover and her son got eye and ear protection, and targets. "For adults," Mastroianni explained, "we use a standard target called a B27, basically it is a black silhouette target of a human torso. Normally, for children we use a bull's-eye target. When I pulled it out, Rhonda asked who it was for. I told her it was for her son, but she insisted that he shoot at a silhouette target. About halfway through the box of ammunition, the boy started screaming, 'Die, you hurt my mom, die!' I told him not to do that, and Rhonda came over and said it was okay. She said that he was upset with his father and was venting."

Her youngster did more than vent; he also displayed a rebellious streak. "Rhonda had just put down a four-hundred-dollar deposit on a gun, and prior to leaving, there was an issue with her son. He wanted to purchase something—I don't exactly remember if it were a gun or something else—and she told him that he couldn't have it. Well, he didn't respond well to that. She must have been having trouble with him, because she approached me at the counter and asked me if I could go back there and discipline her child for her."

As behavioral-modification methods were not part of his job description, Mastroianni balked. "I told her that I felt completely out of place, and I just told [the] child that it was nice of his mom to bring him along, and that if his mom says no, she means no.

"Rhonda was going to buy a gun here but changed her mind," he said, "and got a store credit. She used that to pay the fee for the defensive class, which is one hundred twenty-five dollars."

There is a set lesson plan for the defensive class, but Rhonda Glover wanted specialized instruction. "She was very insistent that she not do that lesson plan. Rhonda said she had a house here and a house in Austin," said Mastroianni. "She said that she wanted to know how to clear her house. She came in about a half-dozen times, and Rhonda went through the defensive class we teach here. She was more concerned about people being in her house, and she wanted to know about clearing the house from the front door. We set the walls, and she said she entered the front door, and there was a room to the right and left. She went to a garage, [and] then she goes into her kitchen. She indicated that walking from the garage to the kitchen, there was a door, a breakfast bar and then another doorway. She asked then how she would shoot someone sitting on her couch. I asked her why she would want to do that—that person's not a threat. She said, well, if they had a gun, and pointed it at her. We did a scenario using multiple targets. One on the couch turning around, one to the side, holding a gun to the child's head, and another to the other side."

Although this detailed scenario was out of the ordinary, the session continued. "Before we did the multiple targets, we did just the couch. When she shot from the breakfast bar, she then wanted to go around to the front of the target and shoot it from the front. I asked her why she would want to do that. I told her that she should have run and got out. She said she wanted to make sure the target was dead. I became concerned about that."

The next scenario was tragically precognitive. "Then she wanted to do the upstairs bedroom. She said the bedroom was at the top of the stairs, and when you opened the door, there was an attic door in the right corner of the bedroom, and there was a bed coming off the wall. She wanted to do a scenario of someone coming from the attic door, and one where someone was on the opposite side of the bed. She wanted to do a reload scenario upstairs."

As a result of Rhonda Glover dictating the training scenarios at Top Gun, policies underwent significant changes following the death of Jimmy Joste. "When she was training, she volunteered that she spent a lot of time in the attic area every day when she was in the Austin home. That day I brought it up to the owner that I was [a] bit concerned, especially after the scenario where she wanted to know about shooting the threat again to make sure he was dead. Top

Gun operates differently now, and now I have full control of the training program, and we have a complete set of guidelines, and what happened with Ms. Glover was part of the reason for that."

The day Rhonda visited Top Gun with her little boy, she had to leave in a hurry. "She said she had to go to the travel agent and get money back from a trip to Cancun. She wanted to leave the ticket open. She came back a little later. She told her son that she got the money back from the trip to Cancun, and told him they were going to do something else. She then bought a holster for a Glock 19, a double mag pouch, an extra ten-round Glock magazine. She asked about—but did not buy—defensive ammo."

During her practices at Top Gun, Rhonda used a Glock 19 handgun that she brought in with her. "Shooting from close range, she was a good shot," recalled her instructor. "Rhonda had mentioned the first time she was in, she was having problems with her ex. She said they were in a custody dispute. She was taught to double tap the target. She practiced a combat reload, where the magazine was dropped and a new one inserted. She seemed well-educated," he noted, "but she mentioned her church a lot."

While at Red's in Austin, Glover said that the person she had been dealing with in Houston was named Rico, short for Americo, Mastroianni's first name. "She liked the Glock pistol better than the Kimber," recalled the Red's employee. "I believe that Glover came in wearing a yellow flower-print dress, and then changed into a black leather outfit similar to something that a biker would wear. She rented a Glock pistol and shot it at the range. After test-firing the Glock, she purchased one, and ten-round magazines.

She asked me about ammunition for home defense, and about hollow-point bullets."

After Glover purchased her Glock, she spent the next hour on the firing range at Red's. "She wasn't a very good shot that day," the employee recalled, "and had bullets placed all over her target. She told me, however, that the Houston range wanted her to be an instructor.

"I helped her with her form, and held her hands around the gun. I also placed my hand on the gun several times while assisting Glover [to] shoot. I provided Glover with speed loaders to assist her in loading her magazines because she had trouble loading them."

Being a responsible and reliable employee, he asked Rhonda Glover why she was buying the weapon. "Home defense," said Rhonda. "My husband has been stalking me. He's broken into my home and cut the alarms."

"Have you called the police about this?"

"No," replied Glover, "my husband knows a lot of people."

When Glover paid for the Glock, she opened her handbag. "She had a lot of cash in that bag," Jeremy Bohac recalled, "a lot of money. She paid cash for the Glock, and then drove away in some sort of SUV."

Glover returned to the Red's Indoor Range on July 21, the same day she shot Jimmy Joste. She entered wearing a dress, and then changed into a tight-fitting black shirt that was so small that it revealed her rather attractive stomach. "I didn't notice what kind of shoes she was wearing," the employee admitted. "I do, however, remember what she was driving that day—a Ford Taurus, like something you would get as a rental vehicle."

Bohac was working on the firing range when Rhonda Glover came in. "I talked to her briefly and asked her if she had been having any more trouble, and she stated that she had not had any more problems. Glover did ask for a speed loader and I provided her one. I am not sure if she returned the speed loader. I noticed that Glover was still shooting from the seven-yard range, and that she appeared to have improved a lot from the time I dealt with her before. From what I recall," he said, "Rhonda Glover always shot from a close range. No farther than seven yards. She had improved dramatically over the weeks of shooting. On July 21, 2004, Glover showed me her target, and she was very proud of her shooting. I remember that all her shots were center mass. All of her shots on the target were in the torso area. She used the range from two oh-seven P.M. until two twenty-nine P.M. She purchased two boxes of S&B ammunition for target practice, which was one hundred rounds."

The targets used by Glover were human-shaped silhouettes. She left Red's in her rented Ford Taurus. Her destination was Joste's residence on Mission Oaks. "It is a very short drive from Red's to the Mission Oaks residence," commented Detective Walker. "It takes only a few minutes to drive from Red's to the house on Mission Oaks, where Janice Van Every showed up looking for Rhonda Glover, and where we found the body of Jimmy Joste."

The identity of the victim was not actually determined and confirmed until the following morning. "Mr. Joste was in a state of decomposition," explained Walker. "You couldn't clearly determine just by looking at him that it was certainly James Joste.

The medical examiner's office believed it was Mr. Joste based on his photograph, and then I had fingerprints requested. I took the fingerprints to the ID section, and based on the fingerprints, we were able to determine for a fact that the deceased was Mr. James Joste."

5

On July 26, 2004, Janice Van Every, Glover's aunt, showed up at Austin police headquarters to give a full statement to Detective Fortune. "Just tell us everything," advised Fortune, and Van Every complied.

"Rhonda has been estranged from her immediate family since Thanksgiving of 2003," Van Every told the detective. "I would describe Rhonda as a person that acts dramatic, flighty, and is very beautiful. I am unsure if Rhonda is working right now, but I do know that last year she was running a personnel-staffing agency. Rhonda has been diagnosed as bipolar. According to her mother, my sister, Sherlyn Shotwell, Rhonda was acting very delusional, and could not care for her nine-year-old son. My sister took Rhonda to court to take custody of the boy in the beginning of 2004, and won custody of him in March 2004, because Rhonda did not show up for court.

"I last spoke with Rhonda in January or February 2004," said Van Every, "and she appeared possibly mentally ill from the way that she was speaking to me. She was very obsessed with healing water from Austin that would cure ailments. Rhonda is originally from Houston and moved to Austin, I believe, sometime between 1995 and 1997. She has had an off-and-on relationship with Jimmy Joste for at least ten years, and Ronnie is their son."

Van Every told detectives that Joste was well-known for giving Rhonda Glover lots of money. "My sister, Sherlyn Shotwell, told me that Jimmy bought Rhonda a brand-new Chevrolet Suburban in March 2004. He paid fifty-seven thousand dollars cash at Landmark Chevrolet in Houston, Texas. Sherlyn received paperwork in the mail from Landmark Chevrolet, and that is how she found out about it, and also that it had OnStar with it.

"The OnStar was activated when Rhonda's mother placed a missing person report with the Houston Police Department," said Van Every. "The OnStar located the 2004 Suburban, with Rhonda and her son, in Michigan by the Canadian border. Apparently, Rhonda was trying to go to Canada, but a technical hang-up occurred due to paper tags on the vehicle and she could not go to Canada. The police in Michigan detained her, but had to release her and the boy because the court order was not final, and she had three more days to return her son to Sherlyn. This was the last time anyone saw Rhonda."

According to Van Every, Rhonda previously confided to her that Joste had a problem with substance abuse. "I believe that Rhonda also has a problem with drugs and alcohol," she said. "I have heard from Rhonda in the past that Jimmy was violent toward her. Rhonda told me that about eight to ten years ago Jimmy dragged her through their house causing rug burns on her. I know of no recent violence, but the police officers at the residence today told me that they have been at the house before for domestic disturbances.

"Sherlyn Shotwell, Rhonda's mother, won custody of her grandson in March 2004," said Van Every, "but Rhonda took off with the boy rather than obey the court." The ruling came down after state child welfare officers, at the urging of Rhonda Glover's mother, checked on the young boy's welfare in November of 2003.

According to records detailing that investigation, officers went to the house and reported back that the child appeared healthy and the couple's house seemed clean. After the visit Glover and Joste called Rhonda's mother and gave her hell for calling the authorities.

The phone call was monitored by police, and Jimmy Joste was heard saying that his son was "Lucifer and God," and that "Lucifer becomes the Holy Spirit." It wasn't unusual for Rhonda Glover to talk like that when off her medication for bipolar disorder. Mental illness is not a character defect any more than any other medical condition, and Glover had been hospitalized due to this brain-based illness on more than one occasion. For Joste to give voice to such delusional ideas was out of character and most troublesome.

When Rhonda Glover's mother heard Jimmy talk about her grandson pulling stars from the sky and putting them in the living room, she realized he wasn't waxing New Age romantic by composing second-rate song lyrics—he was tragically serious. When Shotwell sought custody of her grandson,

Rhonda asked her friend, Patti Swenson, of the Oak Hill Gymnastics Academy, to testify on her behalf.

On the afternoon of July 26, 2004, Patti Swenson sat down with Austin detectives to share what she could about Rhonda Glover and Jimmy Joste. "I've known Jimmy and Rhonda for about three and a half years," Swenson told Austin detectives, "because Glover and Joste enrolled their son in my after-school program. Rhonda and I became friends after a gymnastics competition trip to Indianapolis."

After is not the same as during. The two women had an emotional falling-out when Glover's son tried to accept his gymnastics award in his stocking feet. "Patti yelled at my son about not having on his tennis shoes to accept his award," recalled Glover. "He started crying on the biggest day of his life, at seven years old. There were over fifty boys competing on the trampoline, and she was yelling at him like he had control over his shoes. Jimmy ran back to the hotel and got them, and I confronted her in the coach's area. I said, 'If you ever yell at my child again, you will never see him on your team ever!'"

"Rhonda got upset with me and yelled at me a lot because I was sticking by the rules that were given to us," confirmed Patti Swenson. "Yes, I made him go back to his hotel and get his shoes. That's a fact. Rhonda got really mad at me, but she calmed down. We were on the same flight back. We talked, and she realized that I meant no harm. When she comes to town, she brings her son with her, and I take care of him for the day.

"Last December, Rhonda asked me to testify on

her behalf at the custody hearing because her mother was trying to get custody of Ronnie. Rhonda told me that the reason that she and Jimmy split was because Jimmy had become involved with pot and crack cocaine. The pool man had supposedly convinced him to try it, saying that it was natural and God wouldn't have put it on earth if we weren't supposed to use it. She said that Jimmy got heavy into it, and that's why she left him and went to her mom. Rhonda took a metal box to her mom's that supposedly had some of Jimmy's cocaine or pot in it. I guess her mom turned the tables on her. Rhonda tested positive for cocaine, and said the reason for that was because Jimmy was withholding money from her, and she wanted the money, so [she] did drugs with him, hoping that would encourage him to give her money.

"I was at the custody hearing, and I said that she was a good mother, to the best of my knowledge. As for the stuff about her son being Jesus and her being Mary, she explained that she and her son were simply doing role play. The court granted her, I think, forty-five days' custody if she did everything the court wanted her to do. That was December 18, 2003, at the Montgomery County Courthouse. She was court ordered to live in Houston. On Christmas Eve I called and reported that there was somebody in the house. It turned out that it was Jimmy and his friend Rick Kutner. Jimmy, we thought, was staying at the Houstonian in the Presidential Suite for one thousand dollars a day."

According to Swenson, Rhonda and her son came up and visited her a few times after Christmas. "She was here for the Kinko's Classic in April," recalled Swenson. Glover had an established fondness for high-profile charity events, offering her the opportunity to rub shoulders with Texas's philanthropic elite. The Kinko's Classic of Austin, entering its second year following a successful debut that saw over $100,000 in charitable contributions to more than twenty local charities, was exactly the type of event Glover couldn't resist.

When Rhonda came to Austin for the Kinko's tournament, she dropped by the gym and asked Swenson if Ronnie could hang out for a couple of days. "She took off," said Swenson, "and the kid stayed. Rhonda called and asked me to dinner. She told me to bring her son, and we ate at a restaurant in Lakeway, and then moved to Mulligan's."

"Mulligan's Billiards Sports Grill would be the perfect place for them," commented journalist Jeff Reynolds. "It has appetizers, good food and billiards—but, best of all, it has a video room for the kids so the youngsters can play games while their parents get drunk in the bar."

Swenson and Ronnie had a delightful time playing air hockey and video games. Every so often, Rhonda would check on them to see if either wanted something to drink. The next day Swenson and Glover met at the gym so Glover could drop her son off. "She gave me twelve hundred dollars," said Swenson, "and told me to take good care of him, and take him to Fuddruckers for lunch."

A $1,200-lunch budget is extreme, even for the finest luxury restaurant. Fuddruckers, a Texas franchise restaurant, is not a white-tablecloth and sterling-silver establishment. It is a self-described "Shrine to the Burger Arts." A family of four could eat their fill for under $100. "Rhonda then told me she wanted to give me more money," said Swenson. "Rhonda reached in her purse and handed me a wad of bills."

Such excess in financial generosity is a well-known side effect of uncontrolled bipolar disorder. "One of the most common bipolar mania symptoms is impulsive and irrational spending," said Dr. Ronald R. Fieve. "The lifestyle of the manic-depressive who is in a high tends to be a glorious scattering of money." So important is lavish spending to sufferers of bipolar disorder, that it may be seen as more than a symptom, but also as a form of self-medicating to counter the emotional sensation of other symptoms.

Someone who has this illness has no control over their symptoms. Willpower is useless. "Try using willpower when you have diarrhea," said substance abuse counselor Leonard Buschel, "and that may give you an idea of how useless willpower is in the control of symptoms of illness."

"Rhonda said that there was something she had to do," Swenson told detectives. "She said she would have to pay the consequences, and that I knew what she meant. I didn't really know what she meant." Glover hinted broadly to Swenson, commenting on Joste's nature, behavior and primary personality flaws.

"We were sitting in the parking lot," recalled Swenson. "Basically, she said Jimmy was Satan, and had to be gotten rid of." Glover provided specifics of her plan, and Swenson wasn't particularly comfortable hearing it or recalling it. "She said she was going to get him to take her shopping, and she was going to buy some sexy negligee. She was then going to go to one of the sex stores and buy some toys for, I guess, having sex, and that she would then take him back to the house and seduce him and get him to let her handcuff him to the bed. She was [then] going to cut off his penis and set the house on fire."

Swenson was so rattled by this scenario that she later called the police nonemergency number and expressed concern. She didn't give details, and there was no follow-up. "Then," recalled Swenson, "I saw smoke, and Oak Hill fire trucks were going by, and I got concerned. I went, 'Oh, my gosh, did she do what she said?'"

She and her friend Susan Riley got in her van and drove up to take a look. "We wanted to make sure that it wasn't Jimmy's house, and we were relieved that it wasn't."

If being Satan wasn't bad enough, "Jimmy was also, according to Rhonda, into crack, cloning and child porn. She told me that she found some things around the house that she felt indicated child pornography. Yeah, I know. It all sounds pretty weird."

"How can some things around the house 'indicate' child pornography?" asked investigator Fred Wolfson. "Either she found child porn or she didn't, and child porn isn't something that is easy to find. Quite the contrary. I mean, there are no commercial child porn websites on the Internet."

"The trade in child pornography on the Internet is not characterized by financial gain," said Max Taylor, professor of applied psychology, University College, Cork, Ireland. "It is mainly a process of exchange, either directly through protocols like IRC or ICQ, or indirectly through newsgroup postings."

With no commercial child porn sites, mutual exchange of photographs between "fans" of this type of material is the primary method of distribution. According to Professor Taylor, this is "the most worrying aspect of the trade in child pornography. Exchange acts as an entry barrier, and also gives the process a sense of security. A relationship of mutually assured destruction develops where the partners in the exchange are each dependent on the other for security."

"I'm sure child porn exists in people's private collections," agreed investigator Fred Wolfson, "that being pictures or videos that they either took themselves or got from other individuals, but I dare you to find a child porn Internet site, or even stumble upon one by accident. It would take concerted effort to find like-minded people, convince them you were not law enforcement, et cetera. Now, if Jimmy had a picture of his own son on his computer, and it was a picture taken of his son being cute in the tub with no clothes on, is that child porn? If so, every parent in America who has a picture of their kid with no clothes on when they were little could be arrested for possessing child porn."

The only claim of Jimmy Joste having an interest in child pornography came from Rhonda Glover, who also claimed Jimmy was bisexual and hired male escorts. According to Glover, she was living in the Austin home, while Jimmy lived in Houston. She claimed that when Jimmy and his pals started cooking up crack in her microwave, she kicked him out. She later moved to Houston, leaving the house empty.

"After Rhonda went to Houston," Patti Swenson explained, "Jimmy's friend Rick Kutner stayed in the Mission Oaks house so the home owner's association wouldn't take the house back for being unoccupied. One night she wanted Kutner to leave, and she called the police."

The last time Rick Kutner stayed at the house was around Easter, 2004. Jimmy Joste came into town and told Kutner that he needed to be out by the next day. "Jimmy wanted Rick out," Swenson told detectives, "because Rhonda didn't want Rick there. Jimmy wanted Rhonda to move back in, and he felt if Rick moved out, Rhonda would come back.

"The day she gave me all the money," recalled Swenson, "I kept her son with me all day. I thought she wouldn't be coming back. But about seven-thirty P.M. that day, she called and said she was on her way to pick him up. She did. At the same visit when Rhonda gave me all the money, she also gave me a silver bracelet. She said it was a gift from her and her son because of everything I had done for them. The last time I saw Rhonda, she did not say anything about doing anything to Jimmy. She said she was going to come back the next week, because she needed to take care of some business. The last time I saw Rhonda, I noticed her hair color was darker. It looked dyed. It was real dark with reddish highlights, and I have always known her to have sandy blond hair. I think her son is with Rhonda now, because she loves that boy and would do anything for him."

When Austin detectives asked Swenson point-blank if she thought Rhonda Glover murdered Jimmy Joste, the response was not hesitant. "My gut feeling," she replied, "is that she did it—what happened to

Jimmy—because she told me that she had to get rid of Jimmy because he was Satan."

As for the home on Mission Oaks, Swenson insisted that although it was in Rhonda's name, Jimmy's money paid for it. Swenson also shared things with detectives that she "didn't know for a fact," such as, "Jimmy bought his drug dealer a car, so all he had to do was call and say he needed a car payment and the dealer would deliver the drugs."

When Detective Walker asked Swenson if she knew anyone who would want to hurt Jimmy, she had no trouble answering. "Yes," she said, "Rhonda." Swenson also spoke of other decidedly unsettling behavior by Rhonda Glover.

"One night I met with Rhonda to have the locks changed so Jimmy couldn't get in. That was in about January. She flew off the handle, and insisted that the blinds be kept shut because she thought that there were people watching the house, and if the blinds were open, they could see in. She was obsessed about the aquifer being under the house. She put holes in the walls and looked for entrances in them. She said people thought she was crazy, but she was going to prove them wrong. We were not to flush the toilets, or run the dishwasher, because the water would run into the aquifer. She actually peed outside once so the water wouldn't go into the aquifer. Rhonda said that Jimmy was the one who tore up the bathroom and he did it when he was on crack. Rick was the one who fixed the house back up."

Detectives knew that Rhonda Glover—not Jimmy Joste—sledgehammered the bathroom. She admitted it to Officer Richard Cross in 2003, the same night she complained of people hiding in her sink.

A consistent characteristic attributed to Rhonda Glover was, according to Swenson, a marked propensity for frequently exchanging automobiles. "She was driving something other than her former car—the PT Cruiser. I think it was a Dodge Caravan. She said that was a rental. The Cruiser was white. She used to have a Suburban, but she said that she sold it, and Jimmy bought her an Infinity SUV as a replacement. It was expensive, had OnStar, and she didn't like it. She only had it for a few days before she backed it into someone in a parking lot in Houston.

"She was changing cars constantly," said Swenson. "Rhonda would make a comment that there was something on it she didn't like, and she would change to a new car. She told me that Jimmy was buying them for her. I believe that the reason she switched cars all the time was because she was running from something.

"I think the last time she was here," Swenson told Walker, "was about June twenty-ninth. At that time she told us that she would be back again the next week, but she never showed up."

"Glover didn't have time to visit Swenson when she returned to Austin," opined investigative journalist Jeff Reynolds, "with her busy schedule of shooting targets, shooting Jimmy, returning the Ford Taurus, and taking a taxicab to the home of her old friend Anthony Barder before making a run for Kansas."

"I was working for Lake Travis Taxi," Jeffrey Burke told Detective Walker on July 26, "and on July twenty-first, I transported her from the rent-a-car place to the Barders' home after returning the Ford Taurus.

The ride cost her thirty-seven dollars and fifty cents. She didn't tell me the address," Burke said. "She just pointed to the house and said, 'Right there.' She paid cash for the fare. She had a bag and a purse. She acted like she was looking for a key for the house. I left before she went in anywhere. She had on big sunglasses. She was wearing a cream-colored floral-print dress. She might have had on some open-toed sandal types, I think, with heels. The flowers were pastel-colored flowers. She was kind of quiet. She did not say anything about where she had been, or if she did, I don't remember. I'm not sure what time I picked her up. It was in the afternoon, because I think it was just before I got off of work at four-thirty P.M. She said that would work, anyway, because her son was in the RV asleep."

Detectives Walker and De Los Santos drove to the address where the taxi dropped Glover the afternoon of July 21. There was no one home. "We asked a neighbor walking his dog if he had seen an RV in the past week," recalled Walker, "and said there had been one parked around the corner on Old Mill Road at some time during the week. We started to canvass, asking residents if they knew Rhonda Glover."

Knock on enough doors, and someone will answer. Anthony Barder responded in the affirmative and invited the two detectives into his home.

"We got a call from Rhonda on July 20, 2004," said Anthony Barder. "We've known Rhonda for about ten years. She called to tell us that she was on her way to Austin, and wanted to stay with us overnight."

His wife, Duanna Barder, had an uneasy feeling. "I don't want her staying here," she told her husband. "Something just doesn't feel right," she added.

"She was at our house on July twenty-first, the day that Jimmy Joste was murdered," said Duanna Barder. "She called on the evening of the twentieth, and wanted to come over, but said not today. She had called and asked what we did with our kids for the summer. She called out of the blue. I have not talked to Rhonda for about a year, and the last time we talked, she was angry with me. Rhonda called again on the twenty-first and asked if she could drop off her son. We said okay. She brought some breakfast with her from Denny's. Rhonda was driving an RV and parked it across the street in front of the park."

"Rhonda told us that she had not seen Jimmy Joste for about a year," said Anthony Barder, "and that she had come to Austin to take care of some business, and put her house on the market. Rhonda was going to call for a taxi to take her to a car rental agency, and I told her I would give her a ride. About noon I took her to the car rental agency on 620, by Buster's BBQ. During the ride there Rhonda spoke about Jimmy being Lucifer. She also spoke about her house, a Morrison Home, was built on Cave X, which was owned by Bush. She said President Bush was also Lucifer, and a clone. She said Jimmy had been doing ritualistic things in the house. She said she had been dealing with the city about her house. She said it wasn't zoned right because it was on Cave X."

Rhonda Glover had already been to the car rental agency once early that same morning. "I got to work at seven-thirty A.M. on July twenty-first," recalled the morning-shift employee Brandon Garrett. "There was an RV in the front. It was kind of a beige color, with stripes on it. It had Indiana plates, and had mountain bikes on the back. I noticed it had Indiana plates as I walked by. I noticed the RV had knocked the cable and Road Runner Internet cable down. I unlocked everything, and about seven forty-five A.M., a customer I knew as Rhonda came in and said she wanted to rent a car. I knew her from having rented a car here before.

"I remembered her," said Garrett, "because the last time she was here, she tried to rent a car without a credit card or anything. I asked her for how long. She said two days. She rented a 2000 white Ford Taurus. She asked if she could leave in the car and leave the RV here. I told her no, she had to move it right then, because she knocked the cable down, and it was blocking the drive to where the cars were. She left, saying she was going to go find someplace to put the RV. I told her everything was done. So when she came back, she could just hop in it and go. I didn't see her after that. I don't know when she picked up the car. I wasn't here when she did. I don't think she picked it up before twelve noon."

When Anthony Barder delivered Rhonda Glover to the rental agency, she picked up a Ford Taurus; Barder returned home. Rhonda ran her errands: visiting the firing range, buying ammo, killing Jimmy.

"When Rhonda came back to the house about four P.M.," said Anthony Barder, "she told my wife, Duanna, that Jimmy had bought the house for a reason, and he invested in cloning. She said she hated Jimmy, and she hated Bush. She said she had been hiding from Jimmy. Rhonda had a place in

Houston. She said she thought Jimmy was trying to stalk her or something. When Rhonda came back, she was wearing the same dress she had left in. I can't remember what kind of shoes she had on. She stayed about an hour and left. This was still the same day, July twenty-first. She said she was going to a Christian place, possibly in Arkansas. When she came back to the house, her demeanor was calm, but she was vindictive about Jimmy. Rhonda said something about documents not being in the boxes in the garage. She said something about God had put documents in some boxes."

Duanna Barder recalled her afternoon chat with Rhonda Glover as the content was exceptionally memorable. Glover, calm and composed, shared interesting observations about Jimmy Joste and President Bush. "She said Bush was a clone, and she was convinced that Jimmy was Lucifer. She hated Bush, and said she would bring him down. She also claimed that she had found DNA of Jimmy and another woman. She was totally calm while saying all this, and stayed about a half an hour. Rhonda began quoting Isaiah, something about a child out of wedlock and a woman who had never been married."

Duanna Barder did her best to keep her jaw from dropping on the table as Glover confided astonishing stories about her church in Houston. "It was called the Secret something or other. Rhonda said this church had sent Navy SEALs to her house on a mission, and the SEALs became violently ill on the way there because there was so much evil. Rhonda said they would go in with guns, because there were people inside doing demonic things. Rhonda said she was going to a Christian place in Arkansas, and her church was funding the trip."

Rhonda's church, the Secret Place Church, not exactly flush with funds for a paramilitary operation, found this story hard to swallow. They had never sent SEALs—navy, Easter or otherwise—to Glover's home, but Karol Kyro, emergency contact with the Secret Place Church, told police that Rhonda Glover had said something about setting Jimmy Joste on fire.

"Kyro was erratic during the conversation," recalled Detective Walker, "and she jumped from topic to topic. She said that Rhonda had been drunk one night, and during the conversation she told Ms. Kyro that Jimmy was the Devil, and said something about the Devil being on fire. She said that when women killed men, it was because of the way men treated them. She said Rhonda was not happy with her situation. There were also some personal things Rhonda talked about with Ms. Kyro, but she was not going to talk about that."

Following her posthomicide conversation with the Barders, Rhonda Glover packed up her son in the giant RV. The lovely and enigmatic Rhonda Glover went on her way, wearing a peach sundress and open toed shoes, and possibly wearing a wig or a weave. Her hair was dark brown. In her bag was a recently fired Glock 9mm handgun.

* * *

While Detective Walker and the other detectives were amassing as much information on Rhonda Glover and Jimmy Joste as possible, the postmortem examination by the medical examiner (ME) of the body of James Joste was performed at 3:00 P.M. on July 26, 2004, at the Travis County Forensic Center, Austin, Texas. Deputy Medical Examiner Elizabeth Peacock, M.D., at the request of and authorization of Chief Medical Examiner Roberto J. Bayardo, M.D., performed the autopsy.

"I am a licensed medical doctor in the state of Texas, and I am chief medical examiner for Travis County," explained Bayardo. "In order to become a medical examiner—first, you must be a physician. Second, you happen to have training in pathology. And third, you have to have training in forensic pathology. I finished medical school in 1958. After that, I had one-year internship and four-year residency in pathology in order to become a pathologist. After ten years of practicing in pathology, I decided to go into forensic pathology, so I went back to school for two more years in order to become a medical examiner. I am certified with the American Board of Pathology as a specialist for the practice of anatomic, clinical and forensic pathology.

"As chief medical examiner my primary duty is to conduct inquests and investigations of any death that occurs in Travis County that is considered suspicious, unexpected or violent. We conduct autopsies in order to obtain information as to the cause of death, and in the examination of the deceased person, we follow several steps in doing that. First we have to identify the deceased, and describe whatever the body looks like. We go by the sex, race, height and weight, the color of the eyes, the hair color, and whatever scars or tattoos might be on the body. The next step is to look for any injury, such as stab wounds or gunshot wounds. We make a detailed description of the injury.

"The next step," said Bayardo, "is to open up the body, including the chest, the abdomen and the head, and we remove the internal organs, dissect them and examine them, looking for any evidence of injury. Then we make a list of our findings, which we call our diagnosis. The last step is to render an opinion as to the cause and manner of death."

Dr. Bayardo had personally performed over fifteen thousand autopsies in his career, and Deputy Medical Examiner Peacock followed the exact same protocol and procedure, as did Bayardo. "When you are looking at her work, it could be the same as my work," acknowledged Bayardo. "The only difference being that she physically performed the autopsy."

There was a rumor that there were African-American hairs found in Jimmy Joste's pubic region, a rumor later promulgated by Rhonda Glover. This was simply not true. There were no strange hairs found on Joste's "privates" during the autopsy. There was one hair on the upstairs carpet that had African-American characteristics. "These can easily be postmortem," said Detective Walker. "They tend to float around and can be transferred via the air-conditioning system. A single hair can be transferred from anywhere to a shoe, and then to a carpet, and be there for a long time."

The body is that of a normally developed well nourished white male, whose appearance is compatible with the recorded age of fifty-five, stated Peacock in the autops report. *When unclothed, the remains weigh 161 pounds and is 71½ inches long. Preservation is poor in the absence of embalming. There is advanced decomposition artifact with extensive skin slip, green coloration, and mummification of the fingertips.*

The body of James Joste was photographed prior to autopsy. Crime scene specialist Lee Hernandez also took fingernail clippings, swabbed the hands and checked for hair and fibers. Joste's clothing was cut off in a manner to preserve the bullet holes. There were a total of five holes in the shorts, and three holes in the shirt. "Most of Joste's fingers were too decomposed to get prints off of," said Hernandez. "Prints were retrieved from his right thumb, left thumb and index finger."

X-rays of Joste were taken prior to Dr. Peacock beginning the autopsy, and there were bullets seen in the X-ray. Some were possible fragments. Dr. Peacock narrated that she found six holes in Joste's right elbow from three bullets, entry and then exit. She retrieved five bullets from the body, and labeled each with a brief description of where they were retrieved as follows:

Bullet #A: Right lung—traveling upward
Bullet #B: Left side lower torso
Bullet #C: Left side mid torso
Bullet #D: Left pelvic bone
Bullet #E: Lower left abdomen

The bullets went through and damaged the following organs: spleen, heart, liver, both lungs and the aorta. Joste's body was X-rayed again in an attempt to locate the last bullet, and the X-ray showed it to be in the dissected organs. Dr. Peacock and assistant Mechum tried for a long time to locate the last bullet with negative results. "Let it sit until tomorrow," Peacock told Mechum, "and try again with fresh eyes."

"When Dr. Peacock collects a bullet out of the body, it is taken to a place where it can be photographed, and where the lightbulb won't drown it out, and then it is documented," Walker explained. "Dr. Peacock usually puts them in separate envelopes and marks like *A, B, C, D* and *E*. Once Dr. Peacock does that, the envelopes are placed in our evidence room."

On Tuesday, July 27, 2004, the last bullet was located in the dissected organs, and was collected by the Austin Police Department Crime Scene Unit. Following the autopsy of the decedent, detectives went to the medical examiner's office and took custody of the inked prints taken from the fingers of Jimmy Joste.

Peacock ruled the cause of death as multiple gunshot wounds, and the manner of death as homicide. All information was turned over to Detective Walker, the case agent. The investigation was now moving at freeway speeds. Less than thirty-six hours after Janice Van Every called the police, detectives had put together a theoretical timeline of Glover's activities from the day before Joste was shot until her aunt called the cops. As for Rhonda Glover's mother, Sherlyn Shotwell, she called Detective Walker the very next day at 9:40 A.M.

6

"No one in the family has heard from Rhonda since February," said Sherlyn Shotwell. She explained that Rhonda had been diagnosed in 1999 with bipolar disorder, and again diagnosed with mental illness in 2004. Rhonda Glover received inpatient treatment at more than one medical facility in both California and in Texas.

Shotwell told the detectives that she believed both Rhonda Glover and Jimmy Joste were involved in drugs because they were "out of their heads," and they had various paranoid delusions. Shotwell indicated that Rhonda kept journals, that Jimmy and Rhonda were together, on and off, for fifteen years, and that they engaged in "mutual assaults." Shotwell provided a description of Rhonda's son, offering to send along a photograph.

"I became so concerned about her, and the safety of my grandson, that I went to Austin from Houston to personally see for myself that Ronnie was okay." The motivating factor for urgent action was a strong suspicion, confirmed by a friend of Glover's in San

Antonio who called Rhonda's father, that Rhonda was off her medication and back into illegal drugs.

"I became seriously concerned about her in spring of 2003," said Shotwell. "Rhonda went to visit a friend in San Antonio, and during that time Rhonda had conversations with her friend about Ronnie being the Second Coming of Christ, and that she—Rhonda—was Mary, Mother of Jesus."

The first thing she did was contact the Austin Police Department and Child Protective Services (CPS). "I made both agencies aware of my concerns," she recalled, "and the police department went there that day. They came back and determined that because my grandson was not physically harmed and looked like he had been fed that he was apparently safe, and they came back and said that he was safe."

Tricia Haverin was employed as an investigator with Child Protective Services; she visited the Joste/Glover household on November 13, 2003. "My job is to investigate in response to reports from the community—to respond to allegations from people who express concerns about the safety and welfare of a child.

"Normally," explained Haverin, "we will attempt to contact the school-age child outside of the home first, where he is in a more comfortable environment. In this case Ronnie was not in school, so I went directly to the home and spoke with him outside the presence of his parents. After speaking with him, I spoke with each of the parents individually.

"When I spoke to the child," she recalled, "all his responses to questions were appropriate, and they were not in any way delusional or bizarre. At that point he seemed pretty normal and healthy. In fact, when I went on to speak with his parents, things started off seemingly fine and normal. But then, toward the end of the conversation, things suddenly turned. By 'turned,' I mean that the things they were saying turned into more and more delusional comments."

What triggered the sudden transformation was Haverin coming right out and asking Rhonda Glover, "Do you believe that your son is Jesus Christ?" She asked this because it was "a concern" noted in the original report to CPS from Rhonda's mother.

"Rhonda actually seemed very surprised that I knew this information, and she called Mr. Joste into the room. From that point on, I was dealing with both of them at the same time in the same conversation."

According to Haverin, Joste and Glover continually interrupted each other during the course of the interview. "When he came in, I continued speaking directly to Rhonda," she recalled, "and she was telling me that her mother was from hell, and that her mother had mental-health problems, but she just needed to drink water. Glover insisted that all of the blood and guts from September eleventh had come into our water system, and it was poisoning everyone outside of their home. Joste joined in, and they both talked about their home being on a purified water aquifer, and in looking around the house there were probably eight to ten glasses of water set around the room, some full, some empty."

In the course of the conversation, Joste and Glover talked simultaneously about water and Jesus and the Second Coming. "I became more and more concerned," admitted Haverin. "Rhonda did most of the Jesus talk, while Jimmy mostly wanted to talk about the curative power of the water. That was his big thing—the water. I spoke to them as a couple for about a half an hour."

By the end of the interview, the woman from Child Protective Services was seriously concerned. "I was convinced that Rhonda Glover and Jimmy Joste were delusional. I made my report and brought the entire matter to the attention of my supervisor at that point regarding the safety of the child.

"We made this case a high priority," continued Haverin, "and maintained contact with the maternal relatives. We were going to take custody of the boy. . . ."

The situation was such that the agency itself was prepared to remove the child and accept responsibility for him. Despite having an opportunity to speak about water and the Second Coming, Rhonda and Jimmy were angry at Shotwell for bringing in the authorities.

"I was concerned about Jimmy Joste's mental state," confirmed Sherlyn Shotwell. "I tried to get people to intervene to help him. I called his brother, Kelly Joste, and Jimmy's banker, and Mr. Mike Cook. These were all people that I knew who had a personal interest or involvement with Jimmy Joste. I made them aware of the conversations I had where Jimmy was saying that Ronnie was Jesus Christ and he could bring the stars and the moon down from the sky into the living room, and that people were hiding in the park across the street to kidnap him, agents from the government because of Ronnie being Jesus Christ, and they wanted to kidnap him."

At the end of the CPS investigation, a caseworker wrote: *The parents' capacity to care for [the child] is questionable due to their bizarre behaviors. Parents have made*

*references that the child is the "next coming," "Lucifer" and
"Jesus Christ." Although parents did not overtly state that
they would physically harm the child, the parents' unclear
statements and behaviors place the child at potential risk of
harm.* The report ended with the following conclusion: *Child is unprotected.*

Sherlyn Shotwell was still at the Austin Police Department when her cell phone rang. It was Rhonda
Glover and Jimmy Joste. "I put my phone on speaker
phone, and Rhonda made statements again that my
grandson was the Second Coming of Christ, and she
made threats. She said that her life—all their lives—
would be in danger because I sent the police to their
home, and my life was in danger as well. Well, all this
made me even more alarmed and concerned. I was
also very frustrated that nobody seemed to be able to
do anything to address this problem."

Shotwell contacted an attorney. "My plan was to
take custody of my grandson," acknowledged Glover's
mother. "It was Friday at the police station, and I came
home Friday night to get in touch with an attorney because they were not going to do anything over the
weekend. I filed for custody of Ronnie on the following Monday. In fact, I brought him back with me to
Houston from Austin, and Rhonda followed me back
to Houston and decided to live in Houston, take up
residence there, and Rhonda and I did make a deal,
or an arrangement, on the custody issue," explained
Glover's mother, referring to their joint court appearance on December 18, 2003. "Ronnie could stay with
Rhonda as long as she took regular drug tests, kept

the child in school and didn't take him out of Harris or Montgomery Counties."

There was more to Shotwell's plan than simply assuring the safety of young Ronnie. She also wanted to help her daughter receive appropriate help for her disquieting delusions. Rhonda complained of injuries supposedly sustained by the brutal treatment of Jimmy Joste, so her mother convinced her to make a visit to the emergency room (ER) of Woodlands Hospital.

"What I really wanted was for her to have a psychological evaluation, as well as a drug evaluation. While she was at Woodlands, she had X-rays on her arm and back."

The reason for the X-rays, and the excuse used by Sherlyn Shotwell to get her daughter to the hospital, was Rhonda's insistence that Jimmy Joste had harmed her. Once there, Rhonda Glover spent one evening before being admitted to Rusk State Hospital, where she was treated for cocaine-induced psychosis, paranoia, delusions and possibly bipolar disorder.

"Rusk State is a well-known mental institution here in Texas," said Travis County deputy prosecutor Bryan Case. "It isn't something that needs to be explained to the average Texas resident. Just about everyone knows that Rusk is the hospital for the care and treatment of people with mental-health issues."

"Rhonda Glover had involuntary commitment to Rusk, but they couldn't keep her for long," commented Fred Wolfson. This wasn't the first time Rhonda Glover had been institutionalized for either drug addiction or mental illness. "These are not character defects," commented Leonard Buschel, a licensed substance abuse counselor and founder of Writers in Treatment. "Both mental illness and chemical dependence are regarded as medical issues, and medical conditions are not against the law."

As it was an involuntary commitment at Rusk, they could only keep her if she was suicidal or homicidal. Since she was neither, there was no "reason" to keep her. Rhonda took this to mean that she was just fine.

Released from Rusk, Rhonda Glover was given medication, and young Ronnie was placed in his grandmother's custody. "My mother was furious that I got out of Rusk so fast," said Rhonda Glover. "Mom told people in her CPS files that I would be there six to eight weeks. Mom was so angry when I called her after only two days. She almost refused to come and get me from the bus station. Then she took me to a La Quinta Inns, next to a Denny's, and dropped me off with fifty dollars and no car. She took my truck to my dad's. Neither one of them would come and get me. They had turned their backs on me when I was trying to get away from Jimmy. My mom refused to help me get electricity and a phone in her name so that he could not find me. Yep, ask her. What is really sad," continued Glover, "is that just a few months earlier, I had called my dad on his cell phone. He said he was in Giddings, which is only about an hour from Austin. I was crying profusely. I told my daddy that Ronnie and I were in a lot of danger from Jimmy. I told my dad that Jimmy was doing drugs, and that Jimmy took my car keys."

Rhonda said she pleaded with her father to come and get her, and that she was concerned about her safety, but he refused.

According to Rhonda Glover, she had never in all her years called on her parents for money, or help in any relationship, or been in jail. "When Dad refused to come get me, I thought I was going to die right there. I cried and cried and cried. My son kept saying, 'Mom, that is just how Papa is, you know that. We're never getting out of here.' Well, I got down on my knees with my rosary and said, 'Lord, if you can just send me the answers, I have no way to leave here without getting hurt. Show me what to do.'

"A few minutes later," said Glover, "Jimmy came downstairs and said, 'Will you go get me some Miller High Life, and get you some lunch while you are out?' I went to the store, and when I was in the Suburban, I found the extra set of keys in the ashtray. It was like winning the Lotto.

"I came back, and we all ate, and he lay down to sleep. I started making my plans to escape without him noticing my stuff was being packed. The night I left, my son was crying, saying, 'Mom, we can't just leave him like that. We have to go back.' I just drove around and round in circles. With all my heart I wanted to help him because that was someone else living inside of him. It was not him. I finally went back, and I lay down on the bed beside him, and I felt as if God was taking the very life out of me. My bones started to ache, and I was literally shriveling up and dying."

Glover restated in 2009, "I knew that Jimmy was truly evil. The Lord was telling me that I was in a lot of danger. I had to pry Ronnie off of his dad and force him to leave. He was so upset, leaving like that."

Assumptions of authenticity or accuracy of fact attributed to Rhonda's reminiscences are ill-advised.

The documentation of her behavior, residences and court-ordered arrangements regarding custody of her son are, in comparison, more reliable indicators of events and outcomes.

Having returned to the Houston area, Rhonda Glover and her little boy spent Christmas Day with the Shotwell family and shared Christmas dinner. "The next day," recalled Sherlyn Shotwell, "Rhonda called to tell me that Ronnie would not be visiting on Saturday, the twenty-seventh from ten A.M. to ten P.M., as agreed, because she and her girlfriend were taking their children snow skiing in New Mexico."

When the first scheduled visitation failed to happen, Shotwell wasn't overly concerned. The next arranged date, January 9, 2004, was kept as agreed. "Rhonda voluntarily brought him for the weekend because she wanted to take him to sign up for gymnastics. From the ninth through the twelfth, we took Ronnie to our lake house for the weekend."

Shotwell repeatedly called her daughter the following week. There was never an answer, and voice mail messages were not returned. "On the twenty-third, I finally reached her," Shotwell recalled. "I wanted to pick up Ronnie the next day, but Rhonda said that they both had the flu, and he couldn't visit."

As would any concerned grandmother, Sherlyn Shotwell called Rhonda every day to check on the health of her daughter and grandson. There was no answer at any of Glover's home or cell numbers. "I left messages, of course. I didn't hear a word until the end of the month, when Rhonda called to tell me that she was moving to another apartment over

Super Bowl weekend. She told me that she had met someone who had tickets to the Super Bowl, and she was going."

It was now February 2004. Every day Shotwell called; every day there was no answer. "Some of the numbers had been disconnected, and there was no contact whatsoever from my daughter."

Shotwell was not the only person irritated and concerned by the lack of phone calls. Stephanie Olech, assistant principal at Hunters Creek School, called Shotwell on February 5. "She called me because my name was listed as an emergency number. My grandson hadn't shown up for school since January twenty-ninth, and they hadn't heard a word from his mother. I told Ms. Olech that Rhonda was moving to a new apartment. I also told her that I feared something was wrong. Olech said they would have the police go to both the old and new apartment to check and make sure that Rhonda and Ronnie were okay, and find out why he was not in school." The police went to both apartments. There was no one at either location.

Upset and anxious, Shotwell placed a call to Rhonda's old friend Sean Kelly. "I asked him if he'd seen Rhonda," said Shotwell. "He said he saw her at the Super Bowl, and she was talking out of her head. Rhonda told him that Jimmy's eyes were on the twenty-dollar bill. Sean told her there was no way that the federal government put Jimmy Joste's eyes on the twenty-dollar bill, and she should not be talking about that kind of stuff to anyone else that day. Sean also told me that Rhonda had signed up to work out at his gym, but she had been late several days in a row. She couldn't commit to daily workouts and the scheduled training times."

Kelly also questioned where Rhonda was getting the money to buy a new Infinity, keep her 2002 Suburban, rent two apartments, buy new furniture and keep on spending as if the money would never end.

"Rhonda took Ronnie and vanished," said Shotwell. "I hired a private detective agency and filed a missing persons report. They found Rhonda and Ronnie in Michigan. She had tried to cross the border into Canada, but they wouldn't let her enter. I talked to the police there, and they told me that Rhonda was on her way back to Houston with my grandson. It would take about one day for her to get home. She never showed up."

"She isn't honest, and she isn't trustworthy," stated Danny Davis emphatically. Jimmy Joste's longtime friend had deep doubts about Rhonda's truth-telling abilities, even if her lapses into revisionist history were unintentional. "Rhonda Glover's reputation was never one of honesty. She was known—to be blunt— as a liar."

"Danny Davis has a lot of nerve saying things about me," responded Rhonda. "He's been in big trouble over things himself. He and Jimmy were investigated by the SEC. They raised money on TV in California for bogus oil and gas deals," alleged Glover, "and Jimmy was mad at Danny for getting him involved, and he punched Danny in the face, and almost knocked him through the plate glass window on the top floor of the office building. It was a real treat to see Jimmy stick up for himself, because Danny was always such a bully."

"Isn't that interesting?" commented Fred Wolfson. "Glover says it was a treat to see Jimmy stick up for himself. This fits in with the description of Jimmy being passive, as opposed to aggressive and violent. Glover seems to be of two minds about Jimmy, and neither mind is talking to the other."

Rhonda Glover denied ever having a mental illness. "Don't forget," she said, "I never told any of those psych doctors about my belief I was anything but a battered girlfriend with an evil ex. That is it—that is all. To hear all these accusations of me being crazy or delusional is really aggravating."

Clearly, Rhonda's view of things differed from the perceptions of many others. She claimed she never suffered from mental illness, while others said the opposite. She claimed Jimmy was an abusive boyfriend, while others claimed he was a perfect gentleman. Another person who offered her perspective on that aspect of the relationship was Christy Dillon, of Houston, Texas. "I met Jimmy through my husband who had known Jimmy for about twenty years. We lived about two blocks away from Jimmy. I finally met Rhonda at a nail salon.

"We had a lot of mutual friends," said Christy Dillon. "We moved in the same circles, and I pretty much knew Jimmy and Rhonda as a couple. We were all living in Houston, and we socialized with them."

It was Christy and Robert Dillon who witnessed Rhonda Glover "beat the crap" out of Jimmy Joste. "I remember it quite vividly because she was pregnant," recalled Christy. "We were invited over to their condo for a barbecue. Jimmy was cooking, and she was drinking alcohol, and she wasn't supposed to drink because she was pregnant."

The convivial atmosphere changed for the worst

when Jimmy Joste admonished her on her alcohol consumption. "She punched him in the face, and put him on the ground. She was on top of him, hitting him, and he wasn't fighting back at all. My husband and I pulled her off him."

Despite this episode of violence, the couples still saw each other on occasion. "Rhonda would just pop by the house. She never called first. She would just show up and knock on my door. She came over to my house unannounced about eight weeks before she shot Jimmy, and Rhonda was talking real crazy the last time I saw her.

"I had just finished working out," Christy said, "and I had on my workout outfit. My husband thinks that Rhonda is a bad influence, and there she was at my house."

Not quite knowing what to do, but knowing her husband wasn't thrilled having Rhonda Glover in his house, Christy Dillon came up with a practical solution.

"I know she likes sushi, and there was a new sushi bar down the street, so I suggested that we go out for lunch. I didn't go with her in her car because I was afraid," admitted Christy. "She looked like a drug addict. I mean, I've known her for thirteen years, and she looked like a drug addict, like you see in the movies. She must have lost twenty or thirty pounds, and the way she was talking—she made statements that really concerned me."

The statements that Christy Dillon found disconcerting were the same ones that compelled Glover's mother to seek custody of her young grandson—the stereotypical symptoms of personalized grandiose religiosity, coupled with paranoid delusions of both persecution and exceptionalness. With little appreciation for the gut-level reaction of her peers, Rhonda Glover proudly announced that her son, the offspring of Jimmy Joste, was none other than Jesus of Nazareth reborn, the long-awaited Messiah who, she was proud to note, excelled at gymnastics. "It makes me upset just to think about it.

"After she got all radical and told me how bad things were," continued Christy, "when we went outside of the sushi restaurant—I had to get home and go fix my husband supper—she met her ex-lover Sean Kelly, who is a bodybuilder and has keys to the same complex, and I left her with him."

Prior to hooking up with Kelly, Rhonda Glover also voiced displeasure with her mother. "She went off about her mother too. She was saying how her mother is at fault with all of this, why Jimmy had to plead guilty, why this and why that. It is all because of her mother," Christy stated.

Rhonda was also, according to Christy Dillon, angry with Jimmy Joste because "he wasn't doing enough or paying enough to get a better attorney in getting her back custody of Ronnie." As for Christy's concerns that Glover was abusing drugs, Rhonda allegedly volunteered detailed confirmation. "She said that she was freebasing cocaine, and that there was a cocaine dealer living in their house. I had never been to that house, so I don't know. She never offered me drugs. We didn't do drugs.

"That day," explained Christy Dillon, "Rhonda was doing drugs while we were together. I mean she would go off to the bathroom every fifteen minutes."

Christy was not impressed with Rhonda's behavior or topics of conversation. "I told her that I really didn't want to get into any of this stuff she was talking about. You know, about how everything was Jimmy's fault because Jimmy [pleaded] guilty to that charge of domestic violence against her when he shouldn't have. If he had not [pleaded] guilty, things would be different, and all about how mad she was at her mother for having custody of her son. She said that her son was molested by someone when in her mother's custody. She would go back and forth between blaming her mother and blaming Jimmy."

Former friends of Rhonda and Jimmy's, shocked by Joste's tragic death, came forward to give statements to Detective Walker. "I saw Rhonda shooting up in 1999," confirmed real estate agent Debbie McCall. "My boyfriend and I went out to dinner with Rhonda and Jimmy. Anyway, we were out to dinner, and Rhonda wanted to go to the restroom, and she asked me to go with her. We went into the handicapped stall, and she started shooting up cocaine. You know, with a needle, and she asked me to help her." When asked if Ronnie was there at the time, McCall said that he wasn't. She did volunteer that she had personally seen Rhonda Glover abuse Ronnie Joste.

The investigation was moving with astonishing rapidity, and all indicators pointed to Rhonda Lee Glover as the person who pulled the trigger, the killer who pumped at least ten bullets into the unarmed and defenseless Jimmy Joste.

Within an hour of speaking to Sherlyn Shotwell, Austin's Intelligence Unit was working with Bryan Sheely, of the U.S. Marshal's Office, in an effort to locate Rhonda Glover and Ronnie Joste. They had checked Rhonda Glover's cell phone number, and discovered it had been changed to a Houston exchange, and the name on the account was Rhonda P. Lee. Lee was Glover's middle name. The marshals were advised that Glover provided false information on the ATF form when she purchased the Glock, which was a felony, and the ATF was notified.

"The minute she lied on that form," remarks investigator Fred Wolfson, "she exempted herself from the right to possess a firearm."

Kent Plemons, of the Bureau of Alcohol, Tobacco, Firearms and Explosives, was the agent assigned for the false information case. At 12:25 P.M., a warrant was issued by the ATF for Rhonda Glover. The charge: firearms violation.

"Not murder, you notice," pointed out private investigator Fred Wolfson, "but firearms violation. There was a good reason for this, from an investigative standpoint, as will become clear. The Austin Police Department is a team of true professionals, and they know what they are doing."

At seven-thirty that same morning, Detectives Walker and Hernandez showed up at American Auto Rental. "I want photographs of the vehicle rented by Rhonda Glover," Walker told Lee Hernandez. "I also want lifts of the driver's seat, collection of the drivers' floor mat and latent-print processing as well."

While at American Auto Rental, Walker received a call from Deputy Marshal Sheely. "He advised me," said Walker, "that phone records indicated that Rhonda had called an RV place in Round Rock,

Texas, RV Vacations. We completed processing the Ford Taurus, and I requested photos of the tires with a scale. The tires were not knobby-looking, and did not look like the tire prints from the driveway, but photos were taken for possible elimination."

The car had not been rented since Rhonda Glover returned it, so the ending mileage was the same as when she brought it in. The ending mileage was 82,557. The contract indicated that the beginning mileage was 82,522, for a total of thirty-five miles.

Deputy Marshal Sheely reported back to Walker that a check of the RV place had been made. "They knew Rhonda Glover at American Dream Vacations," said Sheely. "She was a former customer who still owed them money from a previous RV rental a month earlier."

The rental agent in July of 2004 with whom Rhonda Glover did business at American Dream Vacations RV Rentals and Sales was Francis Mund. "I did the contract with her when she came in to rent the RV," said Mund.

"You know, we don't just let people pick one out and drive it away. We have paperwork that must be filled out, and it's a regular rental contract. I would say she came in around lunchtime, or midafternoon. As for the RV itself," Mund said, "it was the biggest one we had. We made out the contract, you know, when she was going to pick it up and when she was going to return it. It was not open-ended. She had a specific date that she was going to return it. At the time she came in, she paid some. She seemed as if she had a lot to do, she was in a bit of hurry and everything. She came back later and paid the rest.

She got the thirty-eight-foot diesel pusher. It will accommodate four people."

"I paid for that RV with my credit card," recalled Rhonda Glover. "And, yes, they knew me there, and the RV had GPS on it. Obviously, if I was intending to hide, I would have rented the RV from someplace where they didn't know me, and I would have paid cash and not used my credit card."

"Rhonda is so full of shit," said one of Glover's more recently disenfranchised former friends, "she was out of her mind for a hell of a long time before she shot Jimmy, out of her mind when she rented that RV, and now she is trying to portray herself as thinking logically? Logical people don't call the cops because there are people hiding in the sink, or shoot their son's father because he is a lapdog of Satan. I don't believe a word she says about anything. She's an attention whore, plain and simple. If she knew that killing Jimmy would get her all over the newspaper and TV, she would have shot him earlier. She will say whatever suits her at the time. She would promise you the moon while stealing the stars."

Glover promised to return the RV on July 28, 2004. That didn't happen. She was arrested in Kansas on July 27. Mund had to send a driver to pick up Glover's RV. "It wasn't in Texas," she lamented. "It was out of state somewhere. I think it was Kansas."

When Rhonda Glover took off from Austin, Texas, she made it as far as Kansas before the authorities caught up with her. She was wearing the same floral-print sundress she had on the day she shot Jimmy Joste.

"When I was arrested in Kansas," recalled Glover

in 2009, "I was pulled over on the side of the road for relief from the wind on the RV, and to get some water and a map. I was going to head back to Texas. Suddenly law enforcement was all around the RV and it was just like the movies. 'Come out with your hands up.' I was supposed to be armed and dangerous. Go figure. Anyway, they were very nice to me. In fact, they were exceptionally polite and friendly to me. When I was taken into their office, I was not even handcuffed in front of my son."

Rhonda had the family dog in the RV, and an officer asked her son the dog's name. "Well," replied the youngster, "his name was Snoopy, but since we are in Kansas, and need to get home, I guess his name is Toto."

"They laughed and laughed," said Rhonda, "I, of course, just sat there looking at him, knowing that I was in big trouble for running. Like Moses did in Exodus 2:11 to 15, I told my lawyer he should use that in the trial—'Well, ladies and gentlemen of the jury, even a man of God killed an Egyptian in self-defense, and then hid the body, which is something my client did not do. She didn't even get rid of the gun. She had full intentions of turning herself in. It just got scary for her in light of the people connected to the victim.'"

Arrangements for travel to Kansas were made by Sergeant Jessica Robledo. "I was informed by Detective Walker that the federal weapons charge had been filed, and that Rhonda Glover had been stopped in Kansas. Walker was coordinating efforts with authorities in Kansas verifying that the child was found safe. I made travel arrangements for Detectives Walker and Fortune to fly to Wichita, Kansas, to follow up with this investigation."

She contacted Assistant District Attorney Dayna Blazey to brief her on the situation involving the child. Blazey advised that she would get Child Protective Services on board, and would coordinate efforts with Kansas.

"I then contacted Assistant District Attorney Allison Wetzel and briefed her on the case," recalled Robledo. "I also instructed Detective De Los Santos to coordinate with Wetzel on the arrest warrant for Glover."

Working with exemplary precision, Robledo made contact with Grace Saragusa, owner of Top Gun in Houston. "I asked her to fax me the receipts of items purchased by Glover. At approximately twelve-thirty P.M., July 28, 2004, I received a faxed copy from Top Gun of all releases, waivers and receipts for purchases."

That was the same day that Rhonda Glover arrived in Wichita, Kansas, in leg irons. It was time to get Rhonda Glover's side of the story.

7

Rhonda Glover was brought into the room where Detectives Walker and Fortune initiated an "informal chat" about travels and other recent events of interest. In truth, Walker and Fortune used established interrogation techniques, and the entire conversation was recorded on video and digital audio.

"Cops can lie to you all they want when they interrogate you," explained Fred Wolfson. "Yes, the police are allowed to lie to a suspect to get him to confess. They believe that an innocent person won't confess. That, of course, isn't true, but it's a big part of the reason why police are allowed to use deception, half-truths or outright lies during an interrogation. The psychological manipulation begins before the conversation even begins. The physical layout of most interrogation rooms is set up to make you uncomfortable, and make you feel powerless. While police may not explicitly offer leniency for a confession or threaten punishment if someone won't confess, they may imply promises or threats in their language and tone."

The interrogation process begins with you being presumed guilty, and the goal is to get you to confess. Once the interrogation begins, a detective may very possibly ignore any evidence of innocence because it doesn't fit the preconceived idea that you are guilty.

"The whole thing is designed to make you nervous," confirmed Wolfson. "And any sign of stress is taken as an indication of guilt. Of course you could be stressed because you are being accused of a crime you didn't commit."

The classic interrogation manual, *Criminal Interrogation and Confessions,* recommends a small, soundproof room with only three chairs—two for detectives, one for the suspect—and a desk, with nothing on the walls. This creates a sense of exposure, unfamiliarity and isolation, heightening the suspect's "get me out of here" sensation throughout the interrogation.

"That 'whole get me out of here' sensation is one of the moral objections to interrogation because someone could make a false confession," said Wolfson. "A process designed to cause someone so much stress that he'll confess, just to escape the situation, is a process that leaves itself open to false confessions. There are plenty of those every year. In fact, there are up to three hundred false confessions per year in the USA."

The more stress a suspect experiences, the less likely he is to think critically and independently, making him far more susceptible to suggestion. This is even truer when the suspect is a minor or is mentally ill, because he may be poorly equipped to recognize or fight off manipulative tactics.

The interrogation manual also stipulates the advantages of putting a suspect in an uncomfortable chair, where he can't control any aspect of his environment, such as lighting, heat, air-conditioning or anything else. The interrogator will also sit in a higher chair than the suspect's. "I used to saw off a small portion of one chair leg," admitted Fred Wolfson, "so the chair would never be even on the floor, and always a bit off."

A one-way mirror is an ideal addition to the room, because it increases anxiety, and other detectives can watch what's going on and figure out what techniques are working, and which ones aren't.

"What you will notice in a classic interrogation, such as the one with Rhonda Glover," commented Wolfson, "is that, right away, Walker and Fortune attempt to develop a rapport with Rhonda. They begin with casual conversation to make everything seem friendly and nonthreatening. Once someone—in this case Rhonda—starts talking about harmless things, it becomes harder to stop talking. Once they start, they usually keep going."

Rhonda Glover was not placed in such a typical interrogation situation. In fact, she was taken into an office, where she sat at the most comfortable chair. She was afforded every courtesy.

"Ms. Glover was brought in and asked to have a seat," recalled Detective Walker. "I identified myself and Detective Fortune, and told her we were from the Austin Police Department. Fortune provided her some water."

Walker told her that he was not there to talk to her about why she was in custody. "I told her she was in custody for a federal firearms violation. She asked what she did, and I told her it was handled through the ATF, and I didn't really have anything to do with that. I told her I had not seen a report or affidavit, and all I knew was it had to do with a firearm, a handgun."

The Department of the Treasury ATF transaction record of Glover's over-the-counter purchase of the Glock asked questions that could impact whether or not she could purchase the weapon. Two of the questions were as follow:

Are you an unlawful user of, or addicted to, marijuana, or any depressant, stimulant, or narcotic drug, or any other controlled substance? Have you ever been adjudicated mentally defective or have you ever been committed to a mental institution?

Rhonda Glover provided false answers and an incorrect address. Her ownership and possession of the Glock was illegal, as she falsified the information on the ATF form.

Walker said that since she was in custody, and even though he wasn't going to talk to her about that, he needed to go through some things. "I then read her the Miranda rights, as required," Walker said. "I explained that if she did decide to talk to us, she could stop anytime."

"Well," said Rhonda Glover, "I don't know what any of this is all about. I'm just on vacation with my son. Actually, I went to audition for a Nashville show. I had my guitar and piano with me, but I chickened out when I got there.

"Then we went to Memphis," Glover continued, "Then we were going to visit some friends in Aspen. It's a long drive, and it's hard driving that big huge motor home. All I know is that I pulled over, and

Kansas police came with guns and got me out of the motor home."

Glover again mentioned having been in Nashville, and talked about recording herself. "I'm glad I didn't audition in Nashville," she said. "These leg irons are so darn tight when I walk."

The leg irons were actually loose, but Glover had pulled them up tight on her calves. "If you let them down," Walker told her, "they will be more comfortable."

"No," replied Glover, "if I do that, they hurt my ankles."

The detectives asked nonthreatening questions that required memory (simple recall) and questions that required thinking (creativity). "When you are remembering something, your eyes will often move to the right," explained Fred Wolfson. "When you are thinking about something, or making something up, your eyes might move upward or to the left, reflecting activation of the brain's cognitive center. The detective makes a mental note about your eye movements."

True to his training, Walker asked nonthreatening conversational questions about where Rhonda was, prior to Memphis. "Oh, we were in San Antonio at the Texas Ski Ranch. We were there for about a week. I got the motor home from American Dream Vacations on I-10. I'm paying three hundred sixty dollars a day for it, but it's worth it."

"I asked where she went from San Antonio," said Walker, and she replied that she went to Austin. "I went to Austin, because I had a home that I sold to my ex. He had given me one hundred thousand dollars in equity on it, and I tried to get all the paperwork switched into his name. He had been a cosigner on it too. I wanted to keep the house."

So far, so good. Rhonda was talking, and that meant she would continue to talk. Hopefully, the talk wouldn't include invoking her right to silence and her right to an attorney. In the United States, as many as 80 percent of suspects waive their rights to silence and counsel, allowing police to conduct a full-scale interrogation. "My ex," Rhonda suddenly announced, "was worshiping the Devil, and he told my mother that Lucifer was going to come into my son."

Things were now taking a very interesting turn in what began as a lackluster travel narrative. "Jimmy was smoking crack," she said. "I called the police in Austin on him many times because of his behavior. I was with him for thirteen years, and his Devil worshiping scared me so bad that I left him about a year ago. I called my mom and told her that there was stuff in the refrigerator he was eating that was not tofu!"

Remarkably straight-faced following her tofu remark, Walker encouraged Glover to continue. "Glover said she wanted to buy another house, but needed her tax returns," recalled Walker. "She rented a car from American Auto Rental. She went to her CPA's office, Mike Hogan, on Bee Caves Road. She said she went to the office of her friend, a realtor named Jeffrey Dochen. She said the house on Mission Oaks was bizarre. She said all the paperwork for the house was erroneous. She said the house was built on what's called Cave X."

"The survey company lied, and said it was on low land," stated Glover emphatically. "I had plumbing problems, and the plumber said that this was a crummy house. He told me to have it inspected.

called in an inspector, and he was terrified by what he found, but he wouldn't tell me what it was."

Perhaps delighted to have such a willing and attentive audience, Glover told more of her adventures in home construction. "She said there was a bow in the walls. She said she took a flashlight, started crawling around and taking pictures. She said she had a picture in Houston. She said it was in her apartment, and she would give us written permission. She said it was in a bag. She said gnats crawled around this bag all the time. She said there was a shaver that Jimmy had shaved up red stuff from the carpet that smelled like blood. She said there were two shoes, a black shoe and a white tennis shoe, with blood. There was a shirt with blood, candy and candle wax. She said God told her to take the plumbing apart. She said she took the plumbing apart, and it looked like her ex had poured all kinds of crap down there.

"Rhonda said that in the beginning she and her ex had been writing a book about water, and how important it was to have clean water," recalled Walker.

"That book was my idea, my book," declared Rhonda Glover. "I wrote two thousand pages of a book based on my own experiences, and with characters based on Jimmy and me. I showed it to the lady from CPS. I was so mad at my mother about that. I was doing what I could to get Jimmy in rehab. I had my own strategy, but she messed with it, and Jimmy flat out refused to go into Betty Ford. You see I went to Betty Ford, and that's when I got clean and sober. So I got hold of Betty Ford's and talked to the top people there. I loved Jimmy, and I wanted to get him into rehab. Anyone who tells you that I was on cocaine, and all that, is wrong. I've been clean and sober since 1998. Now, people may have thought I was messed up on drugs, but the drugs I was messed up on were the ones they gave me to take—lithium, Topamax and Antabuse."

Lithium is used to treat the manic episodes of manic depression. Manic symptoms include hyperactivity, rushed speech, poor judgment, reduced need for sleep, aggression and anger. It also helps to prevent or lessen the intensity of manic episodes.

Topamax is a prescription medication used in the treatment of migraine headaches, but it is prescribed frequently by psychiatrists to treat bipolar disorder, alcoholism and cocaine addiction.

Antabuse is a medication that causes vomiting, if taken with alcohol. This drug is given to alcoholics to keep them from drinking.

Rhonda was long off any of the above medications when she sat chatting amiably with the Austin detectives. "She said," recalled Walker, "that she found out that the city had given Morrison Homes permission to build this house despite failed plumbing, mechanical failures and the framing having failed on the house. Then she asked if we were Christians."

"We replied yes," recalled Walker, "and Rhonda said that in the Bible, in the book of Isaiah—God always told her about the Book of Isaiah. I asked her if God mentioned any particular chapter."

"Isaiah 54," Glover said enthusiastically. "It's about strengthening your stakes."

Rhonda Glover wanted to clarify why she had stakes in her automobile. "Those stakes tied the dogs in the backyard with long chains. The dogs were always running away and squeezing out of the fence because they hated Jimmy. If he was home, they were

let out the back and they ran off. I was always looking
for them. I had those stakes in the car because I had
hired a guy to mow the lawn out back and pulled
them up. I put them on the car because I found them
homes with a family that already had two other
Pomeranians. Jimmy was hurting the male dog because he was peeing on the rug. Everything Jimmy
had, the dogs either chewed it up or peed on. They
hated him so much and I could not figure out why.
He was abusing them. I am devastated to know these
things."

Speaking to the Austin detectives, Rhonda Glover
continued her explanation of Isaiah. "Isaiah 1:29 said
you will be ashamed of the sacred oaks in which you
have protected."

Rhonda became visibly more excited as she explained that the bank that financed the house was on
Briar *Oaks* in Post *Oak* Park. She said the house was
on Mission *Oaks*. She said the bank was the Heritage
bank, and was now Prosperity.

"Poor Rhonda," mused Fred Wolfson, "she placed
incredible significance on *oaks*. She linked the oaks
mentioned in the Bible with her home. I wonder if it
would have made any difference if she'd known that
the actual tree mentioned in Isaiah isn't oak. The
original Hebrew clearly says terebinth, which is a
Mediterranean tree from which we get turpentine.
The King James Version of the Bible was created
specifically for the Church of England. To make the
Scripture more understandable to the British, the
translators decided to change terebinth to oak, a tree
familiar to people in England."

"Jimmy taught me this code," continued Rhonda
enthusiastically, "and even though he was high all the

time, I listened because I was seeing miracles from God. In this code, nine is J. He is JJ. There is ninety-nine on my driver's license. Listen, it's important for you to know what's going on, because he was the ringleader in all of this.

"Jimmy was the one," said Rhonda. "God kept telling me that he was the one. The Bible talks about how men will flee into caves in fear of the dread of the Lord, and 'you sacrifice children in overhanging crags, and your hands are full of blood.' If you read Isaiah, you'll know about this house."

Glover had taken the most typical symptoms of mental illness to the deadly extreme. She took sacred texts revealed thousands of years ago to tribal people in another land, immersed in a cultural milieu as far removed from Texas as Glover was from reality, and personalized them to be all about her, her life, her son and the father of her child.

"There is so much to tell," Glover told detectives. "I'm just a lonely girl who people think is crazy. No one will believe me. They all know each other, and they are all Devil worshipers. They are murdering children in these caves because the house was built on Cave X and they lied about it."

Walker and Fortune listened compassionately as Rhonda Glover gave voice to her version of reality. "On Friday and Saturday nights," she said, "homosexual men line up on Mission Oaks and crawl through those gates there. I have built my case against these people. I can tell you everything. Homosexuals are coming and going, in and out of there, all the time!"

The homosexuals who were crawling into Cave X existed only in Rhonda Glover's imagination. According to a representative of Regents School, location of the only entrances, it required a special key to unlock the concrete grate because the cave was sealed to protect endangered species. Trespassing was virtually impossible.

The Kansas interrogation was not resisted by the enchanting woman in the uncomfortable chains. Encouraged to tell more, Rhonda Glover continued. "When all this started, Jimmy wouldn't let me leave, so I called my dad to come get me, and he told me that I was crazy. Jimmy put on an angel's face, but behind closed doors I was scared of him. When I found out about the homosexuals, I had to get out of there, because I was afraid I could get AIDS, or who knows what."

She said when Jimmy Joste made a remark about "toy-shit-kids," and she saw a little boy by the side of the road, that's when she put the "cave thing together."

"In Isaiah, it talks about the caves and murdering children," Glover explained to Walker. "Did you know that the Texas Film Code is sixty-nine? I've built my case against these people, but I have no voice. No one will listen to me."

According to Rhonda Glover, the cave under the Mission Oaks house was no little dugout in the ground. When she said "cave," she meant something bigger than the Batmobile's garage.

"Cave X is a big cave, a really big cave," insisted Rhonda. "There is an entrance on the Regents School property, and there were constantly cars over there. The house itself was built on state park land, and there was no permit for it to be built there."

All this illegality was manipulated, said Glover, by George W. Bush. "He is the builder," confirmed Glover. "Yes, George W. is the builder. The documents say Travis, Texas, not Austin, and the documents had five 9s on the bottom. I called information," said Glover, "and found Travis, Texas, is a 254 area code, which is Bush. I prayed about it, and asked how I could prove these people were into bondage and child porn and crap. God said He would put it in the news.

"If you look at money, on a twenty-dollar bill," she said, "it says *Satan you nasty nut in Austin.* Seriously."

"Oh," said Detective Walker, "I hadn't noticed that."

"Well," she responded, "it's in code. It's jumbled."

She took her finger and pointed it in the air, moving it around as she recited each word: "*Satan. You. Nasty. Nut. In. Austin.* It's there, but, yeah, it's in code.

"And you know that little green face on the right side? It looks like a bondage mask. Yes, Jimmy has been involved with the Bush family for a long time."

She referred to Isaiah again, recalled Walker. "She said, behind her house there was a gate, and that there's an entrance to the aquifer there too. There was a watchtower there. She said that the Bible Book of Revelation talks about seven golden lamps."

"From my office window," said Glover, "I could see seven golden lights out there, and they moved and shined down into the woods to light the aquifer entrance."

In the process of police interrogation, there is a technique known as theme development. "Walker uses this in his approach to Glover," noted Fred Wolfson. "The idea is to figure out what type of excuse might make her admit to doing it. For example, does she blame the victim? The detective then lays out a theme, a story, a frame of reference, to see if the suspect latches onto it. In the Glover interrogation, Rhonda kept laying out the theme for the detectives. All they had to do was get all soft and sympathetic, speak in a soothing voice, appear nonthreatening, and lull her into a false sense of security."

Detective Fortune, who had been listening in relative silence, now addressed her in a voice filled with compassion. "You've been having a nightmare. No one is helping you."

Rhonda Glover nodded in agreement.

"No one has listened to you."

At last, someone understood.

"Yes, yes," said Glover, "and, in the meantime, all these innocent people were being killed."

"How did you protect yourself?" asked Fortune.

"I got into the high-rise, but evidently Jimmy knew where I lived because he had sent me child support. He has a lot of connections. I don't know how far up he is connected, but he is connected. I never called Jimmy, because I was afraid for my son. I was afraid that Jimmy would kidnap him. That's why I never let my mother see my son, because she let him go off with strangers."

"What was your mother supposed to do with your son?" asked Walker.

"Well," responded Glover, "I showed my mother some stuff Jimmy had been smoking that smelled like flesh. He smoked it in a glass thing. I knew Jimmy had property in Horseshoe Bay, and God told me that he had buried somebody on the golf course. I have all that information in my house, in the bedroom in the high-rise, in the back bedroom."

Although her answer had nothing to do with the question, detectives allowed her to continue on her topic of choice. "In the bedroom there is Styrofoam, where it looked like a little kid had cut a hole. At the Mission Oaks house, I heard noises behind the wall, and I showed the Austin police where Jimmy had taken the baseboards apart. You know, like John Wayne Gacy."

Glover asked Fortune and Walker if they knew about John Wayne Gacy Jr. Even if the detectives didn't, Rhonda obviously saw sinister similarities between Joste and Gacy who, during a three-year period, viciously tortured, raped and murdered more than thirty young men, who would later be discovered under the floorboards of his home.

"I think Gacy was Jimmy's father, and a vice president at Southwestern Bell, and every business they owned was nine-six-six-nine. They could track anybody, and the people who knew the code, the homosexuals and the Devil worshipers, would know that was them. I have it all written in the book. I wrote two thousand pages for God.

"Everyone thinks that because I am on a mission from God that I'm crazy," said Glover. "When I was eight years old, I had the stigmata. You can check. It is in my school records at Oak Ridge Elementary."

"Rhonda told us that Susan McBee, of house 16, knew all about the cars that line up on Mission Oaks," recalled Walker. "And then she talked about Scripture again, and she had built her case. She said no one

would listen to her. Detective Fortune asked who she
went to for help, and she said that she went to God."

The big concern for Glover, she said, was "if my
son were to see Jimmy, and go off with him, I might
not ever see him alive again."

"What do you think would happen to him?" asked
Walker.

Glover looked at him as if he hadn't been paying
attention. "He could be sacrificed in the caves," said
Glover, as if stating the obvious. "The ultimate sacrifice for satanic worshipers is a virgin boy," Glover re-
iterated in May 2009. "I feared he would kill me and
take my son."

Glover explained to detectives, "My son could be
used in the pagan sacrifices. As you recall, in Isaiah,
it talks about the pagan sacrifices. And if they were
doing that in the caves, they could sacrifice my son. I
met a guy who told me that I needed to get a gun."

Glover recounted taking the handgun-safety course
with her son at Top Gun in Houston. "It scared me
half to death to learn how to fire a gun," she said, "but
this was something that I felt I had to do to protect
Ronnie and me. I was also going to take the defensive
handgun course, but the guy never called me back."

Glover jumped topics and time frames with astonishing rapidity. One moment she was breathlessly de-
scribing homosexuals creeping past endangered
species in Cave X to participate in pagan sex rituals,
and then, following the next intake of air, she was
speaking of events in Houston several months
earlier—but not with historical accuracy.

"I called Jimmy because I needed child support.
He ended up in Houston, behind me in a car. This

was several months ago. Jimmy asked me to marry him, and gave me a ring. Well, at first I refused, but then told him that I would think about it. I mean, that was an expensive ring, and I needed the money. I never even took possession of it. Jimmy offered it to me, and I refused it. He took it back to Deutsch & Deutsch Jewelers, not me. It was an incredible-looking ring. So much so that it didn't look real. But I never had it, and I never pawned it. I had other rings that I pawned of my own, but never that one."

Rhonda Glover, remarkably loquacious for a woman in leg irons, spoke to the Austin detectives of target practice at Red's, and how she purchased the Glock. "At Red's they told me that everyone buys the nine millimeter," explained Glover. "I went back to Houston, and when I decided to go on this trip, I wanted to take the gun with me."

Detective Walker asked her where the gun was when she went to Austin. "Oh, it was in the motor home," she replied, and was only partially truthful.

"I would really like to know more about your trip to Austin," said Walker. Glover responded with a recounting of destinations, locales and purposes. Not once did she mention shooting Jimmy Joste. "She said she first went to San Marcos, where they stayed the weekend," recalled Detective Fortune. "She rented the RV on Tuesday the twentieth. She said they left about eight and they spent the night in the parking lot of her friend's car rental place. She said she ended up knocking over a wire she didn't see."

"I got to San Marcos in a rented Dodge Durango. On

Monday, I went to Smithville and picked up documents at Covert Chevrolet and went to Houston. I went to Top Gun, but they were closed, and then ran some errands. I packed all my things, and drove back to San Marcos, to the Quality Inn."

Glover told detectives that whenever she stayed somewhere, she used alias names. "She said on that occasion she used the name Emily Cartwright," said Walker. "Then she got the dog a haircut in San Antonio at Best of Show. That was Tuesday. Then they went back to San Marcos, then to the motor home. She went to Austin, and they stayed at the car rental place overnight. She said she wanted to get a car so she could be at her CPA's office, first thing in the morning. She said she rented a car and the taxi driver was not there. She was going to use a cab to take her son to her friends' house. She identified the friends as Tony and Duanna Barder."

"Jimmy was evil. Did you know," Rhonda Glover asked Walker, "that Jimmy was accused of chopping off his mother's head?" Despite his career in Texas law enforcement, Walker was unaware of Mrs. Joste's tragic decapitation.

"Well, she lived," explained Glover. "That was back in the '70s, and it had been quieted up. That's why Jimmy moved to Austin. I first heard of this from a business associate over lunch. He said, 'Rhonda, do you know who you're dating?' I said, 'I guess I don't, if you have some secret about him.' He said, 'He was the number one suspect in the attempted murder of his mother, and was ousted from

Houston.' I was devastated that I had not heard that before, so I confronted [Jimmy]. He went off on me, but admitted that it was true that they did investigate him, but they never found the weapon used, no one was ever arrested for it, and she lived. Someone came in and chopped her in the head."

8

"Any suggestion that Jimmy Joste attacked his mother is absurd," stated Hal Martin, respected Houston jeweler. "Jimmy was out driving around with me when that happened, and he was as shocked as everyone else."

Barbara Joste was violently attacked, but not by a member of her family. "Barbara Joste was having an affair with a married man," stated a reliable family friend. "The wife found out, and came after Barbara with a vengeance. Barbara did the class thing and kept her mouth shut about who did it to her. No need for scandal or more problems for her, the wife or the man. I think she was just happy to survive. She passed away about twenty years later, and not as a result of that attack."

Rhonda Glover's hopscotch topic trajectory transitioned directly from decapitation to automobile rental. Glover told detectives that she only had the rental car for an hour, as that was all she needed it for. "I went to my CPA's office, and went to Jeffrey Dochen's office of Shelton Properties in West Lake.

That's all I wanted to do, because I wanted to get going so I could be in Nashville by the twenty-fourth or twenty-fifth."

According to Glover, Dochen left her a message that he was back in town, and would help her list the house, or help with the paperwork. "I drove by the house," said Glover, "but I didn't see any lights on or anything. I didn't have a key to the house anymore. I then went to the tanning salon, so maybe I was gone maybe an hour. Then I went back to Round Rock."

"She said her friends, the Barders, were watching her son," recalled Walker. "She said Tony Barder had driven her to the car rental place. When I asked what kind of car she rented, she said she thought it was a Ford Taurus, and that she rented it from her friend Wes, at American Auto Rental in Lakeway."

Despite any emotional or psychological difficulties, or manifest errors of perception, Rhonda Glover couldn't miss the fact that she was in custody in Kansas, bound in leg irons, and talking to detectives from Austin, Texas. This wasn't simply a social call.

"What's this all about?" asked Glover.

"It's about your ex," Walker replied. "Weren't you together for thirteen years? Did you two ever get married?"

"No, we were never married. We never lived together thirteen years. That's not true at all. We only lived together for a year. At one time, several years ago, we lived together in a high-rise, the Park Lane, in Houston, but he tried to strangle me, and I had to call the police and have him kicked out."

Glover then told the detectives that she was actually hiding from Jimmy Joste because he had come to her old apartment and harassed the guards so often that they had called in a criminal trespass charge against him.

"I was terrified of him," said Glover. "I didn't go near him, or answer his phone calls. My attorney, John Green, knows all about him. I have a ton of evidence, like bloody tennis shoes and bloody shirts of his that I got from the house before I left."

Detectives Walker and Fortune suddenly found themselves in the Twilight Zone of interrogations. "We didn't have the slightest idea what she was talking about at this point," confirmed Walker. "Then she went about her mother, and how her mother tried to say that Glover was crazy, but that she wasn't crazy at all."

"My mother sent me to a mental hospital, but they let me out right away because I am not crazy, and my mother had me sent back to Jimmy's custody after I was in the mental hospital. I mean, at the hospital they asked me what happened, and I told them I had a bag of food in the refrigerator that had blood in it, but I'm a vegetarian!"

"Rhonda told us that her ex had lay in bed one night and moaned and screamed, and that she found out that he was a homosexual and had male escorts. She then related some story about Jimmy telling her that George Bush owned the property that their house was on."

"It's true," insisted Rhonda Glover. "Bush owned the property around the house and my son can confirm this, and I can give you the name of a neighbor who can confirm some other things about the house and the people around it, and . . . a cave! Cave X!"

At this point in the conversation, Walker finally asked her, "What in the world are you talking about? What house? What cave?"

"I'm talking about the Mission Oaks house that I still own," said Glover. "I read the thing about the homicide that took place at the Mission Oaks house."

"What thing did you read?"

"The federal marshals had a document saying that there was a homicide at my Mission Oaks house, and I was still the owner of the house. I thought maybe he killed someone there. Did he kill someone? Did you," asked Rhonda, "find a body there?"

"Yes," confirmed Walker, "we did find a body in your Mission Oaks house. What is your ex's name again?"

"Jimmy Joste," replied Glover. "Did you find a kid there?"

"No. Why do you think we found a kid there?"

"Well," she replied conversationally, "one day my son and I were going to Mulligan's, and Jimmy said something that made me turn around. We saw a man and a woman on the side of the road, and there was a child in Barney pull-ups. They were talking to the child as if they were going to leave him there, and Jimmy knew I was going to be gone for hours. So I sat in the median on Southwest Parkway and watched them. They all got back in the car and took off, looking at my house as they made a U-turn. Jimmy said 'toy-shit-kids.'"

"This response to news that a dead body was recently found in her home," commented private investigator Fred Wolfson, "is absurd, incongruous and inexplicable. Listen to her. These cops are telling her that a dead body was found in her home, and she doesn't even ask who it is, or for any information at all. Of course she knows damn well that Jimmy is the body, because she killed him."

"She mentioned that Rick Kutner had lived in that house," recalled Detective Walker. "She said he could be questioned, and that her friend Patti Swenson knew how to get in touch with him."

"I am a very good mother," insisted Rhonda Glover. "And I am very protective, and when all the Devil worship stuff started, I got away from him."

"When was the last time you saw Jimmy?"

"I last saw him at a hotel in Houston, about three or four months ago. Every time I saw him, he looked different. About a year before, he bought me some clothes. My friend Denise had seen Jimmy, and he had been in Europe."

"What do you mean about him looking different?"

"Well," answered Glover, "one time I saw him and his face was round, and then the next time that I saw him, his face was thin. I thought he had AIDS because of his homosexual activity. But, listen, I want to finish the story about the little boy because it bothered me, okay?"

"Okay," said Walker, and Rhonda Glover told the story.

"My friend Rick told me that when he came to the house from Colorado, he found it destroyed. It looked as if Jimmy had lost his mind. I went out to the trash. First there was some bubble gum in the bedroom, like a child would chew, but my son had been with my mom for months. This was last year. I left him in September 2003. Anyway," continued

Glover, "I kept the gum, and then I found a piece of candy in the trash. Then—get this—I found a candle that had been burning in the bathroom that had like a piece of an ear on it."

"What did you say?"

"Did you hear about the ear?"

"Bits and pieces."

"That's right. I said a bit or a piece of an ear."

"Okay," said Walker, "I heard that."

"Well, listen. I took a nail file and put it in a piece of plastic."

"The nail file or the ear?"

"The ear," explained Rhonda. "Then I took it to a DNA place, Identigene, in Houston." (Glover was still stuck on the chewing gum when speaking to the author in late 2009. "It was a big piece of bubble gum," she said, "gum like a kid would chew, not an adult. I took that chewing gum to Identigene. Identigene had my DNA, my son's DNA, Jimmy's DNA, but the DNA from the chewing gum didn't match any of them!")

"While I was at the house," continued Glover, "there were things that popped up in the backyard that looked like body molds. You know, I called police in Austin and they think I'm crazy. Rick Kutner told me that I was crazy too, but I told Rick that I am not crazy at all, and that all this was really going on, and I was going to prove it."

Glover then told Walker and Fortune that Kutner moved into the house in the middle of the year, but then moved out because Jimmy was so crazy.

"He saw Jimmy firsthand in his deranged state of mind—Jimmy was deranged, not Rick. He came down from Colorado and helped Jimmy get somewhat together and presentable. Once I left him, he got worse and had not showered or shaved or eaten. The house was torn up and he said I did it.

"Patti Swenson told me that Rick knew I wasn't really crazy," Glover told detectives. "Rick knew something about Jimmy, about the Devil worshiping. Jimmy tried to get me to believe that Lucifer was coming into my son.

"I ran to my mother, but she sent me back to Jimmy."

"How did she send you back to him?"

"The mental hospital released me to my mother's care, but my mother just dumped me in a hotel with no money or anything. I had to go back to Jimmy because I had nowhere else to go. Jimmy came at me with a sword, and the whole time he was living a double life—looking like a nice guy to everyone, but I found him with homosexuals and Devil worshipers."

When Rhonda wasn't battling homosexual Devil worshipers crawling through Cave X to molest clones and children, she was attending church services at Gateway. "It's a great church," Rhonda said. "On Sunday, I drove all the way from San Marcos to Gateway, and all the way back—that's the kind of Christian I am. Anyway, you can certainly see that I was worried about Jimmy and what he had been up to."

Detective Fortune expressed sympathy for her obviously troubled situation. "It sounds as if Jimmy was a dangerous person," Fortune said.

"Jimmy was very, very dangerous," confirmed Glover. "He went to jail for assaulting me, you know. He pulled a knife on me, and made me go and tell them it had been my fault, and made me take my testimony back. I was scared of him."

There is no known incident of Jimmy Joste pulling a knife on Rhonda Glover. "You can't just take back your testimony in a situation where someone threatens your life with a knife," says Fred Wolfson, "especially in a domestic violence call. The prosecutor would have probably pursued it, and there would certainly be a record of his arrest. To the best of my knowledge, this incident is pure fantasy."

"Oh," Glover suddenly blurted out, "let me finish telling you about this friend of Patti Swenson! I have been just dying to tell someone about this!"

As Glover was so enthusiastic about this friend of Swenson's, the two detectives leaned forward in supportive attention. When she opened her mouth to speak, she said nothing about him. Instead, she returned to the topic of the DNA laboratory in Houston, and the failure of the Houston police to take an interest in her Cave X conspiracy.

"They told me," said Glover, "that it sounded like a matter for the Austin police, as the house is in Austin, and so is Cave X."

At this point in the conversation, Detective Fortune spoke up, communicating the deepest sympathy and compassion. "We know you were terrorized, Rhonda," said Fortune. That was the moment that Rhonda Glover broke down in tears. At long last, Rhonda Glover had two detectives from the Austin Police Department hanging on every word. Finally her story was being told.

* * *

Detective Walker asked Rhonda Glover why she drove by the Mission Oaks house. "Oh, I always do that to see what's happening," she said. "I didn't want to see Jimmy that day. I put an angel in the front yard."

"Rhonda," asked Walker, "did you have your gun with you?"

It was at this point that the interrogation took on a change in tack. "This is where the detective will ask basic questions about the crime," said Fred Wolfson, "to determine if Glover is being truthful or deceptive. Walker pretty much knows the answer to the question. If she answers honestly about the gun, she will be remembering, so her eyes will move right. If she is not being truthful, the eyes might move to the left. If Walker determines that Glover's reactions indicate deception, and all other evidence points to guilt, the interrogation of presumed guilty suspect begins."

"No," she lied, "the gun was in the motor home. After I dropped the car off, I got a taxi ride back to my friends' house, and talked to them for a little while. They asked me if I had seen Jimmy, and I told them that I hadn't."

"So you didn't have the gun with you?"

"No."

"You would think that she would know where this conversation was going," commented Wolfson. "I mean, the lady may be crazy, but she isn't so stupid that she can't figure out that here she is, in leg irons, talking with two detectives who are asking her if she had her gun with her when she went by the Mission Oaks house."

"She did seem nervous," acknowledged Walker. If he didn't "spill the beans," he, at least, tipped over the jar when he asked, "What if I told you that we know that you did have the gun with you that day?"

"Notice how he phrases that," said Wolfson. "'What if.'" He didn't confront her with a statement of fact, but rather a hypothetical one. In this technique the detective presented the implication of evidence or knowledge that might or might not exist. The detective typically stated in a confident manner that the suspect was involved in the crime. The suspect's stress level would start increasing, and the interrogator might move around the room and invade the suspect's personal space to increase the discomfort.

"But I didn't," objected Glover.

"Did you go shoot that day?" Walker asked.

"You mean did I go to Red's that day and shoot? Yes, I did."

"Why did you lie to me about that?" asked Walker.

"I didn't lie," insisted Glover. "I had the motor home with me when I went to Red's."

They looked at her; she looked at them. The lovely lady in leg irons, perfectly capable of buying into the most bizarre fantasies and paranoid delusions, was incapable of denying the real reason Walker and Fortune were asking her questions about shooting, guns and Jimmy Joste.

"I did it!" Glover wailed. "He came after me, and I did it."

"We told her we were there to help her get it off of her soul," recalled Fortune, taking creative liberties with his official job duties. "She said she went to get the camping equipment from the house, and her old golf clubs for her son, because she had hers with her."

"I had called Jimmy," said Rhonda Glover, "and he told me that he was eating lunch at a restaurant. I thought I had time to get in, get what I wanted, and leave."

If Jimmy Joste was dining in Aspen, Colorado, which is what Glover insisted he told her, there would be no concern about whether she had time to get in, get her stuff and leave (as she already established that she didn't have a key to the house).

"I hung up the phone and went to the house," Glover told Walker. "I took the gun with me and went upstairs to the attic to get the camping stuff. That's when I heard the garage door open."

The truth, verified by all of Joste's neighbors, was that Jimmy's blue VW hadn't been out of the garage in days. He was home when she arrived, and dead when she departed. Glover previously told detectives that she didn't have a key to the house. Neighbors said the garage door had been open for a few days. (It is logical to assume that Rhonda Glover entered the house through the garage.)

"I went into the attic by the upstairs bedroom," she said, "and then I heard him come home. I was going to hide there and hope he would just go away. I was on my knees, and when I tried to stand, I fell over a board. That's when he heard me. He came up, and I had my briefcase, and the gun was in the briefcase."

"The two detectives," commented investigator Fred Wolfson, "certainly perceived the glaring absurdities of her narrative. A man comes home, and she is going to crouch in silence waiting for him to leave. As he lives there, he might not leave the house for two days, three days. Perhaps he has nowhere to go, plenty of food in the fridge, and he has guests coming. She could be crouching up there for the better part of the week. She said that she brought the gun with her in the briefcase for protection in case he was home. However, she just spoke to him and ascertained that he was in Colorado. Hence, there was no reason for her to have any concern that he would show up because he is in a faraway state."

Perhaps realizing the incongruity of her statement, she quickly clarified it. "I mean, I didn't have the briefcase out, but I did have it with me. I didn't expect him being there, but I did have the briefcase with me. I just wanted to make sure that if he was there, I could protect myself, because the last time I saw him, he said he would kill me."

The detectives were not buying it. "That doesn't match what we saw, Rhonda," said Walker.

"I didn't want to leave the Glock in the RV because my son knew the box it was in, and might get into it. I decided to hide it," she said. "There was a Christmas stocking in the attic, and the Glock would fit in the bottom of it perfectly. I didn't just want to put the gun in its regular case up there, because if he and his druggie friends went up in the attic to find something to pawn for drugs, they would certainly pawn the gun. I knew that they would never find it if I put it in the Christmas stocking."

Unlike Rhonda Glover, Jimmy Joste was not known to pawn his possessions for drugs, even when down to his last $50,000 in cash.

"There I was, upstairs in the attic, when I heard the garage door open. I thought that maybe Jimmy had made a phone call, telling the men he'd hired to kill me where I was, and that it was time to take care of me. I was terrified. The floor was plywood, and when

I went to move, I tripped over a board and landed with a loud thud on the floor. Well, this was right above the garage. Whoever it was that showed up would know exactly where I was."

Glover then told detectives that Joste came at her, and they struggled. The scenario she described did not correspond to the physical layout of the attic or the forensic evidence. "We were struggling," said Glover, "and I got free and made it to my briefcase and got my gun."

Listening intently, Walker and Fortune merely nodded in encouragement as Glover continued her version of events. "She said he hit her on the head with the gun," recalled Walker. "She supposedly had the gun in her hand when he hit her in the head with it."

"I didn't have my finger on the trigger," said Glover, "because I had been taking a defensive class with a guy named Rico. I bought kickboxing and Tae Kwon Do stuff. I know that stuff, so I kicked Jimmy off of me. I got up and then I was in the bedroom."

"What happened then, Rhonda?"

"He was coming at me, and he was screaming, 'You fucking bitch! I'll kill you!'"

Glover's gaze darted quickly between the expressionless faces of the two detectives before she added a secondary fear factor: "His voice wasn't human! It was demonic!"

Walker and Fortune said nothing.

"It was a demonic voice, like Satan!"

The two detectives kindly encouraged Glover to continue her narrative.

"I emptied the gun into him," said Glover succinctly.

"What did he do when you shot him?"

"He fell over in the hall, but not until I had finished shooting him."

Fortune and Walker already knew better. Forensic crime scene experts could easily tell that the shooter blasted at least one bullet directly into Jimmy's groin while standing over him.

"I just emptied the gun and ran," she insisted. "I was standing in the bedroom when I shot him. I just kept shooting. He finally fell over when I was done shooting."

"But, Rhonda," said Walker, "that doesn't match up with what we saw."

Glover denied having shot in the hallway, saying it was only in the bedroom. "I'm not a very good shot," she said, "and I hadn't been shooting long."

"Why did you go to Red's that day?"

"I always practiced," Glover replied. "I mean, if I am going to have a gun, I should know how to use it if I have to."

Detective Fortune inquired as to when she went to the Mission Oaks house. "Was that before or after you went to Red's?"

"I went to Red's that morning, in the motor home. I can't remember if I went from there to the house. I think I went to get the rental car first."

Walker asked her where her son was during all of this, and she told him that the boy was asleep in the motor home. "I told her I knew it helped to get it off of her chest," recalled Walker. "I then brought up that I knew she had been practicing in Houston on different ways to shoot someone. I told her one of the ways she practiced was in the bedroom with the attic door."

"This wasn't premeditated at all," Glover quickly explained. "That was my house, and I had a right to be in my house and protect myself. Jimmy Joste was a murderer! I was scared of him, and I practiced all sorts of scenarios. There were things in the house I wanted, and I told Rico that I wanted to go back. I'm guilty of protecting myself and my son," said Glover. "I hid upstairs, and he found me upstairs."

With tears streaming down her face, Rhonda Glover finally said the magic words that brought the casually framed interrogation to an end: "I want a lawyer."

She was offered a tissue and water. "I told her the interview was over," said Walker. "I told her I was going to give her my card if she wanted to talk to us again. I let her know that we could not initiate contact with her, since she had asked for a lawyer."

"Am I going to be sent home?"

"Well, we are dealing with a federal warrant," Walker explained, "so I'm not sure, but I believe that you're going to see a judge on Friday."

"Wait," said Glover. "I don't want you to leave until I give you the names and phone numbers of witnesses to the things I want investigated. I don't want you to lose any time investigating the cave, and all the evidence I have about that."

"She said she would give us permission to go to her apartment," recalled Walker. "I left the room to advise the marshals what was going on. Rhonda then began giving information to Detective Fortune."

"In my house," she told Fortune, "in the crawl spaces, there is a formaldehyde smell. I found a little girl's hairbrush. My mother has the hairbrush," said Glover. "Look in those crawl spaces!"

She wrote out a "consent to search" for her apartment on Allen Parkway, and told detectives that another serious issue was that the Houston Forensics Lab was closed, so she didn't have anyone to take the evidence to. "You will find the candle wax with the DNA, the candy, pants with semen, and in the bag of evidence you will find some pictures that my son and I took, and . . ."

The pause was beyond pregnant; Walker prompted Glover to release whatever she was holding back.

"And what, Rhonda?" he asked softly, comfortingly.

"You can see an outline of a body in the air hoses."

Detectives made a mental note of the body in the air hoses.

"The entire house was redone by the 9/11 company," Glover said, and gave detectives contact information for Patti Swenson. "All this information is in the motor home. Ask Patti Swenson. She'll tell you."

"Thank you, Ms. Glover," said Walker. "I know this was tough for you to do."

"I never wanted it to come down to this," she explained. "I just wanted to be left alone. I really didn't think he would be there. It was him or me. He was coming at me."

Rhonda Glover wiped away more tears, then looked up at Walker and Fortune. "You know, I called the police so many times for help, and they did nothing to him. Go look," she encouraged, "there are tons of police reports on him—just look at all the times the police came out to that house."

Walker and Fortune already knew how many times Austin police responded to Rhonda's calls, and al calls ended with the responding officer determining whether or not this emotionally disturbed person was a danger to herself or others. Having delusions is not criminal, but medical. It only becomes a matter for law enforcement if there is a perceived and/or verifiable danger resulting from the delusions.

"Delusions," explained counselor Leonard Buschel, "are false beliefs that someone firmly clings to. For example, the delusions that one is famous or publicly important or is a god, believing a spouse or partner is unfaithful when it is not true, believing one is being followed, spied upon, secretly listened to, or thinking that random events contain a special meaning for you alone. Then there are other even more bizarre delusions, such as believing things that are actually impossible, such as having the delusion that there are dolphins serving on [the] state supreme court, that your husband is a gerbil, your rabbi is the pope, or that there is a rat living in your mouth with whom you communicate. Delusions are one aspect of the psychotic features of psychosis, bipolar disorder, schizophrenia and schizoaffective disorder, as well as some other psychiatric conditions [that] can be made worse, of course, by use of alcohol or other substances that alter mood or perception."

It is difficult to say when something is a delusion, and when it is simply a different view. "For instance," said neuropsychologist Max Coltheart, from Macquarie University, "it seems to me that if you believed two thousand years ago that the earth was round, that's a delusion. It's a delusion because nobody else believes it and you've got no evidence for it. It happens to be true, but you can have delusions that are true. The crucial thing is, do you have real evidence for this?"

Rhonda's delusions about pagan homosexuals performing human sacrifices in the underground refuge of translucent, little arachnids outstrip alien abductions in the absurd-delusion category. There is at least a scientific and sociological explanation for the delusion of alien abductions.

If a person awakes from sleep feeling paralyzed, and has the sensation of floating up to the ceiling, they are experiencing a remarkably common phenomenon technically termed hypnagogia, or hypnogogia. Thirty percent of all people experience this combination of sensations, but some people are eager and/or willing to believe that these physical sensations mean that they are being abducted by aliens. For other people who have this experience, the idea of alien abduction never occurs to them.

The explanation is very basic, and easy to understand: The people who claimed to have experienced alien abductions had believed in UFOs all of their lives. Their mental model of the world included invading and intrusive aliens. Someone whose mental model of the world doesn't include visitors from other planets dropping by their bedrooms would never even think that the twin sensations of numbness and "floating" were related to visitations from outer space.

You can explain to a person who holds such beliefs that there are other explanations, but it is unlikely that you will convince them that aliens, gremlins, ghosts or demons are not responsible. When related to religious beliefs, delusions are more difficult to deal with, because religions have long traditions, devout followers and continual reinforcement of a particular view of reality.

Rhonda Glover's delusions found their origins in a forced convergence of biblical passages, paranoia, grandiosity and local geography. In the long-standing tradition of mental patients personalizing sacred texts to bolster self-image and/or exceptionality, Glover envisioned herself on a mission from God to deal with Satan, now conveniently located in Austin, Texas.

In a model of dualism unfamiliar to Jesus and His Disciples, Rhonda Glover had become the Lord's "Terminatrix" in the battle between a good god and a bad god. The good god, not quite able to fend for himself, needed Rhonda Glover. She would save her son—save the world—and reveal the sordid truth. All she needed was someone willing to listen. She found willing listeners from the Austin Police Department's homicide division.

"What's going to happen to me now?" asked Glover.

"There is still some work to do," replied the detective. "You will have to go through the legal process, and that would include appearing in court."

"Can I get a bond?"

"Yes, but the judge has to agree to that. I can't guarantee anything."

"I need to talk to an attorney," said Glover. "I haven't been allowed my phone call yet."

"I can't give you one because you are in federal custody, and I have to abide by their rules. They'll have to tell you what is going to happen from here, as far as the federal stuff goes."

* * *

Before Rhonda was transported to the Travis County Jail, she gave Walker written permission to search her Houston apartment and "retrieve certain things that she claimed would validate her story of pagan sacrifices, sexual abuse of children, murder and clones."

Detectives were authorized by her to seek out specific items, including DNA material in an Identigene box, and men's shoes with what she believed was blood on them. "She told me to ask for Natalie, the manager," Walker recalled. "We didn't suggest any of this. It was all Rhonda Glover's idea."

The deputy marshals came in, handcuffed Glover and removed her from the office. Glover was held on a million dollar bond. The interview ended; the investigation continued. "Our next destination," said Walker, "was Hays, Kansas."

9

Walker and Fortune drove to Hays first thing in the morning of July 29, 2004. "As soon as we arrived, we met with Trooper Doug Rule of the Kansas Highway Patrol. He was the man who actually arrested Rhonda Glover."

"I was advised," reported Rule, "of a possible murder suspect driving a white RV, with Indiana plates, in the area. I found a matching vehicle at the Golden Ox truck stop. [I] ordered the driver to step out, and it was Rhonda Glover. She was placed in custody on the outstanding federal warrant. Her son was in the RV, and I verified that he was unharmed. After that, Social Services took custody of the boy, and placed him in temporary foster care."

Trooper Rule told detectives that the RV was a white Gulf Stream motor home with the aforementioned Indiana plates. "He also gave us the VIN number from his handwritten report," said Walker, "and told us where the RV was stored on West Fifty-fifth in Hays, Ellis County, Kansas. Rule arranged for a Kansas Bureau of Investigation agent, Delbert Hawel, to process the vehicle for us."

Agent Hawel, Detectives Walker and Fortune, and Trooper Rule convened at one o'clock that afternoon with the county attorney Tom Drees. "Mr. Drees reviewed the draft of the search warrant affidavit," said Walker. "He made a few minor changes, and then graciously assisted me in preparing a return order to have any evidence seized in Ellis County, Kansas, returned to Travis County, Texas."

Under Kansas law, Texas law enforcement could not actually execute the search warrant, although they could be present to assist. Agent Hawel, a Kansas peace officer, would be the one to execute the warrant.

If this sounds like a tedious and time-consuming process, that is because law enforcement personnel must be the first to abide by the law. Violations of law in the process of a criminal investigation can have horrific consequences.

The affidavit, warrant and return orders were then presented to Judge Edward Bouker, of the 23rd Judicial District, Ellis County, Kansas. At 2:32 P.M., Judge Bouker approved the affidavit, and a search warrant was issued for the 2002 Gulf Stream.

"Agent Hawel left to pick up some equipment to process the RV," recounted Walker. "Fortune and I followed Trooper Rule to the Ellis County Drug Enforcement Unit. The building was inside a fenced area with a locked gate. The building itself was also locked and alarmed."

Once inside, Walker saw a motor home with the license plate confirming it was Rhonda Glover's. "It was the only one in the building," commented

Walker, "and Rule said that it was the one that she was in when he arrested her."

There was an evidence seal on the RV's entry door. "I put that there myself," said Rule, "and I had custody of the keys as well. I drove the RV to the impound area, and I'm the only person who's entered it. I didn't search or tamper with anything. Once I got it to the impound building, I locked the door and sealed it."

Agent Hawel showed up fifteen minutes later and executed the warrant five minutes after that, starting with overall photographs. On site with Fortune and Walker for the search were Hawel, from the Kansas Bureau of Investigation; Doug Rule, of the Kansas Highway Patrol; and Deputy Scott Braun, who was with Rule when Rhonda Glover was arrested.

When Agent Hawel opened the exterior compartments on the sides of the RV, Walker noticed minor collision damage on the left-hand side. After photos were completed, Hawel began searching the RV's exterior compartments.

"In the forward compartment, right side," said Walker, "there was some luggage. In a black bag were several items of interest, including two photographs of James Joste with a male child."

The first cursory search also yielded a pink floral dress, two pairs of open-toed sandals and, in another bag, a short black top with a black halter top. "Then we broke the seal on the RV. Using the keys provided by Trooper Rule, Hawel unlocked the door, entered and took overall photos of the interior.

"When I looked inside the door," said Walker, "I saw a brownish stain on the floor next to the entry step, on the right side of the RV below the passenger seat. I asked Agent Hawel if he had any Hemosticks to test for blood, but he did not. I asked for a swab of the brownish stain."

Walker collected the rental contract for the RV. "The license plate wasn't correct, but the name on the contract was Rhonda Glover. The RV was large, approximately the length of a bus. The interior was as follows—driver's seat and controls left side front, with swivel driver's seat. On the forward dashboard there were several maps, none of which were marked with a route. There was a Styrofoam cup in the drink holder of the dash that had cash in it. There was a pack of Marlboro Light 100's on the dash as well."

Opposite the driver's chair on the right side was the entry area with steps, noted Walker. "On the right was a passenger's swivel chair. It was below this chair that I had observed the brownish stain. Between the driver's and passenger area was a walkway to the living area of the RV. The carpet was tan-colored, and the walkway portion was covered in plastic."

Hawel started searching from the back of the RV to the front, and he found another brownish red spot in the bathroom area, and a sock nearby with a similar stain. Then he opened a drawer to the left of the bathroom vanity, and inside he found several wigs. "They all had similar-colored dark brown hair," recalled Walker, "and I requested samples from each of them. Agent Hawel found a brown key fob with two keys on it. One of them looked like a house key, possibly to the Mission Oaks house."

In a sack in the bedroom closet was a black leather Glock holster, and in the right-side closet, rear of the galley refrigerator and forward of the bedroom, there was a paper bag stuffed up in the top left corner of the closet. "An unusual place," commented Walker. "In the bag were a black short top and a pair of black jeans. These clothes matched the description of the clothing Ms. Glover changed into at Red's firing range on July twenty-first."

Walker also tagged as evidence a pair of yellow shooting glasses located in the passenger compartment, plastic bags with three .22-caliber expended cartridge casings, six 9mm casings and one .45-caliber casing. "There was also a black leather Bible with pages marked for passages on those that commit murder and manslaughter," recalled Walker. "I found a large amount of cash in a handbag on the rear left side of the kitchen area in a cabinet. The money was later turned over to Kansas Highway trooper Rule to secure."

One peculiar item of interest found in the RV was a U.S. Postal Express envelope. Inside was a letter written to the RV rental company, and a large amount of cash. The letter stated that it was written by a friend of Glover's named Katherine Banks, and that Glover had been involved in a fatality collision on a motorcycle accident and that she was recovering. The money was sent to cover the rental expenses for Glover not returning the RV on time, and it covered the rental fee for an additional three days.

"Even if Ms. Banks exists," commented Jeff Reynolds, "Rhonda Glover was not in a fatality accident with a motorcycle or anything else. It would seem that Rhonda wrote that letter herself to buy time and explain why the RV hadn't been returned."

Inside the mobile home was a brown purse, the rental documents for the RV, various other receipts and a card for the Wig Mart in Houston. There were also wigs seemingly matching the one described by those who had seen Glover in Austin at the time of Joste's murder. Evidence was shipped to Austin, and in the secure evidence-viewing area, detectives opened the paper sack containing the brown purse. Inside were several items, including a perfume bottle, coins, and a fired 9mm shell casing, which was packaged separately. This item was then submitted to ballistics for testing.

On the day they searched the RV, it had been exactly eight days since Rhonda Glover pulled the trigger on her Glock 9mm, killing her son's father. She didn't tell Ronnie the true circumstances of his father's death. She told him that his dad had died of a heart attack.

"Ronnie is going to grow up knowing that his mother killed his father," commented Bryan Case, Travis County assistant district attorney, "and not only that, but someday he is likely to find out the real circumstances under which it was done, the manner in which it was done. It is going to be horrible for him."

Sherlyn Shotwell, a woman who had devoted so many years to dealing with her daughter's problems, now concerned herself with the emotional well-being of her grandson. "There is a special place in heaven for women such as her," said Fred Wolfson. "She has devoted her entire adult life to meeting the needs of others."

"When her grandson reaches puberty," commented counselor Leonard Buschel, "he will predictably struggle with a love/hate relationship with his mother, and the loss of his father will affect him even more when the full implications of his mother's act sink in. There will be tremendous anger, resentment and frustration—much of it inner directed or misdirected. Counseling to deal with these issues is more available now than ever before."

According to Rhonda and Jimmy's son, the story told in the media basically made this entire horrific event into a cliché in which his mother was portrayed as a gold digger and his father as a sucker for beautiful women. He insisted that this was not the case, and that Rhonda Glover was not after his father's money. After all, he pointed out, if money was her motivation, all she had to do was take him to court the day her son was born, and compel him to pay child support—no doubt a large sum of money.

He also asserted that the public did not know that he was the true victim in this case, as he was there through the entire madness of what his parents were going through. He saw everything, day in and day out. By his own admission, he saw things that a child should never have to see in an entire lifetime, much less at the ages of six to ten years of age. His side of this story was never heard, and he was never allowed to tell what both his parents had put him through with all of the drugs and insanity that he was forced to live with every day with them as his parents. Still a minor, Ronnie must follow the guidance of his guardians. He hoped to tell the entire story some day from his perspective, in hopes that it might help others heal from similar trauma.

According to research by a team of doctors and psychologists in the United Kingdom, children seemed to find it less difficult to accept the death of the father at the mother's hands than the reverse. This might be due to complexities in attachment and identification with the mother as a victim of chronic domestic violence, either real or represented.

"If the mother repeatedly tells the child that Daddy is mean and evil," commented Donna Mc-Cooke, "even if he isn't, the child will obviously see themselves, and mom, as victims." These children may be more difficult to treat for post-traumatic stress disorder and other psychological problems, as their symptoms may be less evident to their caregivers.

Children might not grieve for the loss of a father perceived, rightly or wrongly, as violent and dangerous. They might even be relieved at his death and instead grieve for the loss of their mother by imprisonment.

The further removed in time the mother's arrest is from the incident, the more shocked and numb the children seemed to be, stated the British study, *whether or not they witnessed the killing. In five cases where the mother killed the father, the crime was not immediately detected.*

When a father kills a mother, the children's contact with the father usually comes to an end. When a mom kills a dad, the child/mother contact continues in 95 percent of the cases. Contact with the mother tends to reduce over time. All current research seems to contradict the common practice of turning the child over to relatives of the person who did the killing.

"Returning the children to the perpetrators or their relatives in cases where the father killed the mother," stated crime researcher Travis Webb, "has not been associated with a positive outcome for the children. Also, kids whose father killed the mother have worse outcomes when they have many different foster placements. When it comes to children whose mother killed their father, those placed with the mother's relatives after the killing are poorer in terms of health, schooling and longer-term social and emotional adaptation than those who were placed in foster care. None of the children where one parent killed the other did well when returned to the care of the perpetrator or their relatives."

Children of mothers who killed their fathers may also do less well in therapy, as keeping loyal to the killer—their mother—makes it difficult to acknowledge angry or sad feelings. Rhonda Glover repeatedly stated that she wished she could be a mother to her child, and perhaps there exist mother/child relationships post prison that have some semblance of health. So far, researchers have not found any. *We doubt,* wrote the UK research team, *that a man or woman who has killed can be an effective parent; deal with unspoken fears, compliance or rebellion; and provide a reliable model for dealing with aggression.*

Mental-health–care professionals believe it is their duty to advise civil courts that are asked to return children to a parent who has killed that they must consider not just the debt to society, nor the risk of further homicide, but the need of the children for competent, trustworthy parenting.

"Competent" and "trustworthy" are not adjectives associated with Rhonda Glover, and her parenting skills already resulted in her loss of parental custody of her only child.

"Rhonda's son is no dummy, and he hasn't been totally in the dark about his parents," commented

Fred Wolfson. "He knows what it was like being with his mother and father when they were both at their most delusional. After all, she ran off with him more than once when she was not taking her medications. He is a bright young man, and his biggest challenge isn't going to be dealing with this tragedy—the challenge is to avoid the illusion of exceptionality. There are plenty of people who have faced horrific situations, tragedies and nightmares. That doesn't reduce the pain, but he is not alone."

Glover's son fortunately has a strong support system because of the active and loving involvement of his grandmother, aunt and other relatives. Other youngsters in his situation are not so lucky.

Criminal behavior is not in someone's blood just because a parent is convicted of a crime, although crime can perpetuate across generations. Quite often, the sins of the parents fall on the offspring. The behavior of Rhonda Glover is no reflection on her son, and there is no stain on his character based on blood relationship.

"Rhonda said there were bloodstains on shoes that we would find in her Houston apartment," Detective Walker said. "We had her permission to enter that apartment. We showed Natalie Santibanez, the apartment manager, the written consent from Ms. Glover, and she confirmed that no one had entered the apartment since Rhonda left. She told us that the week of July twenty-first, Rhonda had been loading personal items into a Dodge Durango. Rhonda, according to the manager, said that she was giving the items away to Goodwill, including golf clubs."

Allowed into Rhonda Glover's apartment, Walker easily found the Identigene box located in the entryway. "There were several sealed items in the box," recalled Walker, "but nothing that was obviously related to James Joste being involved in criminal activity. The items were photographed, but not collected. The box was left secured in Ms. Glover's apartment."

In the master bedroom there were two walk-in closets with numerous shoe boxes. "As one of the items we were given consent for was a pair of men's shoes, we opened those boxes after we initiated photos."

On the counter in the master bathroom was a pair of men's athletic shoes, size-10 Skechers. "These could be the shoes that Glover was talking about. They were not obviously bloody, but there were a series of brown spots on them that could be dried blood."

Walking through the apartment, Walker found an envelope containing several torn-up photographs of Rhonda Glover with a male later identified by Glover as Eric Zimmerman, soccer coach. "I met him one night at a restaurant," recalled Glover. "We got talking, and he wound up coaching my son at soccer for two years. Eric and I vacationed together in the Caymans, and he was an Eagle Award winner two years in a row. He is a great athlete and a super great guy. We had problems with Jimmy and his jealousy, so we broke up, but I would have probably married Eric."

According to Glover, Jimmy Joste was afflicted by extreme jealousy. "Jimmy was jealous of any man who befriended me." If Joste had a jealous streak, it was news to those who had known him all his life. Rocky Navarro and Danny Davis both characterized their pal as a man with endless tolerance and patience with Rhonda's freewheeling lifestyle.

"Hollywood Henderson's attention to me was another one that provoked Jimmy's rage," insisted Glover. "I didn't know that Henderson had been a crack smoker, and wrote a book called *Out of Control*."

Henderson's fame didn't derive simply from smoking crack or writing a book. A former star with the Dallas Cowboys, Henderson had an ignominious departure from the NFL, and squandered what fortune he had on drugs and booze. He went from sports stardom to a prison cell in California, and then gallantly rebuilt his life, image and sense of purpose. An outspoken advocate of recovery from drug and alcohol addiction, Henderson garnered headlines again in 2000 when he won the $28 million Texas Lottery.

"Anyway," continued Rhonda, "we met and he got my number, but not from me. He called, and Jimmy threw a fit. He also threw his Daytimer and hit me in the nose with it. Jimmy had a real problem with jealousy."

Rhonda Glover could wax conversationally about Joste's alleged jealousy, drop into terrified, hushed tones when uttering allegations of the generous Jimmy Joste murdering people and burying them on golf courses, or even attacking his mother with an ax. Detectives Walker and Fortune looked for evidence of illegal activity by Joste in Glover's Houston residence. They didn't find any.

"The television in the living room was turned to the Sci-Fi Channel," noted Walker. "There was a damaged prescription bottle for Rhonda on the kitchen counter, and it had white powder in it. It appeared to be ground-up prescription meds. The lab marking could be seen on the larger pieces. This was noted, but again it was not collected."

Strolling amidst the abandoned luxury of Glover's impressive high-rise condo, Walker saw a membership packet for the Secret Place, the religious organization that Rhonda Glover had mentioned. "I walked into the utility room," said Walker, "and I saw another item of interest. There was a book sitting on the edge where the washer and dryer were next to each other. The book was *The Ethics of Cloning.*"

"Rhonda said that Jimmy was into cloning," said Patti Swenson. Rhonda Glover also said that President Bush was a clone. How this was accomplished, of course, was never explained.

Accompanying Detective Walker on his tour of Glover's high-rise was Detective Fortune. "In a large box next to the entertainment center in the master bedroom," he recalled, "I found some papers that referred to letters and numbers similar to the so-called codes Ms. Glover had invented. In a box large enough to contain shoes, I found some typed sheets referring to threats against George Bush and Dana Bateman.

"Ms. Bateman," explained Fortune, "was a woman who had a child, and had been stranded on the side of the road. Apparently, Mr. Joste made a comment that Ms. Glover took with having some sort of significance."

That witch, wrote Glover. *She is in on it too. Dana Bateman. I think she was the woman I caught with that little boy the day my son and I were going to the movies. She had a man and a little blond boy on the side of the road with only a diaper on. When she saw me, she panicked and took the boy back into the truck. I think that may have been one of the clones of my child. Oh, my word! He was adorable. How and why can they feel okay about this? Dana Bateman, I know where you are. And what you look like. Watch out. Look around you. I am watching you. Be afraid. Be very afraid of ME and my GOD.*

Detectives contacted Dana Bateman and advised her of this threat against her, but also assured her that Rhonda Glover was in police custody. These rants, written by Glover, were found in abundance—as promised—in the Houston condo.

We have once again been sacrificed by Satan for the good of mankind, wrote Glover. *And this is the last time in history that we will have to be walked on by the Devil. You see, GOD has been working on this plan to catch Satan for years, and it took the real estate in Austin, and my income level, to get me into the house over that aquifer. You see, GOD has made other people aware of these crimes, and there has been no one strong enough, or fearless enough to come out against Bush. But I would like to see him face to face, fagot little scrawny bully! I would like to rope and tie him like I did when I was a cowgirl in the rodeo. I hope I have a chance. Bush, come after me. Try it, you queer, and I will use my power to annihilate you in seconds. You cannot stop GOD this time, Satan. Satan stands for Sexual Aquifers Taken All Nations. You are nothing but a punk, a freaking cannibal. Blood thirsty beast masquerading yourself as the most innocent and caring person in the world. I only wish I had been meaner to you.*

Detective Walker notified the United States Secret Service of Glover's threats against President Bush, although her ability to harm him seemed insignificant. All threats of this nature must be investigated by the

Secret Service. The United States Secret Service visited Rhonda Glover three times following her arrest, and each time they allegedly got an earful about the nefarious activities of George W. Bush and his henchman, Jimmy Joste, in Cave X.

Her assertion that Jimmy stalked her, and tried to get into her Houston apartment, turned out to be true. The Houston cops were called on more than one occasion specifically to keep Joste away from Glover's residence.

Rhonda Glover repeatedly claimed that she called police at least once a month because of Joste's physical abuse; yet there is no record whatsoever of any such calls, or any charges against Joste for abuse other than the one controversial Barton Creek Incident.

"There is no evidence at all that Jimmy Joste was a violent and abusive man," said Assistant District Attorney Bryan Case. "The only person who says Jimmy Joste was violent is Rhonda Glover. Ask anyone else about Jimmy Joste and they all tell you that the aggressive one in the relationship was Rhonda."

10

"I drank with Jimmy Joste," said Danny Davis. "I got intoxicated with Jimmy Joste. I never once saw him violent or aggressive when intoxicated. Never. When he drank, he was a very happy, easy, loveable drunk. He was never violent. Never. But I'll tell you honestly that Rhonda used to be violent toward him. In fact, back in the mid-1990s," recalled Davis, "maybe 1995, he showed up beaten up by Rhonda Glover. He had been worked over pretty good. He took a lickin' and kept on tickin', up until the last licking when he got shot ten times."

"No one thought Rhonda would murder Jimmy, but . . . ," said longtime friend Joyce Imparato, pausing to reflect on the unpleasant side of the Joste/Glover relationship, "I'd seen Jimmy show up with bruises and lacerations before. We figured that that Rhonda was hitting him, but Jimmy would make excuses, and say that he walked into a door. Personally, I only saw that a couple of times, but I did see it."

Jimmy Joste wasn't the type of man to repeatedly walk into doors. He was the type of man, however who would let Rhonda Glover abuse him and cover for her. In the world of domestic violence and abuse, men such as Jimmy Joste seldom seek shelter from the storm of a violent and dangerous female.

A review of published academic literature by Martin Fiebert, Ph.D., at the University of California, Long Beach, found seventy empirical studies, fifteen review and/or analysis and eighty-five scholarly investigations that demonstrate that women are as physically aggressive, or more aggressive, than men in their relationships with their spouses or male partners.

According to numerous studies in America and abroad, ignoring violent women, and concentrating solely on inhibiting violent men, contributes to the cycle of violence for the next generation. Most domestic violence is mutual, and most wouldn't happen if there was not a history of such violence in the family of origin.

Boys who come from violent homes are one thousand times more likely to beat their wives; girls who come from violent homes are six hundred times more likely to beat their husbands.

For the most part, there are few, if any, resources to which the abused man might turn. There are virtually no crisis lines, support groups, media recognition and, in most cities, no shelters.

"Animal shelters get more of a budget than women's shelters," stated domestic violence expert Susan Murphy Milano. "Men's shelters are almost nonexistent."

Jimmy Joste didn't need a shelter. He could stay in a fancy hotel, or one of the homes he purchased for Rhonda Glover. But being rich, or formerly rich, doesn't protect anyone from domestic violence.

* * *

The Joste homicide was, in some ways, remarkably similar to that of the plot hatched in 1998 against Chicago millionaire Albert Goodman by ex-wife April Goodman.

Portraying April Goodman as motivated by "evil obsession," a judge sentenced the once-aspiring actress to thirty years in prison for hiring an undercover police officer to kill her wealthy ex-husband, Albert Goodman.

"The defendant's homicidal plot was premeditated, well-organized and planned," said Cook County Circuit Court judge John Moran. During the trial the defense depicted April Goodman as a troubled woman who was twice hospitalized for psychiatric illnesses due to bipolar disorder. The judge noted that April Goodman was receiving medical treatment for her illness prior to her arrest and that a court-ordered psychiatric exam showed she was "symptom free" after her arrest. "Sadly, in our society today," said the judge, "many people have grievances against other people—real or imagined. . . ."

Rhonda Glover's imagined grievances against Jimmy Joste, centering on the human sacrifices in Cave X underneath the Austin home they once shared, were absurd, but she believed them with a deadly certainty in 2004. Five years later, she alternated between denying that she ever believed it, and asserting that it was all true.

And as far as the Cave and all, she wrote the author in 2009, *it is real and no joke. Me and Rick Kutner in Austin have done our homework, and been there. It is dangerous for me to know about it and I want to move ahead in life not get caught up in that. If you decide to print this, it could also get you in some trouble too. Just leave that crap alone. It was not mentioned in my trial for a reason. Do you understand? Don't talk about that anymore until we see each other face to face, and I tell you why it is dangerous ok? I never want to get involved with this I just want out to go home and be a mommy again. If you do print it, I'll have to turn my evidence over to whomever. Just forget it.*

Cave X is not easily forgotten, and it is a real place. Yes, Cave X really exists, and so does the aquifer that Rhonda was always mentioning. An aquifer is simply an underground body of water. It is a less glamorous way of saying "artesian well." It just refers to underground water that's under enough pressure to be tapped with a well or bubble up by itself.

Underneath Austin is the Edwards Aquifer, "one of the most prolific artesian aquifers in the world." The Save Our Springs Alliance was formed in Austin in 1990 to fight against development practices that were viewed as potentially harmful to the aquifer.

Driving through Texas, you always see signs about aquifers and watersheds. This is a subtle way of reminding people of ecological concerns, and to avoid allowing pollutants to leak into the ground and pollute the water in aquifers. This polluted groundwater ultimately ends up in people's kitchen sinks.

Cave X is an underground limestone cavern where insects have mutated over countless years, adapting to the darkness. It got the name Cave X simply because there was an X on the map noting its location. The name stuck, and Cave X remains Cave X. Rhonda Glover insisted that homosexuals were sneaking into Cave X through an entrance at Regents School to perform pagan rituals.

There are two entrances to Cave X on Regents School property. Considering the nature and purpose of Regents School of Austin, Glover's allegations of immoral and illegal behavior became exceptionally incongruous.

We are a school community seeking to serve mankind and honor God, reads the official statement of Regents core beliefs. *By engaging in our classical and Christian program, students develop an appreciation of truth, goodness and beauty.*

Austin entered into an agreement with the Regents School in November 1999 regarding Cave X. Under the agreement the school constructed a one-lane paved road accessible only to emergency vehicles and water-quality pond maintenance crews over a portion of the cave's footprint. Regents School was responsible for monthly inspections, including looking for evidence of tampering or vandalism. The school was also responsible for removing any accumulated trash or debris, vegetation management and biannual fire ant control. The agreement between Austin and the Regents School was implemented primarily for the protection of the federally listed Barton Springs salamander, which is dependent on the Edwards Aquifer. There are only two places on earth where the blind spider, *Cicurina cueva,* is known to exist, and one of them is Cave X. The spider is a protected species. The Regents School gated Cave X and fenced a small area around the cave entrance to protect it from unauthorized trespassing and vandalism.

The idea that people could somehow sneak into

Rhonda Glover's physical beauty and outgoing personality immediately captivated Jimmy Joste. *(Photo courtesy of Rhonda Glover)*

Rhonda Glover

Jimmy Joste as friends and family remember him—good natured and optimistic. *(Photo courtesy of the Austin Police Department)*

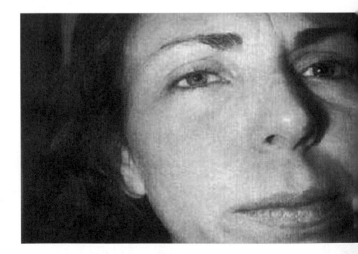

MISSING PERSON

Date:	3/15/2004
Case #:	040439804 Y
Name:	RHONDA GLOVER
Address:	ALLEN PARKWAY
	HOUSTON , TX
Height:	5 Feet 6 Inches
Weight:	120
Age:	37
Sex:	F
Eyes:	BLU
Hair:	BLN
Race:	W
BirthDate:	7/26/1966

OTHER INFORMATION BELOW

LISTED MISSING PERSON (MP) WAS LAST SEEN ON 01-17-04 WITH HER 9YR OLD SON, CHANDLER JOSTE, BY HER MOTHER, AFTER HE WAS DROPPED OFF TO MP AT HER APARTMENT AT N POST OAK BY HER MOTHER. MP'S MOTHER LAST HEARD FROM MP ON 02-11-04 ON THE PHONE. MP ADVISED HER MOTHER SHE WAS TRYING TO GET AWAY FROM HER SON'S BIOLOGICAL FATHER, WHO WANTS TO KIDNAP HIM. MP HAS BEEN DIAGNOSED WITH MENTAL DISORDERS. MP BELIEVED TO BE DRIVING A 2004 CHEVROLET SUBURBAN WITH PAPER TAGS.

ANY INFORMATION AS TO THE WHERE ABOUTS OF MP, PLEASE CONTACT HOUSTON POLICE DEPT. MISSING PERSON OFFICE.

ENTERED: 03-15-04   HPD MISSING PERSON OFFICE.

Missing Persons poster for Rhonda Glover.
(Photo courtesy of the Austin Police Department)

Rhonda Glover following domestic violence incident with Jimmy Joste.
(Photo courtesy of the Austin Police Department)

The Joste/Glover Austin residence as seen from the rear. *(Photo courtesy of the Austin Police Department)*

ntrance to the Joste/Glover ustin residence. *(Photo ourtesy of the Austin Police epartment)*

Police approached the stairs via this hallway. *(Photo courtesy of the Austin Police Department)*

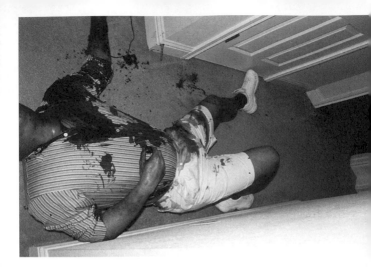

Jimmy Joste died of ten gunshot wounds at close range.
(Photo courtesy of the Austin Police Department)

Spent shells from a Glock 9mm were found near the body.
(Photo courtesy of the Austin Police Department)

Each shell casing was numbered and noted.
(Photo courtesy of the Austin Police Department)

Four more shell casings were discovered in the bedroom.
(Photo courtesy of the Austin Police Department)

Shots fired from the bedroom were embedded in the hallway wall.
(Photo courtesy of the Austin Police Department)

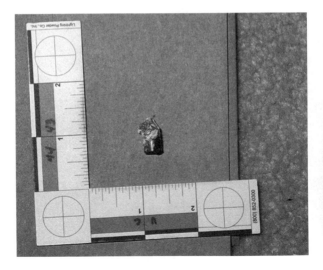

Glock 9mm shell recovered from the wall.
(Photo courtesy of the Austin Police Department)

Detective de los Santos found this card for the Top Gun handgun training and shooting center. *(Photo courtesy of the Austin Police Department)*

Glover purchased her Glock 9mm from Red's Indoor Range in Austin, Texas. *(Photo courtesy of the Austin Police Department)*

Rhonda Glover drove her RV to American Auto Rental where she rented
a Ford Taurus. *(Photo courtesy of the Austin Police Department)*

The Ford rented by Glover from American Auto Rental.
(Photo courtesy of the Austin Police Department)

Detectives measured the car's tires and photographed the tread to confirm identification of the vehicle. *(Photo courtesy of the Austin Police Department)*

The mileage on the Ford's odometer was also carefully verified.
(Photo courtesy of the Austin Police Department)

Police found Glover's business card, and that of her attorney, with picture of her son. *(Photo courtesy of the Austin Police Department)*

234

WE HAVE BEEN ONCE AGAIN SACRIFICED BY SATAN FOR THE SAKE OF MANKIND AND THIS IS THE LAST TIME IN OUR HISTORY THAT WE WILL HAVE TO BE WALKED ON BY

THE DEVIL. YOU SEE GOD HAS BEEN

WORKING ON THIS PLAN TO CATCH SATAN FOR YEARS AND IT TOOK THE REAL ESTATE IN AUSTIN AND MY INCOME LEVEL TO GET ME INTO THE HOUSE OVER THAT AQUIFER. YOU SEE GOD HAS MADE OTHER PEOPLE AWARE OF THESE CRIMES AND THERE HAS BEEN NO ONE STRONG ENOUGH OR FEARLESS ENOUGH TO COME OUT AGAINST BUSH.

BUT I WOULD LIKE TO SEE HIM FACE TO FACE , FAGET LITTLE SCRAWNY BULLY. I WOULD LIKE TO ROPE AND TIE HIM LIKE I DID WHEN I WAS A COWGIRL AND RODEOED.

I HOPE I HAVE A CHANCE. BUSH COME AFTER ME. JUST TRY IT YOU QUEER AND I WILL USE MY POWER TO ANIHILATE YOU IN SECONDS. YOU CANNOT STOP

GOD THIS TIME SATAN. SATAN

STANDS FOR SEXUAL AQUIFERS TAKEN ALL NATIONS.

YOU ARE NOTHING BUT A PUNK. A FREAKING CANNIBAL, BLOOD THIRSTY BEAST MASQUERADING YOURSELF AS THE MOST INNOCENT CARING PERSON IN THE WORLD. I ONLY WISH I HAD BEEN MEANER TO YOU.

"God has been working on this plan to catch Satan for Years," wrote Glover. She believed she was part of the plan. *(Photo courtesy of the Austin Police Department)*

Glover was convinced that her son was being cloned, and that Dana Bateman was somehow involved. *(Photo courtesy of the Austin Police Department)*

THAT WITCH SHE IS IN ON IT TOO DANA BATEMAN. I THINK SHE WAS THE WOMAN I CAUGHT WITH THAT LITTLE BOY THE DAYJC AND I WERE GOING TO THE MOVIES. SHE HAD A MAN AND A BLONDE LITTLE BOY ON THE SIDE OF THE ROAD WITH ONLY A DIAPER ON AND WHEN SHE SAYW ME SHE PANICKED AND TOOK THE BOY BACK INTO THE TRUCK. I THINK THAT MAY HAVE BEEN ONE OF THE CLONES OF MY CHILD OH MY WORD HE WAS ADORABLE. HOW AND WHY CAN THEY FEEL OKAY ABOUT THIS? I AM COMING AFTER YOU DANA I KNOW WHERE YOU ARE AND WHAT YOU LOOK LIKE. WATCH OUT LOOK ARUND YOU I AM WATCHING YOU... BE AFRAID BE VERY AFRAID OF ME AND MY

GOD.

Rhonda Glover's black leather Bible was taken as evidence.
(Photo courtesy of the Austin Police Department)

The Houston home of Glover, paid for by Joste, offered a stunning view.
(Photo courtesy of the Austin Police Department)

Expensive furniture and the best of everything in Glover's Houston home.
(Photo courtesy of the Austin Police Department)

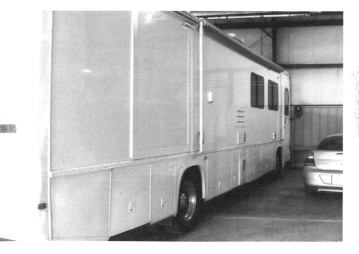

J66635937A
AGAIN THE MARK OF THE BEAST 666 JAMES
JOSTE AND GEORGE BUSH
F2 10 - FCK BAK /
"**F**" = CHRIST KING BAK BECOMING A KING OR
COMING BACK

J96G6G6G3D5F9J3D7HA=
9/JESUS AND 6/GOD
JAMES AND GEORGE
JOHN GACY
9J+6G=1B5F=15=1+5=6=1-5=4=6+4=10=A=10-
=6G=6+4=10+10=20+1=21=M=21+6=27=2+7=9J=2
+2=2C9J=29=U=2-9=7=7+7=14=1-4=3=29-
=26R=2X6=12=1+2=3D=3+1=4E=4X3=12+12=24=
4=2=24+2=26R MURDER JCJ HA

"The Mark of the Beast," Glover believed, was a biblical reference to
President Bush, John Gacy and Jimmy Joste. *(Photo courtesy of the Austin
Police Department)*

The enormous RV/motor home in which Glover made her "getaway."
(Photo courtesy of the Austin Police Department)

Assistant District Attorney Bryan Case. *(Author photo)*

Assistant District Attorney Gail Van Winkle. *(Author photo)*

The Travis County Courthouse where Rhonda Glover testified in her own defense. *(Author photo)*

Rhonda Glover back in her rodeo days. *(Photo courtesy of Rhonda Glover)*

Rhonda Glover: how she appeared when she met Jimmy Joste. *(Photo courtesy of Rhonda Glover)*

Cave X via the Regents School property was pure fantasy. "You couldn't break in with a crowbar using all your might," confirmed a Regents School employee. Concrete grating and a locking system impervious to break-in secured Cave X against intruders. "There are no incidents of trespass because trespassing is impossible. It is seldom that anyone enters the cave, except people from the Texas state agency that oversees the caves and the endangered species situation. One time they came to get in and we had misplaced the key. Well, even with the key, getting in is an elaborate security procedure. It took hours and hours using high-powered equipment to get that heavy concrete gate open. Anyone who thinks folks can sneak into Cave X is entirely mistaken. It simply can't happen. No one from the general public gets in Cave X."

According to Rhonda Glover, she and Rick Kutner investigated Cave X, and she proved that she wasn't crazy. "Rick moved to Texas to be with us, and saw Jimmy firsthand in his deranged state of mind. He would be able to correctly portray the danger I was in and felt that it would be me dead before too long. Rick came down from Colorado and helped Jimmy get somewhat together and presentable. Once I left him, Jimmy got worse and had not showered, shaved or eaten. The house was torn up and he said I did it."

Rhonda apparently forgot that she admitted taking a sledgehammer to the bathroom, and explained this to Austin police during one of her numerous emergency calls to 911. "Being as she said there were people hiding in her sink," remarked one officer, "I'm not surprised she took a sledgehammer to it."

"There are other entrances to Cave X that they are not telling you about," insisted Rhonda Glover in 2009. "Devil worshipers were entering it then, and I am sure that they are still doing all those evil things in there, to this day. I know what I know," insisted Rhonda. "These are satanic Devil worshipers, and Jimmy was the one."

"If Jimmy Joste was worshiping the Devil," commented a religiously devout woman affiliated with a Protestant denomination, "I could see why Rhonda would feel the need to protect herself and her child, especially with domestic violence running rampant."

Domestic violence is more prevalent than Devil worship, especially considering that the type of satanic cult activity described by Rhonda Glover was found primarily on movie screens and in fevered imaginations. Over twelve thousand accusations of Devil worship in America were investigated by Phillip Shaver, a psychologist at the University of California. There was no truth to any of them.

"What truthfully amazed me the most," admitted Rocky Navarro, "was that no matter how Rhonda acted, or what sort of nonsense was going on in her head, Jimmy loved her unconditionally. She may have been crazy, but Jimmy was crazy about her."

So dedicated was Jimmy Joste to preserving their tenuous family bond, he was ready, willing and fully prepared to take both Rhonda Glover and Ronnie and leave the country. Based on information shared with Detectives Walker and Faithful, Jimmy was fully anticipating the arrival in Austin of Rhonda and their little boy. He wasn't waiting to hurt them, but for all three of them to run away from home.

"That certainly seems to be the truth," agreed Danny Davis. "When you look at the stuff Jimmy did just before Rhonda killed him, it sure seems as if he was in the process of getting everything sort of in order for the three of them—Jimmy, Rhonda and Ronnie—to take off together. Hell, ask Joyce Imparato, she'll tell you what Jimmy was doing."

"I've known Jimmy Joste for about twenty years," said Imparato. "I have known Rhonda Glover for about fifteen years. Their relationship was very on and off. She was always taking his child and leaving, and he was always trying to keep her happy with money so she wouldn't leave. It was that way until he ran out of money. That was the pattern that had been going on for many years.

"I saw Jimmy a week before he died," she told Austin detectives. "He came to my door and rang the doorbell. He handed me a bag with a couple of items in it. These were gifts that I had given him over the last ten years. He said that he wanted me to have them, because he didn't want anyone else to get them."

"I'm going away," said Jimmy. "I don't know what is going to happen to my stuff, and I want you to have back this stuff that means a lot to me, so that I know that it's safe. I am worried about the disposition of my items after I leave, and if I give this to you, I know what you gave me is safe."

Imparato looked at the items, and felt a bit confused. "It was a couple of blankets that I had given him as a housewarming gift a number of years ago. Maybe one cost four hundred dollars, but it was an old blanket, for the most part, so I was confused on what he was talking about and why he would bother to bring it back to me. He said that he was leaving with Rhonda, and that he wanted to make sure that he got this stuff back to me, and it was important to him."

Joste began sharing some of his new business ideas. "He gave me a long laundry list of his business ideas," she confirmed, "and half the time I didn't pay much attention to his ideas, because they were all so grandiose most of the time, but he said he was leaving with Rhonda, and that he didn't know what was going to happen to the items in his home once he and Rhonda left.

"He said he was leaving, and that he was going to France to start a water company. Well, I knew Jimmy real well. And he knew that I knew that he tended to exaggerate some things. He started to laugh about it, and I didn't confirm with him if he was telling me the complete truth or not."

Joste left, but she saw him again about a half hour later coming out of the bank. "I was making a deposit late on a Friday afternoon, before four because that bank closes at four. We hugged, and I said that I would see him at dinner. He was acting as if everything was fine, but I sensed trouble. I tried to get him to have dinner with me," she recalled, "because I felt that something was wrong. Oh, he acted like everything was great. He was supposed to go to dinner with two other friends, but he didn't go. Instead, he returned to Austin. When he got there, he went around and gave other friends some things he wanted them to have, because he was definitely planning on leaving with Rhonda."

Alberto Hernandez, a carpenter who worked for Imparato and several of Joste's friends, also received an unexpected visit immediately prior to Joste's murder.

"Jimmy told him that he needed Alberto to come get everything in the Austin house, and that Alberto could have it all," related Joyce Imparato. "Well, Alberto said he would gladly store it for Jimmy, but Jimmy insisted that he wanted Alberto to have it. That is exactly like Jimmy. Jimmy's been like that for the twenty years I've known him. He was always incredibly generous to everyone. Jimmy also told Alberto that he was moving away.

"You know," added Joyce Imparato, "when I saw Jimmy later that same day that he came by my house, the Friday before the murder, he said that he had to get back to Austin because he and Rhonda were leaving together for Canada."

"Yeah, poor Jimmy thought he and Rhonda and Ronnie were all going to leave the country together," said Danny Davis. According to Imparato, Joste was expecting Rhonda and Ronnie to arrive precisely when they did. "He had withdrawn the last of his money, perhaps fifty thousand dollars out of the bank, and would use it to get them into Canada, out of the country, and establish residence."

Jimmy Joste's visit to Joyce Imparato explained many things, according to Bryan Case. "It sheds some light on the depletion of his assets. It sheds some light on why Rhonda would be coming to Austin, or he thinks that Rhonda would be coming to Austin in an RV—why he would think Rhonda would be coming over to the house. It explains any number of things as to what he was thinking was going to happen to their relationship. Jimmy was wanting or trying to get her to go away, and the three of them would have a family together. Jimmy believed it, but Rhonda knew it was never going to happen. Jimmy wanted to get back with Rhonda, and she let him continue in his belief."

This scenario is further validated by John Thrash, a wealthy retired Houston physician turned CEO of a thriving energy company, and executor of Joste's estate. "I knew Jimmy because I met him in the Houston area through my father, who is also in the oil and gas business. He knew my father first, and that's how I came to know him.

"He was a very dear friend," Thrash explained. "We socialized together often, up until I got married, then not as frequently. I met Rhonda through Jimmy, and we saw and socialized sometimes, but not as often as with Jimmy."

The very fact that Joste and Thrash were close friends further exemplified the personality and social circle of Jimmy Joste. "Philanthropy is an important and highly valued characteristic of their shared social circle," stated Houston journalist and author Steven Long. "John Thrash and his wife, Becca, are an excellent example of the high-society philanthropy of petroleum millionaires. Some folks in that social strata fund hospitals, education, engineering and technology research, or social services. John is one of the most respected men in Houston, and Becca is a relentless fund-raiser for the arts, board member for the Houston Grand Opera, the Contemporary Arts Museum and American Friends of the Louvre. The long-standing friendship between Jimmy Joste and John Thrash bespeaks volumes of their shared values, interests and common concerns."

Thrash, whose "cozy" home is a remarkably comfortable twenty-thousand-square-foot manse, sat in the Travis County Courthouse discussing the affairs of James Joste. "Jimmy and I discussed the idea of me serving as executor of his estate," said Thrash. "I learned definitely that he had done that after his death.

"Jimmy made an investment of five hundred thousand dollars in 2000 or 2001, in one of our companies in New York State," explained Thrash. "In 2004, that project was in intense multilateral litigation with AIG and the bank that was involved and a number of other partners, including us.

"This was not an asset that Jimmy could easily liquidate," said Thrash. "It was a private limited-partnership ownership, and it was not liquid. Liquid would be stock, publicly traded stock that could be sold on an open market. These were private interests in private companies, and so establishing their value, particularly in an instance where there is litigation going on, would be virtually impossible.

"It might have been two to four months before his death that Jimmy came to me and told me that he wanted to sell about a hundred thousand dollars of his share in that investment because he was getting married."

Thrash explained to Joste the difficulties involved in his request, and that it wasn't feasible at that time to anticipate being able to liquidate any of that investment. Jimmy Joste wasn't the only person in the

Joste/Glover relationship to approach Thrash about money.

"Some months before I saw Jimmy, I was on my way out of the office when I was told by one of our receptionists that Rhonda was in the lobby and wanted to talk to me. Since I was on my way out, I just walked to the lobby and we met in a conference room off to the side. I was surprised to see her. If we didn't have an appointment or had talked, it would not be customary for her to just swing by."

According to Thrash, Rhonda came by his office to request a favor. "She wanted to see if I would consider lending her some money. She was kind of vague as to the reason," he explained, "but it had something to do with taking care of her son and some other expenses. She wanted about five or ten thousand dollars, but I told her that I really didn't feel that I could do that and just kind of quickly excused myself."

Eventually, after Jimmy Joste's death, litigation was resolved, and his estate went from zero to $650,000, not counting the $350,000 diamond ring that was on consignment at Deutsch & Deutsch Jewelers in Houston.

On October 7, 2004, Austin police received a message from Susan Oswalt, an assistant district attorney in Travis County assigned to the 167th District Court. Ken Schaeffer, attorney for Deutsch & Deutsch, advised Oswalt that James Joste had purchased a ring on special order to give Rhonda Glover.

According to Schaeffer, the five-carat diamond ring was valued at $275,000, and Joste placed a deposit on the ring. This was consistent with pieces of a check found in the laundry room of Joste's house. That check, written to Deutsch & Deutsch, was for $27,768.25. When Rhonda turned him down, Joste tried to resell the ring back to the jeweler. They declined, but they did agree to try and resell the ring. Schaeffer thought it was still at the store, and advised Austin police that the jeweler had a claim against Joste's estate for the balance due on the ring.

Rhonda Glover did go to Deutsch & Deutsch and attempted to resell some other jewelry that Joste had given her. They refused, and she sold it to jeweler Hal Martin in May 2004. "Rhonda sold a TAG Heuer watch, a diamond bracelet and some junk jewelry," said Martin. "She also sold us two 2-carat oval diamonds. This was on two different dates. We gave her a total of eight thousand seven hundred twenty-nine dollars for those items."

If Rhonda was, as she claimed, a successful businesswoman in her own right, and Jimmy was kicking in $10,000 a month, it didn't make sense that she needed to pawn her jewels. "I returned a ten-thousand-dollar watch that Jimmy got me, and while I was doing that, I asked for my old watch back, which I had pawned, but they had already sold it. There were times when, just like everybody else, I needed money."

"Jimmy's will made lifetime provisions for Rhonda," said Thrash. "Rhonda Glover was to receive five thousand a month for life. Of course, she doesn't get the money if she murdered him."

11

It would make sense, at least in the mind of Jimmy Joste, for him to take the last of his available funds and head off to Canada with Rhonda and Ronnie. Canada protects people from being shipped off to face charges in countries that may not be as fair and just as Canada. Extradition law seeks to allow the surrender of an individual to criminal prosecution by another country for only the most serious crimes.

"The extradition process from Canada is designed to protect people from unfair and unjust prosecution," explained Fred Wolfson. "Whatever they want you for in the other country has to also be a crime in Canada, and punishable by two or more years in prison, or five years if committed in Canada. For example, in 1910, when Dr. Hawley Harvey Crippen was arrested in Quebec City for the well-publicized murder of his wife in England, he waived his right to extradition proceedings in Canada and agreed to return right away to England to face trial. He was tried and ultimately executed before the year was out."

Canada would have been a safe haven for them, or at least one can see how Jimmy would think so. Rhonda Glover tried to cross the border in Canada herself, following her vanishing act from Houston. The only thing that kept her from getting into Canada was paper tags on her vehicle. If she had successfully crossed the border, her family may never have heard from her again.

"Perhaps she figured she could go to Canada, and then have Jimmy send her money," offered one acquaintance. "Then again, if she were as nutty as she seems, she probably wasn't making rational long-range plans any more than she was when she took off for Kansas."

Arrested in Kansas, and transported back to Austin, Rhonda Glover's stay in the Travis County Jail coincided with the memorial service at St. Martin's Episcopal Church for James "Jimmy" Martin Joste. According to his published obituary, he was the perfect host who often cooked for up to twenty people at his mother's home several nights a week. He was known for his great sense of humor, and his ability to tell vastly amusing jokes.

"Oh, those dinners were spectacular," recalled Danny Davis. "Jimmy was really a fabulous cook. His mother was a wonderful, outgoing and charming woman. She was also feisty as hell. If you ever saw *Auntie Mame,* that's exactly what she was like. Generosity was a hallmark of the Joste family. No one, friend or stranger, went hungry if they came in contact with the Jostes. They were incredibly kind, outgoing and giving."

Jimmy's amazing love and devotion to his son, said the

obituary, *was evident to all his friends*. His brother, Kelly, asked that donations be made to the educational fund established for Jimmy's son.

In real life, "should" is often an unrealistic expectation based on flawed assumptions. "The criminal justice system is based on the premise that people understand there are rules, why they have to be obeyed, and if they aren't obeyed, then society has the right to come up with any number of options," said Legal Aid Commission lawyer Kearney Healy. "All of those things are irrelevant to [a certain segment of the population]. It's got nothing to do with good or bad—they just don't see it the same way. Planning, organizing and learning from past mistakes are not in their repertoire. They are egocentric, impulsive and very concrete in their thinking. Typically, they do not make connections between cause and effect, anticipate consequences or take the perspective of another person."

Cheryl Meyer, professor of psychology at Wright State University in Dayton, Ohio, is well-versed in Texas laws regarding insanity. "The insanity defense in the state of Texas is pretty well-defined. Did she know right from wrong? But even the most psychotic individual knows right from wrong. It's disappointing and points to the flaws in the insanity defense. It leads me to wonder, who is insane? What does that have to be for someone to actually be successful with this defense? Jeff Dahmer, for example, killed people and then ate his victims, and he was found sane, and he had no history of mental illness. But here's a woman with an extensive history of mental illness and who does something that defies any motivation, but she's not insane either."

One of the ironies is that individuals such as Rhonda Glover often make model prisoners. In terms of the justice system handling individuals with treatable mental illness, one of the things they fail to understand is that these people do very well in structured environments. Often people are fooled in the early stages of treatment into thinking somebody is doing really well, not realizing that they're doing really well because all the opportunities for them not to do well are taken care of in a structured program. There is a point where the individual with mental illness, if not monitored closely and correctly treated, falls apart again.

Being crazy isn't against the law, but murder is a capital offense. When the one accused of murder is mentally ill, a variety of factors immediately come into play.

"Popular misconceptions about mental illness are partially responsible for the railroading of mentally ill persons through the criminal justice system," stated Jeff Reynolds. "From arrest to the determination of competency to stand trial and beyond, a person's mental illness affects every stage of passage through the criminal justice system."

"Behavior associated with mental illness is often perceived as bizarre and suspicious," insisted private investigator Fred Wolfson, "thus drawing police attention, even if the person has not committed a crime. Untrained to recognize and handle mental illness, arresting officers and other staff inappropriately assume the arrestee understands such things as their Miranda rights. Mentally ill people are more likely to give a false confession, especially if they are delusional."

The concept of culpability is an important aspect of criminal law. Culpability signifies qualities such as consciousness, reason and responsibility. It is precisely these qualities that are disabled and distorted by mental illness, and therefore a gap exists between a mentally ill offender's behavior and his culpability.

"In cases such as Rhonda Glover's," said Wolfson, "the issue of mental illness can be raised in Texas as a mitigating factor. Mitigating factors are particular circumstances that are legally recognized to decrease a defendant's culpability and result in a non–death penalty sentence. Since untreated brain disorders can cause individuals to act in inappropriate or criminal ways, certain aspects of mental illness, such as a defendant's diminished capacity to appreciate the criminality of his conduct, and to conform his conduct to the requirements of the law, are codified as mitigating factors in capital cases."

The way that the criminal codes in Texas defined legal responsibility had to do with whether or not Rhonda Glover knew what she did was "wrong." This is a very difficult standard to meet, or explain. It grows out of a nineteenth-century understanding of the mind, and was crafted in an era in which doctors did not know even the vaguest things about the nature of mental illness.

The first famous legal test for insanity came in 1843, in the McNaughton, or M'Naghten, case. Scotsman Daniel McNaughton (often spelled M'Naghten) shot and killed the secretary of the British prime minister, believing that the prime minister was conspiring against him. The court acquitted McNaughton "by reason of insanity," and he was placed in a mental institution for the rest of his life. However, the case caused a public uproar, and Queen Victoria ordered the court to develop a stricter test for insanity.

The McNaughton rule created a presumption of sanity, unless the defense proved *at the time of committing the act, the accused was laboring under such a defect of reason, from disease of the mind, as not to know the nature and quality of the act he was doing, or, if he did know it, that he did not know what he was doing was wrong.*

The McNaughton rule became the standard for insanity in the United States and the United Kingdom, and is still the standard for insanity in almost half of the states, despite obvious flaws. "They didn't know much about any illness back then," added Jeff Reynolds. "They knew nothing about bacteria, and it never even occurred to them to wash their hands before performing an operation. Medicine has progressed since that time. And we now understand that one's suffering from mental illness, and even profound mental illness, such as psychosis, often leaves one unable to control her acts, even though she understands that they are wrong."

Realization of this fact led to what is known as the Durham rule, or "irresistible impulse." Monte Durham, age twenty-three, was in and out of prisons and mental institutions since he was a teenager. He was convicted for housebreaking in 1953, and his attorney appealed. Although the district court judge had ruled that Durham's attorneys had failed to prove he didn't know the difference between right and wrong, the federal appellate judge chose to use the case to reform the McNaughton rule.

Citing leading psychiatrists and jurists of the day, the appellate judge stated that the McNaughton rule was based on "an entirely obsolete and misleading conception of the nature of insanity." He overturned Durham's conviction and established a new rule. The Durham rule states *that an accused is not criminally responsible if his unlawful act was the product of mental disease or mental defect.* Alcoholics, compulsive gamblers and drug addicts successfully used the defense to defeat a wide variety of crimes, as it was too broad.

In response to the criticisms of the various tests for the insanity defense, the American Law Institute (ALI) designed a new test for its Model Penal Code in 1962. Under this test *a person is not responsible for criminal conduct if at the time of such conduct as a result of mental disease or defect he lacks substantial capacity either to appreciate the criminality of his conduct or to conform his conduct to the requirements of the law.*

The Model Penal Code test is much broader than the McNaughton rule and the Durham rule. The Model Penal Code test asks whether defendants have a substantial incapacity to appreciate the criminality of their conduct or to conform their conduct to the law rather than the absolute knowledge required by McNaughton and the absolute inability to control conduct required by the irresistible impulse test.

The ALI test also requires that the mental disease or defect be a mental diagnosis. In this way it manages to incorporate elements of all three of its predecessors: the knowledge of right and wrong required by McNaughton, the prerequisite of lack of control in the irresistible impulse test, and the diagnosis of mental disease and defect required by Durham.

Such a broad-based rule received wide acceptance, and by 1982, all federal courts and a majority of state courts had adopted the ALI test. While some states have since dropped the ALI test, and it no longer applies at the federal level, eighteen states still use the ALI test in their definitions of insanity. Texas is not one of them.

In 1984, the U.S. Congress passed, and President Ronald Reagan signed, the Comprehensive Crime Control Act (CCCA). The federal insanity defense now requires the defendant to prove, by *clear and convincing evidence,* that *at the time of the commission of the acts constituting the offense, the defendant, as a result of a severe mental disease or defect, was unable to appreciate the nature and quality or the wrongfulness of his acts.* This is generally viewed as a return to the standard of "knowing right from wrong," or as some term it, "a return to the ignorance of the 1800s."

There are some states where insanity is never a defense. Idaho, Wyoming and Utah have abolished the insanity plea. In general, people who are found not guilty by reason of insanity usually spend more time in mental hospitals than they would have in prison. People who lose spend more time in prison than they would if they had not pleaded insanity. The average sentences for those defendants are 22 percent longer than those who never claimed the insanity defense. Sixty-seven percent of unsuccessful insanity pleaders went to prison, compared to 11 percent of all felony arrests.

"At the time of her arrest, and after being returned to Austin to face charges," noted an Austin officer, "Rhonda Glover was incredibly delusional. Her grasp of reality, if it existed at all, was tenuous at best. In her mind she had been attacked by the Antichrist, defended herself and feared Joste's Devil-worshiping associates more than she feared prosecution under the law."

In a majority of cases, dangerous or violent behavior exhibited by persons with brain disorders is the result of neglect and inappropriate, or insufficient, treatment of their illness. Therefore, mentally ill offenders are by definition not the worst of the worst offenders.

What is exceptionally problematic is that crimes are primarily committed by criminals, and criminals share certain thought disorders common to sociopaths. Among these are traits of manipulation, dishonesty and lack of empathy. They never recognize the rights of others and see their self-serving behaviors as permissible. They feel entitled to certain things as "their right."

"Verbal outbursts and physical punishments are normal for them," commented UK health care professional Donna McCooke. "Based on my experience working with convicted criminals, they don't really see others as people—they see them as either targets or accomplices—and both of those become victims. They also tend to have no sense of guilt or remorse.

They are unable to empathize with the pain of their victims, having only contempt for others' feelings of distress and readily taking advantage of them."

Sociopaths are not concerned about wrecking others' lives and dreams, are oblivious or indifferent to the devastation they cause, do not accept blame themselves, but blame others, even for acts they obviously committed. Psychopaths, of course, are an even worse and more severe version and comprise a minority of sociopaths.

Most parents of children with sociopathic or psychopathic behavior are aware that something is wrong even before the child starts school, according to Dr. Robert Hare. "They are different from normal children—more difficult, willful, aggressive, and deceitful. [They are] harder to relate to or get close to. The parents are always asking themselves, 'What next?'"

Dr. Hare, who conducts training seminars for the FBI, pinpointed certain school-age traits as prime indicators of behavior indicative of sociopathic or psychopathic conditions—some of which are also manifested by correlated mental conditions.

"As I mentioned in my book *Without Conscience*, these hallmarks include repetitive, casual and seemingly thoughtless lying, apparent indifference to—or inability to understand—the feelings, expectations or pain of others, defiance of parents, teachers and rules, continually [being] in trouble and unresponsive to reprimands and threats of punishment, among others."

* * *

All the punishment or imprisonment, electric chairs and gas chambers, put together won't bring Jimmy Joste back for a joyous reunion with family, friends and his beloved son. If determined competent enough to aid in her own defense, Rhonda Glover would stand trial in the 167th Judicial District of Travis County, Texas, for the murder of Jimmy Joste, and could possibly face the death penalty.

12

No matter what the criminal charge against you, you don't have to prove your innocence. You are presumed innocent. The burden of proof is on the prosecution to prove guilt beyond a reasonable doubt. There is no burden of proof on the defendant. We begin with the assumption that the defendant is not guilty. That is what the American system of justice is all about.

"There is a gender bias when it comes to capital punishment, probably stronger than a race bias," said Victor Streib, a law professor at Ohio Northern University who tracks death penalty cases involving female offenders.

Women account for about one in eight murder arrests nationally, but only about one in seventy-two people on death row. Of more than seven hundred people executed in the United States since 1976, only seven have been women. Even advocates of capital punishment sometimes balk at the notion of executing women.

Considering Glover's history of mental-health issues

in the context of brain-based and/or hormonal-based conditions relative to criminal prosecution, the fact that if deemed competent to stand trial, she could possibly be sentenced to death, life or sixty years in prison is rather remarkable.

Christine English, for example, confessed to killing her boyfriend by deliberately ramming him into a utility pole with her car. She was freed, however, because she had PMS—apparently a valid excuse. Sandie Smith, a woman who murdered a coworker, was put on probation—with one condition: she must report monthly for injections of progesterone to control symptoms of PMS.

Sheryl Lynn Massip placed her six-week-old son under a car, ran over him repeatedly, then did it again to make sure he was dead. She claimed postpartum depression, and was given outpatient medical help.

"It's like there's something more valuable about women's lives," Streib said. "Women are also treated differently when they're victims. You always hear about the women and children killed in fatal crimes."

John Junker, a University of Washington criminal law professor, doubted that prosecutors would hesitate to charge women with aggravated murder, when warranted. "But they might be reluctant to ask for the death penalty, either because of their own attitudes about women or because of their assessment of what community attitudes might be," he said.

Other death penalty experts insisted a gender bias did not exist, claiming the discrepancy is more due to the kinds of murders women tend to commit. "They rarely murder in the course of violent crimes against strangers," said Elizabeth Rapaport, a University of

New Mexico law professor, and one of the nation's foremost experts on women and the death penalty. "I am not going to argue that there never has been a break cut for somebody because she's a woman, but the huge explanation is eligibility. Women very rarely commit the kinds of murders that statutes treat as aggravated."

Juries have traditionally been less likely to sentence women to death because of juries' and judges' preconceived ideas of women. In some of the older cases, noted Victor Streib, judges from the bench would say, "If you had committed this crime as a man, I would have sentenced you to death. But women are the source of all life—so how can I take your life?"

Lesbians don't get the same breaks as straight women, research has shown. The less traditional the woman, the less special consideration she received for her femininity. In some countries, Streib said, it is illegal to execute women. Russia is one of them.

As of 2009, Texas was still executing people, but the oft-told joke that Texas has a death penalty express lane didn't match reality. "It took a Dallas jury only fifteen minutes to convict Ronald Chambers of murder in 1976 after he robbed and shot two college students," stated Texas journalist and author Ron Franscell. "He was sentenced to die, but more than thirty-one years and three trials later, Chambers is Texas's longest-serving death row prisoner, and he's been there three times longer than the U.S. average of ten-ish years between sentencing and execution. In Texas, fifteen of the three hundred ninety-one condemned inmates have been on death row more than twenty-five years.

"Yes, Texas has the death penalty," commented

Franscell, "but it also staunchly maintains the rights of defendants such as Rhonda Glover. Texans are patriots, and the Bill of Rights of the U.S. Constitution, and the Texas Constitution, guaranteed Glover certain important rights during the criminal process."

These rights are not "legal technicalities," as some might suggest. They are a fundamental and vital part of a democratic and truly free society, and they have existed in some form for hundreds of years. They were developed over a substantial period of history as a response to tyrannical rule and unfair court systems. Such systems were used to jail or execute those who dared oppose the government or the state-sponsored religion.

The legal concepts and basic rights about which we are speaking came to America with the early colonists in the seventeenth and eighteenth centuries. Bold, freedom-loving heroes of the American Revolution, when forming a new government, insisted that these rights be included as a part of the basic governing rules of the United States. Essentially, the same rights were also adopted as an important part of the Texas Constitution after Texas gained independence and later became a state.

These rights include the rights to an attorney, the right against self-incrimination, the right to the confrontation of witnesses, the right to a public trial by an impartial jury, the right to a presumption of innocence and the right to a grand jury indictment in felony cases.

"You also have the right to *not* be prosecuted if you are mentally incompetent," remarked investigator Jeff Reynolds. "You can't prosecute someone who can't aid in their own defense or understand what's going on."

After three months of being locked up in the Travis County Jail, and not receiving any medications, Rhonda Glover was finally scheduled for mental evaluation in late October 2004.

Dr. Mary Anderson, a frequent court-appointed psychiatrist for purposes of competency evaluation, was appointed by the court to examine Rhonda Glover in October, and gave her report on November 2, 2004.

"For a competency hearing," explained Anderson, "I gather as much information as I can from as many sources as possible. First of all, I find out what they are charged with, and then pull together what information is available, such as their medical and psychiatric records, previous diagnoses, and I check out their chart from the jail. Then I personally interview the person, perform a psychiatric interview and perform what we call a mental status examination. [This] has to do with how a person holds conversations, and how they answer certain questions, such as do they know what the date is, the year, their name, where they are, and that sort of thing.

"I evaluated Ms. Glover October 19, 2004," Anderson testified. "It was determined that she was not on any medications, hence her condition was not the result of any inappropriate medications that could cause her symptoms. The problem I encountered in interviewing Ms. Glover," explained Anderson, "wasn't that she couldn't respond to the questions, or that she didn't make any sense at all, but rather that

I couldn't get her to focus on the topic. Her thought process was fragmented and she would go off on tangents.

"Ms. Glover has a history of being diagnosed with bipolar disorder and psychotic disorder, NOS," Anderson explained. (NOS is the medical acronym for "not otherwise specified.") "I reviewed various records from a hospitalization she had at Rusk State Hospital in 2003 for a couple of days. Rhonda Glover claimed that Rusk said there was nothing wrong with her, but records from Rusk Hospital indicate otherwise.

"Rusk reports that she experienced paranoid delusions," said Anderson. "She believed that others were out to harm her, and that her significant other and the president of the United States were out to poison her."

Anderson also commented on Glover's previous diagnosis of bipolar disorder. "Bipolar disorder is a mood disorder and there can be psychotic symptoms that go along with that disorder, be it mania or depression. Bipolar disorder is a treatable condition, however. The records from Rusk indicate that she was there only a short period of time, and there was not enough time to completely discover the exact specific nature of her psychotic disorder, which is why it is termed Psychotic Disorder, NOS. . . .

"Glover also has a history of substance abuse," commented Anderson. "Glover acknowledged a past history of alcoholism. She is clearly intelligent, and when structured, she is able to give factual responses, but if you give her more time, and a little more room, she promptly regresses. Her thinking becomes more disorganized and she keeps saying the same things over and over. In fact, once she regresses, it becomes increasingly difficult to get her to focus on relevant issues—for example, her defense in this case."

The court asked Anderson to explain. "She went off on a lot of tangents that were difficult to understand," said Anderson. "She talked about having to call the police, and that the police thought she was crazy. Her significant other was involved in cannibalism and she was convinced that he was involved in murder. It was all tangential and disconnected. She was so obsessive on disconnected items, such as her neighbor finding a shoe in the snow, and how this somehow proved that her significant other was involved in cannibalism and murder, that it was impossible for her to address the important issues of how her defense should be addressed."

Anderson showed the jury excerpts from Glover's videotaped conversation with Austin detectives in which her delusional thoughts and fragmented thinking were blatantly obvious.

"Do you need to narrate this video," asked Assistant District Attorney Bryan Case, "or shall we just play it as is?"

"Well, I've watched this tape several times, and this is just a short excerpt that will give a good example of the type of disjointed thinking that I'm talking about," she said, and the jury watched the videotape.

When it was over, Case said, "Dr. Anderson, please tell us what we just saw."

What they saw was Glover, in response to questions from Austin detectives, begin babbling about Cave X, the Bible, children in caves, her significant other and George W. Bush. "At some point you just go, 'Wait a minute. What does this have to do with what they asked her?' So you can see where it becomes hard to follow what the point is. How do these things connect? Well, if you try hard enough, you can perhaps see how some of the remarks could be related, and even if there are facts involved, it all has a delusional quality. What does the house construction have to do with what she is being asked? How is it that if we read the book of Isaiah in the Bible, we will know about her house in Austin, Texas? This is an example of a thought disorder, and that is something that is hard to explain, but when you see it, that is kind of what it looks like."

According to Anderson, Glover understood the charges against her, and the basic facts of the case, but Anderson did not believe that Glover was capable of working with her lawyer and actively participating in her own defense. "I think she has significant impairment. I don't think she is able to stay focused on the things she needs to tell him. She just can't keep from going off on all these delusional tangents. She keeps focusing on things that, in her mind, have great importance, but as far as her case goes, they are of no importance at all. In conclusion," said Anderson, "she is clearly not competent to stand trial. It is possible that with some treatment, she may be competent to stand trial in the future."

Incompetent to stand trial, incompetent to aid in her own defense, incompetent to communicate effectively with her lawyer, Rhonda Glover was sent off to North Texas State Hospital, originally named North Texas Lunatic Asylum. This is the largest state hospital in the Texas mental-health system, and provides psychiatric services for both the mentally ill and mentally retarded in North Texas, as well as the entire state of Texas.

It was possible that Rhonda Glover could have remained an inmate, or patient, at Texas State Hospital for the rest of her life—had she not been able to, against her most sincere desires, keep her mouth shut. Even with medical treatment, it took quite a while before Rhonda Glover became mentally stabilized to the point where she was deemed competent to stand trial.

"And it must be kept in mind," commented her attorney, "that Rhonda Glover was certainly not suffering from drug-induced psychosis while receiving mental-health care during her extensive period of treatment following her arrest. Drugs were not part of the equation of her mental-illness symptoms."

It was significant that the videotape of her confession to Detective Walker played a major role in the jury recognizing that Rhonda Glover was mentally incompetent. "The jury saw what she was like when arrested," commented Jeff Reynolds. "And it was pretty damn obvious that she was more than EDP. She was OOHFM, as in 'Out of Her Friggin' Mind.'"

Texas has one of the most restrictive insanity defenses in the nation. It is rarely used and almost never successful. If Rhonda Glover's attorney wanted to claim that she was insane, he would have to prove that she suffered from a severe mental illness, and that she was incapable of knowing right from wrong. Texas, however, does not give jurors definitions of "knowing" and "wrong."

"This lack of definitions," said Houston attorney Fred Dahr, "contributes to a vague standard, and often jurors are reluctant to find insanity when a defendant has some minimal appreciation of having committed a crime."

Texas, like many states, restricted the insanity defense after John Hinckley Jr. was acquitted by reason of insanity of shooting President Reagan in 1981. Hinckley claimed that he shot President Reagan to impress actress Jodie Foster.

The Mental Health Advocate, a publication of the Mental Health Association in Texas (MHAT), took a strong stance when examining proposed legislative actions pertaining to a plea of "not guilty by reason of insanity."

Accounts of individuals with mental illness committing violent crimes periodically fill the headlines, stated the *Advocate. In many cases, these men or women are found "Not Guilty by Reason of Insanity" and are sent to a state mental health facility for treatment rather than to a prison for punishment.*

The insanity defense is invoked in less than 1 percent of all criminal trials, and it is rare that there is a repeat violent offense. These cases, despite their rarity, or perhaps because of it, receive widespread publicity.

These rare situations often contribute to public misperception and stereotypes that stigmatize and label people with mental illnesses as dangerous and unpredictable, stated the *Advocate, even though the vast majority of people living with mental illnesses are not threats to the community and have never had contact with the criminal justice system.*

In 2004, the Senate Jurisprudence Committee of the Texas Legislature was officially charged to study insanity defense laws, specifically evaluating the impact of changing the defense of "not guilty by reason of insanity" to "guilty, but insane."

This initiative paralleled a movement in other states to change the insanity defense laws to make it possible to send the mentally ill to prisons and jails instead of mental-health facilities. Prison is for criminals, and there is no doubt that an overwhelming number of criminals' violent behavior is directly related to confirmed brain-based injury or illnesses. Rhonda Glover's violent behavior is not, however unique to a particular segment of the "mental patient in prison" population.

This group has been the subject of extensive scholarly study. *Rage or anger, overwhelmingly directed toward intimate or familial relations by the use of a firearm or sharp object, was the most frequent motive for murder,* reported Phyllis L. Solomon, Ph.D., in her published work *Characteristics of Persons With Severe Mental Illness Who Have Been Incarcerated for Murder. Most had been raised in households with significant family dysfunction, and/or extensive histories of substance abuse and criminality, and had received little treatment for their mental and substance use disorders.*

In the words of deputy prosecutor Gail Van Winkle, Rhonda Glover was a woman who did not fit that category as defined by Solomon. "She has known that she has had an illness since 1999. She has had treatment. She has been prescribed medication, but in her own words, she has admitted to you that she often did not take her medications. She didn't take her medications on July 21, 2004."

In framing Rhonda Glover's defense, the issue of her past history of mental illness, and medical treatment for her condition, could not be referenced. It could only be introduced as a mitigating circumstance when determining punishment if she were found guilty of murder.

The prosecuting attorney viewed Glover's illness as a nonissue. "Yes, she has a mental disorder," conceded Van Winkle, "a mental illness, but I submit to you that she is a scary individual, and you would not want her in your community. Her mental health, under these circumstances, and the opportunities that she has had, and her refusal to take her medication, and to mix her medication with illegal drugs, is actually aggravating."

Prisons are not an appropriate placement for someone suffering from mental illness, asserted the MHAT: *The prison system is not designed to provide an array of mental health services, and does not have rehabilitation as a primary goal. Individuals with mental illness need treatment, not punishment, in order to recover from their illness and integrate safely back into their community.*

There was another reason why the revision in the law was so strongly opposed by the mental-health professionals. A guilty conviction of any kind would make it more difficult for the individual to find housing or employment after release. *The stigma associated with a "Guilty" conviction could last a lifetime,* said the official position paper, *long after the individual's illness may have stabilized.*

The Mental Health Association in Texas opposed efforts to eliminate the "not guilty by reason of insanity" defense and replace it with any option that involves forcing an individual to be found guilty in order to get treatment. Instead, MHAT advocated for changes to the insanity defense laws that would more accurately take into account the impact and effect of serious mental illnesses on individuals who commit crimes while impaired by their illnesses.

"Some of the changes they proposed," remarked Denise Brady, MHAT public policy director, "included changing the current insanity law to allow the jury to consider whether the person's mental illness made them unable to comply with the law, or to understand and appreciate the moral wrongness of their action. We also wanted to eliminate the provision in state law that prohibits juries from being informed of the consequences to the defendant if a verdict of 'not guilty by reason of insanity' is returned."

The Mental Health Association in Texas also advocated for Jail Diversion Programs for persons with mental illnesses who come into contact with the law. *A revision of State laws that assures that mental illnesses are treated as any other illnesses,* said the Association, *will help remove the stigma associated with these disorders.*

What exactly constitutes "sane" or "insane" isn't always immediately obvious, as illustrated by the case of Andre Thomas. In 2004, Thomas cut out the hearts of his wife and her two children and put them in his pocket. Prior to his murder trial, he plucked out his right eye. Found guilty, and placed on death row, Thomas ripped out his other eye and swallowed it. Thomas is *clearly "crazy,"* a judge on the Texas Court of Criminal Appeals wrote in a concurring denial of his appeal, *but he is also "sane" under Texas law.*

"Here you have another classic example of crazy versus insane," commented Fred Wolfson. "After Thomas was arrested, they gave him medication and treatment to the point where he could communicate with his lawyer. Because he could do that, he was determined to be mentally competent to stand trial."

Inmates such as Thomas, sentenced to death, can only be executed if they understand what "execution" means, and the reason why they are being executed. Sometimes they must undergo mental-health treatment simply to get them well enough to be executed.

The whole concept of knowing "right" from "wrong" as the standard by which sanity is determined has at least one incredibly obvious flaw: Some defendants, such as Thomas, know killing is wrong but say God is telling them to do it. They know it is "wrong" by society's standards, but they are behaving in conformity with, they firmly believe, a higher standard— the Will of God. They honestly believe what they did was morally "right," because they were acting righteously on behalf of God.

Rhonda Glover claimed that she was never mentally ill, only overstressed and overmedicated, and that her psychosis on previous occasions was due to her ingestion of drugs. The reason she used drugs, claimed Glover, was to deal with the insanity of Jimmy Joste.

The way Glover portrayed the situation, and the way Texas law is written, it would be impossible for her lawyer to use "not guilty by reason of insanity" as a defense for shooting Jimmy Joste. The only possible way to deal with it would be to claim self-defense, that she was protecting herself. She certainly said that she feared for her life when Joste confronted her in the Mission Oaks house.

The United States Supreme Court, many experts agree, will have to make further rulings on the entire issue. So far, the court has ruled only that an inmate must be competent to be executed. The high court also ruled a mentally ill defendant cannot represent himself in court. The court has not ruled on whether an inmate may be forcibly medicated to render him eligible for execution. That issue may be ripe for the U.S. Supreme Court to decide. The court may also have to decide if it is unconstitutional to impose the death penalty on someone who is sane but mentally ill. So far, only a handful of states are even considering a ban on executing the mentally ill. Texas is not among them.

"There is something just horribly wrong," said Maurie Levin, an adjunct professor at the University of Texas School of Law, "with a system that permits somebody severely mentally ill to be found competent to stand trial or sane at the time of that crime."

"We need to change the law," agreed Bryan Shannon, a Texas Tech law professor, "because a mentally ill person may know their conduct is wrong but be unable to fully comprehend the situation because the illness affects his emotional state and thinking and reasoning ability."

"The presence of so many people with mental illness in prison calls into question the ethical and moral basis for society's assigning criminal responsibility to people with mental illness," said Jennifer Bard, of Texas Tech Law School. "Thus, the problem of adjudicating mentally ill people who violate society's criminal laws should be approached as a public-health problem." To deal with this problem from a public-health crises standpoint requires developing a global plan to address mental-health needs both before and after a crime has been committed.

13

With Rhonda Glover temporarily in a mental institution, those outraged over Jimmy Joste's death expressed concern that Glover was "getting away" with murder. The more hot emotions run, the less likely the appearance of justice.

Many people have the mistaken idea that if someone is found "not guilty by reason of insanity," they just walk free. That is simply not true. If the jury believes that, they will be reluctant to render the verdict of "not guilty by reason of insanity." What really happens is that the defendant is sent to a mental hospital. Admittedly, under current law, the length of that hospitalization is not determined by the court because the court cannot make rulings on medical matters.

Prosecutors oppose efforts to broaden the "not guilty by reason of insanity" defense. "The people who are truly mentally ill, to the degree that their functioning is impaired, I think they are protected by the existing system," said Karla Hackett, a Texas prosecuting attorney.

For two simple reasons, Rhonda Glover, even though mentally ill, could not use insanity as a defense for shooting Jimmy Joste, despite her delusions about Cave X, clones, human sacrifices and demons in her walls. She knew it was against the law to kill him, and she had a history of illicit drug use and drug-induced psychosis. Under Texas law if the illness is caused or worsened by "voluntary intoxication," such as drug or alcohol abuse, you don't get to claim insanity. "The majority of people with mental illness self-medicate with alcohol or other mood-altering drugs," noted Leonard Buschel. "Right there, you eliminate the ability to claim mental impairment by one of the symptoms of it!"

In 80 percent of the cases in which a defendant is found "not guilty by reason of insanity," it is because the prosecution and defense have agreed on the plea before trial, according to the American Psychiatric Association (APA). *The vast majority of people with a mental illness would be judged "sane" if current legal tests for insanity were applied to them,* the APA notes in its insanity defense fact sheet. *A mental illness may explain a person's behavior. It seldom excuses it.* Mental health is one of the most complicated areas of criminal law, poorly understood not just by the public but by most defense lawyers as well.

Theodore the "Unabomber" Kaczynski was mentally ill, and part of his mental illness was the inability to recognize or admit that he had mental illness. He was found competent to stand trial, fired his attorney, eventually pleaded guilty with counsel and was sentenced to life in prison. Similar to the Unabomber, Rhonda Glover also insisted that she was never mentally ill, when it couldn't be more obvious that she suffered significant mental instability.

Dr. Mary Anderson evaluated Rhonda Glover again in May of 2005. Glover's new attorney, Joe James Sawyer, was there for the evaluation, and Anderson spoke with him as well. "I also examined all the medical records from Texas State Hospital," said Anderson. "Glover was there from December 2004 until March of 2005. Her discharge diagnosis was psychosis, alcohol dependency and cocaine abuse. She was discharged with prescription for one hundred fifteen milligrams of Seroquel, an antipsychotic medication, to take at bedtime."

Medication has become a critical part of an effective treatment regimen for bipolar disorder and schizophrenia. Mental illnesses such as schizophrenia and bipolar disorder are serious, biological-based brain disorders. Physicians who treat these disorders need a range of options in order to find an appropriate treatment for their individual patients.

Mental illnesses such as bipolar disorder and schizophrenia cannot be overcome through "willpower" and are not related to a person's character or intelligence. Without adequate treatment the consequences of mental illness for the individual and society are staggering and can include: disability, unemployment, substance abuse, homelessness, inappropriate incarceration and suicide. General understanding of these illnesses and their treatments has improved in recent years as science has progressed.

"Glover thought of reducing the dosage," said Anderson, "because of the sedative effect, but decided to stay with the medication, and said that she was committed to a regimen of medication to relieve the symptoms of psychosis and also her bipolar condition, whether she felt she needed them or not."

On March 1, 2005, Rhonda Glover was again interviewed by Dr. Anderson, and, despite harboring the exact same delusions as the day she arrived at Texas State Hospital, she was determined to be competent to stand trial.

"Her speech patterns were normal," said Anderson. "She didn't seem suicidal or homicidal. She was able to acknowledge that some of the thoughts expressed in her letters to her mother and others could be considered crazy by many other people. Although she hadn't abandoned these thoughts, she had discussed with lawyer Mr. Sawyer that she believed that she could keep these thoughts to herself if her defense attorney advised her to do so."

By Anderson's admission, Glover still had the same bizarre delusions that made her incompetent. The only difference between Glover being competent and incompetent was the probability of her being able to hide her incompetence.

During this interview Glover obsessively and repeatedly talked about her previous attorneys and her mother's view of them. When she was told to put that aside, and focus on other issues, such as the charges against her, she was able to answer questions regarding the legal process.

Anderson reviewed documents from Texas State Hospital where Glover was interviewed for fifty minutes, and again for thirty minutes on February 5. Her medical records from previous hospitals were reviewed at Texas State, and they inquired if Glover was aware of any head injuries she may have sustained.

"She has no knowledge of any head injuries. She acknowledged that she had developed a problem with alcohol, and that she sought treatment for her alcoholism by going to the Betty Ford Clinic in 1999. She was arrested for driving while intoxicated in 1989. She told Texas State Hospital that she was an active member of AA, and denied any use of illicit drugs. Her mother, however, reported that Glover's treatment at Betty Ford in 1999 was for cocaine, as well as alcohol, and that more recently Ms. Glover had been using crack cocaine. She was involuntarily admitted to a psychiatric hospital on November 23, 2003, and she tested positive at that time for cocaine."

This was Glover's only known previous psychiatric hospitalization, and was triggered by her mother's concern for Glover's delusional thinking, including paranoid and grandiose content. Glover was kept for two days after which the court decided that she did not meet the criteria for continued involuntary commitment, although she had been prescribed Risperdal, an antipsychotic medication, and she had promptly stopped taking it.

More and more, Risperdal is not being prescribed for just schizophrenia or other severe mental illnesses, but for behavioral disorders in children and in elderly patients with dementia and Alzheimer's disease, including delusions, aggression and anxiety. (The Public Citizen, a consumer group, is worried by the safety implications that have arisen in various clinical trials, showing the dangerous effects of Risperdal.)

Glover sought outpatient treatment in 2002, and

continued staying in contact with mental-health services until 2004. She was diagnosed with bipolar disorder in March of 2003, and this was later changed to psychotic disorder, NOS.

"She received no medication while incarcerated," said Anderson, "but at Texas State Hospital she was placed again on Risperdal, but that was changed to Seroquel. She has been compliant with the program. She denied any mental-health problems, and denied ever being diagnosed bipolar. She was cooperative during the interview, but did often provide excessive and unnecessary details. She denied having any psychotic symptoms, such as hearing voices or having special powers."

Even though Anderson was now determining Glover to be competent to stand trial, she admitted that there remained characteristics to her thinking that Anderson defined as "of a suspicious nature."

Anderson revealed that "Glover knew who and where she was. She did, however, misidentify the season of the year. The report concludes with her diagnosis, once again, of psychosis, with alcohol and cocaine abuse, lingering delusional thoughts and moderate psychological impairment displaying ongoing grandiose delusions. Glover's social skills are impacted by her inability to be sensitive to the needs and feelings of others.

"Glover's new attorney, James Sawyer, had reservations about his client's ability to interact with him," reported Anderson. "She has an established history of treatment for serious mental illness. She is not retarded. It is essential that she receive ongoing psychiatric care. Failure to follow these instructions will result in a deterioration of her condition and a return to incompetency."

"In other words," said Fred Wolfson, "take her to trial as fast as you can before she stops biting her tongue and shows just how incompetent she still is."

One might think that if Glover was mentally incompetent on the day of her arrest, and for several months after, that she was also obviously mentally incompetent on the day she pulled the trigger. That might be true, but that was not the way the law worked.

Dr. Anderson's apparent standard for competency was that Glover could refrain from revealing the true degree of her incompetence. In short, hiding the symptoms was equal to not having the illness. (This sheds light on Glover's postconviction statements that there were important things that her lawyer would not allow her to talk about.) She was every bit as delusional as the day she was arrested, and to this day holds the same delusions as true and valid representation of reality.

"Had the rules regarding the insanity defense been different," commented one observer, "I'm sure the plea would have been one of 'not guilty by reason of insanity,' or 'guilty and insane,' whichever was allowable in the state."

In August of 2005, Rhonda Glover's attorney made a motion to suppress the videotape of her confession. She did not want that tape played at her trial. The argument was based on Texas law that says: *A statement made by a defendant during an examination or hearing on the defendant's incompetency, the testimony of an expert*

*based on that statement, and evidence obtained as a result
of that statement may not be admitted in evidence against
the defendant in any criminal proceeding.*

Douglas K. O'Connell, of the district attorney's
office, countered that argument, saying, "It is clear
that this law applies only to statements made by a defendant during a mental-health examination or
during a competency hearing. The statements in
question were made during an interview with Austin
police detectives."

Excluding statements made to a mental-health
provider preserves a defendant's Fifth Amendment
protection. In this case Rhonda Glover wasn't speaking to a mental health provider. In addition, Glover
agreed to the admission of the tape at her competency trial, yet now sought to prohibit its use at a trial
on the facts.

"A jury found the defendant was incompetent to
stand trial on November 2, 2004. No verdict or ruling
has ever held that the defendant was incompetent on
July 27, 2004, the day she gave her confession to Detective Walker. Dr. Anderson testified that a portion
of the video shown to the jury was an example of the
tangential thinking displayed by the defendant. Dr.
Anderson never testified that the defendant was incompetent as the time she gave her confession to
Detective Walker. Nor did Dr. Anderson testify that
she relied solely on the videotaped confession. Furthermore, Dr. Anderson did not testify that tangential thinking is definitive proof of incompetence. No
further discussion of this issue is warranted," said
Douglas K. O'Connell, assistant district attorney.

At the time of Rhonda Glover's arrest and trial,

Texas law required tests of mental competence at several stages:

1. Before trial: Defendants must be able to understand the trial process and be able to communicate with their attorney and understand the proceedings. A judge may make the determination at an examining trial where the defendant is represented by an attorney and may present evidence from experts. The defendant may request a jury decision.

2. At the time of the crime: If the defendant claims at trial to be not guilty by reason of insanity, he must prove he did not know his conduct was wrong while committing the crime. As in any criminal trial, he may request a judge or a jury.

According to a new report by the United States Department of Justice (DOJ), entitled "Mental Health Problems of Prison and Jail Inmates," more than half of all prison and jail inmates—including 56 percent of state prisoners, 45 percent of federal prisoners and 64 percent of local jail inmates—were found to have a mental-health problem. Many suffered from treatable disorders such as bipolar disorder.

Whether or not Glover's altered mental state on several occasions was due to overmedication or lack of medication is hotly debated, but the debate is between Rhonda Glover and everyone else.

"There is no real problem with being bipolar if you simply take your medication. If you neglect it, you have trouble," commented Fred Wolfson. "This isn't some big mystery, or some bizarre unknown in the field of mental health. There are bipolar folks functioning perfectly in all walks of life. You would never know they had a condition or an illness for the simple reason that they take their medication, just as people with a heart condition take their medication."

Travis County deputy prosecutor Gail Van Winkle agreed, and cut Glover no slack for her condition— a condition Rhonda Glover denied having at all.

"Think of what she did on July 21, 2004," said Van Winkle. "It was cold and calculated. Yes, she has mental illness. We all agree. There are many people in our community living with mental illness. There are many people out there in our community—our neighbors, our friends—who are bipolar, but they do not commit violent crimes. They do not take the lives of human beings."

Los Angeles prosecutor Robin Sax shared similar sentiments: "Everyone who commits a murder must have a personality disorder. The personality disorder makes him a murderer who should be punished."

Famed true crime author and journalist Steven Long took a divergent view. "I absolutely believe it is essential for the jury to know about the defendant's mental illness, history of mental health problems and treatment, or lack of it," Long said. "Suzy Spencer and I covered the Andrea Yates case together. If telling the jury the details of her treatment, and its absolute and utter failure, didn't prevent a Texas jury from sending her, of all people, to prison, how on earth can it taint a prosecution?"

Andrea Campbell, author of *Rights of the Accused,* and a diplomat and fellow with the American College of Forensic Examiners International, has admitted to being torn on this issue. While she believed that the mental condition of the defendant should be made known during trial, she didn't think they should be "cut any slack" for heinous crimes or felonies. The goal, she asserted, is to keep dangerous people out of society, be it by putting them in prison or in a mental institution.

"We are talking about far more than a cranky personality disorder," commented researcher Travis Webb. "What I've seen, Glover has a documented history of severe mental illness, intervention by Austin Police's EDP personnel and medical prescriptions for mental-health medications."

Crime author Kathryn Casey has taken the position that if people know right from wrong, and are capable of working with their attorney, the issue of mental health should not be raised when the jury is considering guilt or innocence. If raised at all, it should only be during the punishment phase.

There is no comprehensive basis of agreement on this issue due to significant gaps between what people believe, what the law states and what brain researchers have learned in the last few years. As for the entire issue of "right and wrong," murderers with antisocial personality disorder, narcissistic personality disorder and even borderline personality disorder understand the difference between what is right and what is wrong.

Outspoken journalist/filmmaker John Semander was not reticent to share his opinion on the topic. "I personally think a jury is too often shielded from pertinent details that would make their civic duty of assigning guilt or innocence a whole hell of a lot easier," said Semander. "Yes, I am aware that in all likelihood I am siding with the defense on this one. Odd for someone like me who is so vocal in his zero-tolerance rants against the insanity that is our nation's criminal justice system.

"The example [of the Rhonda Glover trial]," stated Semander, "seems to lean toward a prosecutor wanting to hide mental illness from a jury out of fear that it would elicit sympathy. For the same reason I could see a defense attorney wanting it brought up as an excuse for his client's criminal behavior. How many times do you hear about a poor victim getting their name dragged through the mud in an effort to establish some sort of pattern that might possibly cast a shadow of doubt on a defendant? Same thing as wanting a jury to hear about someone who thought they were doing 'God's will' when they machine-gunned a crowded bus stop. So, lay it all out for the jury and let them decide for themselves whether or not to totally disregard it. The bottom line is that too much information can work both ways. So if I'm on a jury, tell me everything there is to know about who's on trial and who they wronged. Tell me straight up so I can make an educated decision about their fate, based on the facts-as-they-are and not the facts-as-I-know-them."

Caitlin Rother, author of the best seller *Body Parts*, is an investigative journalist who has grappled with this same issue on more than one occasion. "The murder cases I find most fascinating to write about are the ones with complex psychological aspects to the crime and/or to the defendant," said Rother. "Yes, I think it's important for the jury to know all about a defendant's mental-health issues and history of commitments. How else can the jury determine the defendant's state of mind at the time of the crime?"

Rother has maintained that the jury should know of the defendant's mental issues during both the guilt/innocence and punishment/mitigation phases.

"Although some judges might disagree," she said, "I believe this would be even more important when the defendant believes God has commanded him to kill, which clearly shows deep delusional thinking, especially if that thinking is resolved after medication."

Rhonda Glover never received focused and comprehensive psychiatric treatment specifically for the reduction or elimination of her paranoid and delusional thinking. Her visits to mental institutions were either involuntary commitments or court-ordered commitments for the purpose of making her competent enough to stand trial for murder.

The involuntary commitments resulted in diagnosis, but as she was neither homicidal nor suicidal, she could not be held for treatment against her will. After her arrest the goal was not to eliminate her delusions, but rather to get her medicated to a point where she could agree not to mention them. "The ability to not mention your delusions," said Fred Wolfson, "is apparently the standard of competency in Texas."

"I am beyond competent," said Rhonda Glover. "I am on a mission from God. That's why people say I'm crazy."

14

Once Rhonda Glover was determined competent to stand trial, the process picked up where it left off. Everything would play out in the courtroom of Judge Mike Lynch. Both the defense and the prosecution started pulling together their witness lists. One witness that the prosecution felt was most important was Patti Swenson.

Prior to the trial Patricia Swenson received a telephone call from Rhonda Glover, who was inside the mental hospital. "She said that she knew that I was going to be a witness," recalled Swenson, "and Rhonda demanded to know what I told the police. I told Rhonda that I told the police that I believed that she murdered Jimmy, because she said that she was going to do it. Rhonda denied having said she was going to do anything."

"You did too," countered Swenson.

"You were drunk," said Glover, "you don't remember what we were talking about."

"I do, too, remember," insisted Swenson.

"We were at Mulligan's and you had been drinking,"

Glover reminded her, "so you don't remember what we talked about."

Swenson didn't mention Mulligan's. She didn't say where or when the conversation took place. Rhonda Glover, however, specifically identified Mulligan's, pinpointing exactly where and when she told Swenson that she was going to do something to Jimmy Joste.

"That is really tragically humorous," said Jeff Reynolds. "Rhonda calling Patti to tell her, 'You don't remember that night at Mulligan's when I told you I wanted to kill Jimmy.' If she didn't remember before, this phone call would certainly bring it all back home."

The trial of Rhonda Glover for the murder of James Martin Joste would take place in the courtroom of Judge Mike Lynch, a man of vast experience eager to explain what it was like to be a judge in Travis County.

"I have served as the judge of this court since 1993," said Judge Lynch. "Before that, I practiced law as a criminal defense attorney for nine years and as a prosecutor for five years. The One hundred sixty-seventh District Court is a felony criminal court. We handle cases for which a person, if convicted, could receive sentences ranging from six months in a state jail to life in prison, or in a capital murder case, the death penalty.

"This court has approximately eight hundred pending cases at any given time," explained Lynch. "Most of these are disposed of through plea bargain agreements—the defendant agrees to plead guilty and the state agrees to recommend a lighter punishment than if the case proceeded to trial. This process, while criticized at times, is the only way to move a massive docket like the one we have. As the judge, I preside over the actual plea of guilty to insure that the defendant understands his rights and exactly what he is doing. I also have the right to reject any agreement that I believe is unreasonable or not in the interest of justice."

A defendant can also plead guilty even without an agreement with the state and ask the judge to sentence him to less time than the state is requesting. In this scenario he must accept the judge's decision, even if it's not what he wanted.

"A defendant can plead 'not guilty' at arraignment and have his case tried before a jury," Lynch explained. "In a felony case there are twelve jurors selected, and the verdict must be unanimous. If convicted, a defendant has the right to have either the jury or judge assess his punishment. He must make this decision prior to trial. A defendant may also waive a jury, with the agreement of the state and have his case tried on all issues before the judge."

During a jury trial it is the judge's duty to oversee the proceedings, including hearings on pretrial motions, jury selection, presentation of evidence and argument of counsel, as well as provide the jury with the applicable law and instructions to guide their deliberations.

"In addition," said Lynch, "it is the judge's duty to maintain proper decorum in the court and to insure that a fair and orderly trial occurs. The judge must be impartial and evenhanded, regardless of the facts or situation, and he must exhibit this fairness at all times during court proceedings."

A district judge in Travis County also has several administrative duties. In addition to overseeing a docket of several hundred pending cases, each judge serves on a board that oversees the adult probation department and a separate board to govern the juvenile court system. Judges also serve on the Community Justice Council, Bail Bond Board and many other boards and committees dealing with criminal justice issues. District judges also oversee the formation, empanelling and operation of grand juries.

The position of district judge is an elected office in Texas. Each term is for a period of four years. In order to be eligible to serve as a district judge, a person must meet the following qualifications established by the Texas Constitution: be a citizen of the United States and the state of Texas, be licensed to practice law in Texas and have been a practicing lawyer or judge for four years before the election, and have resided in the district (Travis County) for two years preceding the election.

The 167th District Court has jurisdiction to hear any felony criminal case arising in Travis County, and that covers all manner of cases outlined above. With so many years on the bench, Judge Lynch had heard all manner of delusional nonsense. Part of his job in the trial of Rhonda Glover was keeping delusional nonsense away from the jury of Ms. Glover's peers.

Representing Ms. Glover were attorneys Joe James Sawyer and Dierdre Darouzzet. Attorneys for the state of Texas were Gail Van Winkle and Bryan Case. It was Case who read the indictment against Rhonda Lee Glover, which in part said that she *intentionally and knowingly caused the death of an individual, namely, James Joste, by shooting him with a firearm*. It was also

noted that during the commission of this offense, she
used and exhibited a deadly weapon.

    "How does the defendant plead?"

    "Not guilty, Your Honor," said Rhonda Glover, and
the trial was under way.

15

"Opening statements," Judge Lynch told the jury, "are not evidence in the case. They are kind of a setup or preview of what the lawyers believe the evidence is going to indicate to you. The idea of opening statements is to give you an overview, and put things in context. At this time for the state, Ms. Van Winkle, you may proceed."

Well-prepared and professional, Gail Van Winkle confidently outlined the case against Rhonda Lee Glover. She established the background of the Joste/Glover relationship, their fluctuating living situations, and told jurors of the Barton Creek Incident. "Jimmy Joste took responsibility for that," said Van Winkle, "and their relationship continued pretty much as it had before."

The state established that Jimmy worshiped Rhonda and showered her with material possessions. "By late spring or early summer of 2004," Van Winkle explained, "Jimmy Joste's financial situation had taken a turn for the worse. He was living in the Austin home he purchased for Rhonda, and she was living in a luxury condominium in Houston."

In the matter-of-fact tone with which Van Winkle calmly laid the foundation of the Joste/Glover relationship, she also put forth the premise of premeditated homicide. "During that same time period," said Van Winkle, "Rhonda Glover began planning Jimmy's murder."

The state then detailed Rhonda Glover's firearms training in both Houston and Austin, and her purchase of the Glock 9mm before getting to the all-important matter of Glover's conversation with Patti Swenson in the restaurant parking lot. This was the conversation where Glover ranted about her plan to seduce, mutilate and murder Jimmy Joste because he was satanic and a cannibal who was murdering children in pagan rituals with George W. Bush.

The jury of her peers before whom Rhonda Glover appeared never heard about Satan or pagan rituals. Everyone, including Rhonda Glover, agreed that the true nature of things leading up to her pulling the trigger were never made public.

"We didn't really want to get into all that," said the prosecution team several years later, stating that Rhonda's justification for murder was irrelevant. "The simple fact is that she absolutely did not shoot him in self-defense. It was murder, plain and simple. She killed him."

Joe James Sawyer, Rhonda Glover's attorney, was determined to convince the jury that it most certainly was self-defense, and that Rhonda Glover had every reason to fear for her life. The jury would have to see

Jimmy the way Rhonda saw him—a cruel and evil man with a marked propensity for life-threatening violence. One legal stumbling block to this portrayal was the ruling by Judge Lynch that there could be no elaborate detailing of drug usage by Jimmy Joste, or other negative portrayals of the victim beyond what was a matter of record, such as the Barton Creek Incident. This was because the state had made a motion in limine.

"This is a motion made before the start of a trial," explained Bryan Case, "asking that the judge rule that certain evidence may not be introduced to the jury in a trial. This is done to keep the jury from hearing possibly inadmissible and unfairly prejudicial evidence. In this case there was a motion granted by Judge Lynch that there would be no mention of bad acts about the victim."

Sawyer was barely two minutes into his opening statement when he said, "Jimmy Joste loves to drink and do drugs, and as in any relationship where drink and drugs are involved, or too many of them—"

Gail Van Winkle was on her feet in a heartbeat. "May we approach?"

"This was in our motion," Van Winkle said to Lynch, "any bad act about the victim. There is no evidence of anything in his system on the date of his murder."

"There is no evidence of anything yet," countered Sawyer. "This is an opening statement. I am absolutely allowed to reference that."

If Sawyer was going to say such things, he better have evidence that was both relevant and admissible. "This is his opening statement," said the judge to Van Winkle. "He is a lawyer who has practiced for twenty years. You have to proceed in good faith, Mr. Sawyer."

Sawyer believed his evidence would come in, and be admissible because "they go directly to motive. Ms. Van Winkle suggests that she killed him in cold blood. I need to link that up to why she got a gun and why she got the RV."

"Because he was using drugs?" Van Winkle was being sarcastic.

"There is a difference," countered Sawyer, "between reacting in fear and reacting in hate. As for Rhonda Glover always going back to him, it was him coming back to her."

Sawyer continued his opening statement in which Jimmy Joste was portrayed as a man of proven violence and abuse, a man who struck fear into the heart of Rhonda Glover, and a man whom Glover shot in self-defense. The evidence, Sawyer told the jury, would speak to them, and it would loudly and clearly say that Rhonda Glover was innocent of murder.

The trial's first day saw a rapid procession of prosecution witnesses as the state presented their evidence in logical order. One by one the secondary players in this tragedy took the witness stand. The jury heard the story from the beginning, starting with Paul Owen telling about his mother, Janice Van Every, and he going to the Mission Oaks residence to find Rhonda Glover, returning the following day and summoning the police.

When Van Every summoned police to the Mission Oaks home, she feared the dead body inside was that of Rhonda Glover, not Jimmy Joste. Rhonda's mother even asked if there was a dead child inside as well. The implication being that she and Van Every believed it possible that Jimmy Joste would murder both Rhonda and his own son. The reason they considered that possibility was because of all the horrid things said about Jimmy by Rhonda in the past year or so. Joe James Sawyer did his best to get this fear of Jimmy in front of the jury when Van Every was on the witness stand, but when he raised the question, the state objected on the grounds that it was irrelevant.

"Objection sustained," said Judge Lynch. Rhonda's aunt and mother fearing that Jimmy might have killed Rhonda and her son was not relevant to the jury deciding whether or not Rhonda Glover fired the Glock 9mm in self-defense on that date, at that time and under those circumstances.

Glover's cousin, aunt and mother were not allowed to mention the reason why Van Every and her son were looking for Rhonda Glover because she had run away with her son rather than surrender him to her mother as ordered by the court. The fact that Glover had been on the run for many months, with her whereabouts unknown, was not revealed during the guilt/innocence phase of the trial.

Austin police officers and crime scene personnel testified about finding Jimmy Joste's body, and jurors were provided numerous visual aids detailing the location of the residence and the layout of all the rooms. Photographs, including aerial views, Google Earth pictures, and crime scene pictures were all entered as evidence, as were the logs of Rhonda

Glover's visit to Red's and Top Gun, the contracts for both the auto rental and the RV rental, and every other conceivable receipt or piece of paper relevant to the case. The Glock, shell casings, and the flower-print sundress were all entered into evidence.

Everyone from the taxi driver who brought Glover back to the Barders' home, to the employee who sold Glover her final box of bullets, told their story in Judge Lynch's courtroom. The state also called Rocky Navarro and Danny Davis to the stand, eliciting testimony about Jimmy Joste's personality, character and complete love and dedication to Rhonda Glover.

Rocky Navarro testified that Jimmy Joste was submissive and "worshiped" Rhonda Glover. Rhonda's attorney, eager to portray Joste as a dangerous man, confronted Navarro on cross-examination.

"You would agree with me that someone who worships a woman," asked Joe James Sawyer, "certainly would not beat her?"

"That is correct," agreed Navarro.

"I'm sure you know that on at least one occasion Mr. Joste was hauled off to jail for doing exactly that?"

"No," replied Navarro, "I didn't know that. It would be hard for me to believe."

"Awfully hard," agreed Sawyer, "because the guy you know was an easygoing, very open, warm human being. You thought he was a pretty submissive guy, and laid-back."

"Yes, sir."

"Of course," concluded Sawyer, "it might stand for the proposition that people wear two faces all the time, the face we present to the public world and the one we wear when we are alone or with our families."

Joe James Sawyer was bolstering his original concept, put forth in his opening statement, that Jimmy Joste was two-faced, giving the public a persona of gentle kindness, but a drunken, abusive brute in private. He took the same approach with Danny Davis, and Sawyer's sidebar sparring with Bryan Case provided additional courtroom drama.

"Did Jimmy like to hunt?" asked Case.

"No," replied Davis.

"Did Jimmy own guns?"

"No, sir. He hated guns."

"And regarding Jimmy's personality," asked Bryan Case, "was he an aggressive or passive person?"

"Passive," answered Davis.

"Can you say that with complete confidence?"

Sawyer was on his feet. "I don't care with what confidence he says it. How on earth is that question relevant or probative to this jury? Object."

"Sustained," ruled Judge Lynch, and Case rephrased his question.

"Would you describe him as a docile person?"

Sawyer objected, calling out, "Same question with sunglasses on!"

On cross-examination Joe James Sawyer picked up on the entire docile issue, asking Danny Davis, "Docile, decent, good men don't go around beating the hell out of their wives, do they?"

"I don't think Jimmy could beat Rhonda up, sir," responded Davis.

"Then I think it would be an absolute shock to you—"

It was Bryan Case's turn to voice objection. "I object to any trashing of the victim. There has been no evidence that he did such, except through the mouth of the defendant!"

"The wicked flee who none pursueth," said Sawyer, paraphrasing Proverbs 28:1. "Your Honor, I'm going to ask a question that is in evidence."

"I will see if there is evidence." It wasn't the judge answering—it was Case.

"Yes, we will," snapped Sawyer.

Judge Lynch had enough. "Listen, listen, listen, lawyers! Address the court, not each other from your seats. Address the court. You may carry on, Mr. Sawyer."

"Now, I suppose it would shock you . . ." Sawyer picked up exactly where he had left off.

"Your Honor, I object," proclaimed Case, "to these sidebar remarks, and I think that it is improper—"

Judge Lynch's aggravation was increasing exponentially. "I'll see the lawyers at the bench for what I hope is the last time . . . with this witness, anyway." Lynch stopped the trial more than once to lecture the attorneys regarding their interpersonal sparring, and the lack of progress in moving the trial forward. It seemed as if no witness could speak more than a few words without the need for another huddle at the bench, or the jury being sent from the courtroom.

* * *

The entire trial was an uphill battle for Rhonda Glover's lawyers, but they did have the Barton Creek Incident on their side—the one indisputable record of Jimmy Joste pleading no contest to a charge of domestic violence against Rhonda. They would need to raise reasonable doubt, and Joe James Sawyer knew it was only a matter of time before Gail Van Winkle would call Patti Swenson to the witness stand. He knew what was coming and he didn't like it. The prosecution previewed Patti Swenson's testimony in their opening remarks, asserting that it would establish that Glover planned the murder far in advance. Sawyer strongly objected to the jury hearing only about the threat, not the reason behind it.

"The state's closing argument in this case," complained Sawyer to Judge Lynch, "is going to be that she had the intent to kill Jimmy Joste as early as the time that she spoke to Swenson, and that the only thing she changed was the method of execution. They're going to say, in fact, she was contemplating murder from probably even before the time she spoke to Swenson all the way through July. That would mean that there was continuing intent and plan to kill Jimmy. This is how they're going to use it. That is going to mislead the jury because they will never have a chance to understand whether this was a statement made out of simple exasperation, whether it was a statement made as a result of the anger of the moment, and whether it constituted any real plan or intent. This is the way in which it is going to mislead the jury. They're going to say there is no question of self-defense in this case. They are going to say that this woman always planned to kill him, and that she was just determining the method of execution, but when she went in there on July twenty-first, it was finally the culmination of this plan that she had made, this continuing course of conduct that culminated in the murder."

Sawyer argued that the jury was entitled to hear all the conversations Glover and Swenson had that day in order to put Glover's scary comments about cutting off Joste's penis into perspective. "I believe the jury is entitled to hear all the conversations," said Sawyer, "so that they can sort it out, separate it out, and determine that there wasn't an ongoing plan. Without it, obviously, the state has the advantage of saying that the only thing she changed was the method in which she executed him."

Glover, in her conversations with Swenson that day, said many more things other than her idea of cutting off Jimmy's penis. "I noticed a change," Swenson said when questioned outside the presence of the jury, "a dramatic change in her behavior and her ideas by the things she was saying to me that day. Rhonda said she was scared because there were things going on in her life regarding Jimmy that she didn't have any control over, and they were affecting her and her son, and she was concerned for their safety. She told me that she learned that Jimmy was the Devil, and that he was into child pornography, and that he had sexually abused their son. Again she said Jimmy was a demon, and she feared that he was harming young children, and that she had some pictures or something that seemed to validate that."

"So, basically," said Joe James Sawyer to Judge Lynch, "Rhonda was telling her that Jimmy was the Devil, that he was into porn, hurting kids, and this other stuff—and that was the reason why she wanted to cut off his penis."

"There was another conversation I had with Rhonda," elaborated Swenson, "where she said other things that were strange too. It was when I went to Montgomery County to be supportive of her in custody of her son. She opened the back of her Suburban and showed me some pictures she had taken of the ductwork in the house."

The photographs of ductwork, Glover told Swenson, showed there was possibly the body of a child hidden in it. "Rhonda became increasingly erratic every time I saw her, and by 'erratic' I mean that now she was saying stuff like Jimmy was into cannibalism and Satanism. Well, this obviously concerned me. I was concerned for her, for her son and for Jimmy. I mean, it was so strange what she was saying. It didn't sound at all like the Jimmy I knew. And the whole time Rhonda kept saying how afraid of him she was. How afraid she was of Jimmy because of the cannibalism, Satanism and all that."

Bryan Case and Gail Van Winkle did not want the jury hearing any of Rhonda Glover's bizarre statements, other than the one about cutting off Jimmy Joste's penis. Sawyer wanted the jury to know the entire conversation so they would get a clear idea not only of the conversation in full, but for a clear idea of just how irrational his client actually was.

"Tell me," said Judge Lynch to Case and Van Winkle, "is there a rational reason why you don't want the jury to hear the rest of the conversation? Why don't you want it in?"

The reason was this: In a case of self-defense, there is what is called the "reasonable person standard."

The questions put forth in the "reasonable person standard" are "What would a reasonable person do in this situation?" and "Would a reasonable person have shot Jimmy Joste at that time, and under those conditions?"

"If her irrational thoughts rise to the level of insanity," said Van Winkle, "then she should plead insanity, and if they do not, then she is held to the reasonable person standard."

"Exactly," agreed Judge Lynch.

"Or," continued Van Winkle, "if she really believes that he was into child porn and child sexual abuse, that isn't a defense to kill him."

Sawyer was adamant about having the whole conversation in front of the jury, and kept hammering away at the issue with all his might. "Meanwhile," said Fred Wolfson, "Rhonda was complaining to her lawyer that the jurors were not being told how much Swenson and she drank that night."

"Let me cut to the quick so that we all know," said Sawyer. "Ms. Van Winkle elicited from Swenson the statement about cutting off Jimmy's penis. I think I am entitled to the entire statement, not just part of it."

"What is it?" asked Lynch.

"She thought Jimmy was a devil. She believed that he was a cannibal! Yes, a cannibal! And they were engaging in satanic worship!"

That's what Sawyer wanted the jury to hear, that's what he wanted the jury to know. "It is part of the same conversation," he argued, "the same ongoing conversation."

This was Sawyer's way of getting the whole bizarre picture before the jury. Not only would the entire conversation give a sense of perspective to Rhonda's scary plan, but would also certainly put the reality of Rhonda Glover's paranoid delusions in front of the jury. He was forbidden from telling them directly about Glover's strange beliefs. If it were to come out in the guilt/innocence phase of the trial, it had to come out in a manner such as the conversation with Patti Swenson.

The situation faced by Sawyer is one that many experts find troublesome. "When I was a psychiatric resident," said Dr. Marc Feldman, clinical professor of psychiatry, and adjunct professor of psychology at the University of Alabama, "I was taught that mentally ill individuals had no greater propensity toward violence than normal people. But that is now known not to be true. It is still the case that the best predictor of violence is a past history of violence, but mental illness—especially when involving hallucinations or delusions—does serve as a potential warning sign. Therefore, it seems to me that in order to understand a case fully, a jury needs to have complete information about any history of serious mental illness, particularly if it has led to police detention, commitment, et cetera. It is vital," insisted Feldman, "that the jury has this information during the guilt/innocence phase."

In Feldman's view, if the criminal behavior was driven by religious delusions, and if serious mental illness had been "a kind of background music in her life, [then] to exclude this information could result in an unfair verdict."

Judge Lynch understood what Sawyer was upset about, and turned to Case and Van Winkle. "How is he supposed to defend against what you elicited from the witness?" he asked, referring to Swenson telling of Rhonda wanting to cut off Jimmy's penis. "How is he to defend and say that is not what she intended to do? You put it in to show intent."

"Yes," said Van Winkle, "she intended to kill him."

"She said she was going to kill him," added Case.

"She did kill him," confirmed Van Winkle.

Judge Lynch agreed with Sawyer 100 percent as to his reasons, and his concerns. The problem, according to Lynch, was that because Swenson took Glover's threat seriously, probing more into the conversations of the day was not going to advance Sawyer's understandable agenda that it was all part of one big irrational blathering binge by a mental patient. For that reason, and despite the judge's sympathy for Sawyer's position, he ruled in favor of the prosecution.

Lynch's ruling on the issue upset both Sawyer and his client. "I think the jury needed to know the whole story. The judge," complained Rhonda Glover, "flat out refused the opportunity to tell the entire conversation we had that night. Patti is no friend. My jerk lawyer let her get up there and say lies about me. That whole thing about cutting off his penis was something she made up to get even with me. Patti had been drinking all day and night, and she closed the bar down. My lawyer could have picked up on that and said, 'Okay, how is it that you can drink all day and night and still say you recall all of what you heard Rhonda say?' That right there," Glover insisted, "would have put that in the jury's mind. They should have heard the whole story, and they should have known how drunk Swenson was, and all that. They could have made a note of that," complained Glover, "but the jury was not allowed to take notes."

"The state," said Judge Mike Lynch, "is opposed to

note taking because of the distraction, and because a number of instructions are required, and because we didn't allow voir on it as required by the rules."

Glover's attorney, the prosecutors and the judge all had a little conversation off the record. End result: no notes. "One more example," said Glover, "of how things were not fair. I am very perceptive. I notice things, and I'm certainly not crazy, dishonest or delusional. Jimmy was the one who was out of his mind on drugs."

Other than the allegation in Sawyer's opening remarks that Joste was a heavy drinker, drug user and abuser behind closed doors, negative remarks about Jimmy Joste were off-limits. It wasn't Jimmy Joste who was on trial, and whether or not he consumed drugs, drank heavily or had child pornography on his computer was meaningless to the jurors whose job it was to determine whether or not Glover shot him in self-defense. Any attempts to portray Jimmy Joste as an evil man who "needed killing," or impugn his reputation beyond any arrests or convictions for domestic violence committed against Glover or their son, were strictly verboten.

Friends and family of Joste and Glover knew full well that drugs had taken their toll on the couple well before Rhonda pulled the trigger. "I've known Rhonda for a long time," said Marty Snitkin, "and can tell you that with her being bipolar, and mixing drugs, and Jimmy too, that she became totally delusional. Jimmy turned into toast."

"The whole issue of past deeds and bad behavior was a continual battle throughout the entire trial," recalled Wolfson. "Even though there was not supposed to be any mention of the drug stuff, or some of the rather disturbing yet unverified allegations Rhonda wanted brought up, these things kept creeping in. If there was even the slightest possibility that a witness was about to touch on a forbidden topic, the attorneys were on their feet, voicing objections."

Another battleground was the interpretation of crime scene evidence. Where Rhonda was standing when she pulled the trigger was a matter of much contention. If she was pursuing Jimmy down the hall, or standing over his dead body when she shot him, the credibility of self-defense would suffer greatly. Taking the stand were the recognized experts on analysis of bloodstains and ballistics, including William Gibbons, who, at the time of the trial, was lab director with the Austin Police Department.

"I've been with the Austin Police Department for nine and a half years," said Gibbons. "And I've been director of the crime lab for three years. The crime lab consists of seven disciplines. Firearms, toolmarks—we have a crime scene unit. We have forensic chemistry, which is narcotics analysis. We have DNA labs. We have a polygraph section and an evidence room. Personally, I am a bloodstain pattern analyst."

One doesn't become a bloodstain pattern expert in two weeks or two years. "I was nine years at the Nueces County Sheriff's Office in Corpus Christi, Texas," Gibbons said. "Then I went to the Corpus Christi Police Department, where I was a crime scene investigator and assistant supervisor for about six years, until 1996, which is when I took the job here as the manager of the Crime Scene and Latent Print Unit for the Austin Police Department. I have approximately thirty-two hundred hours of clock-hour training in crime scene investigation, and two hundred of those hours are in the area of bloodstain pattern analysis."

Gibbons spent two years in a mentorship program with an experienced bloodstain analyst in order to become proficient in the discipline.

"What I would like you to do, Mr. Gibbons," said Bryan Case to his witness, "is explain to the jury some of the key concepts of bloodstain analysis, along with a short explanation so they can understand why you make the determination of where the victim was shot, what direction they were going—and that sort of thing."

"By using calculations," said Gibbons, "we can measure a bloodstain and determine at what degree that that bloodstain struck the surface, and then find a point of origin where that bloodstain originated from. We also look at the size of the stains. The size of the stains tells us the type of force that was involved when the bloodstain was produced. And a large stain," explained Gibbons, "was usually the result of gravity and sustained blood loss in one place. There is also what we call medium-velocity impact spatter. It is smaller in size. In high-velocity stains we can determine from the shape of the stain what the point of origin was."

"If the bloodstains look random, it is because somebody is moving," Gibbons testified. "If the spots are elongated with tails pointing a certain direction, those are high-impact stains. In other words, we had the few stains of the door of the bedroom, and then as you go through the hallway, you start to have more blood. Putting it in layman's terms," said Gibbons, "what we have is a victim moving to the hallway as he started to lose more blood, and so, you know, common sense tells us that [the big pool of blood] is where he came to rest. At some point, before he fell to the ground, he was standing, dripping blood, and then he fell over. I can tell you that because of the drip patterns of the bloodstains on the carpet. I can't tell you how long—how many seconds or whatever—that he stood before he fell. If you look at the picture of the bloodstains, you can see that they start at the bedroom door, and then they get more random as he goes down the hall, and then more concentrated when he finally falls over. We can, from the movement made inside the scene, make an opinion what the occurrences are in that scene."

Gibbons was asked to deliver some ballistics testimony, but Mr. Sawyer objected. "If we're going to have ballistics testimony," said Sawyer, "it has to come from someone with ballistics knowledge who is qualified to give answers, so I'm going to object to it."

Bryan Case then showed Mr. Gibbons pictures of the bloodstains and asked him to explain them. According to Gibbons, Joste was first shot in the bedroom, near the entry door. The bloodstains indicated that Joste then moved from the bedroom into the hallway as the shooting continued. "Basically, the victim," said Gibbons, "was in an upright position or near an upright position in or around the doorway. He started to work his way through the hallway. We see that from the increased blood concentration. At some point there was a bullet that went through him and into the wall while he was traveling down the hallway. Basically, he was shot in the hallway, and that is what caused the high-velocity impact stains. He starts to slow down, which is indicative of a gunshot injury. He actually stopped, staggered a little forward, stops for a few seconds, and then he goes to the ground."

16

Roberto Bayardo, M.D., the chief medical examiner for Travis County, testified regarding the autopsy performed by Dr. Peacock. "There were a total of thirteen gunshot wounds to Joste's chest, abdomen, arm and groin areas. Of the thirteen wounds," Dr. Bayardo said, "three were exit wounds. This indicates that Joste was shot ten times.

"Gunshot wound number one was in the chest," Bayardo testified, "and this was through and through. The bullet exited out the back. There was a gunshot wound on the right side of the abdomen, and there was another one, that makes three. There was a gunshot wound to the right lower portion of the abdomen, just above the genitalia. This makes number four there. There were two gunshot wounds together by the left groin. There was also a gunshot wound on the right hip. Gunshot wound number eight was through the right hip, and wound number nine was through and through the left wrist, and there were three gunshot wounds over the right elbow with one of those being an exit wound. There was another gunshot wound of the right upper back that was the exit wound from the chest area."

Gail Van Winkle asked Bayardo if during the course of an autopsy, there was an attempt to determine trajectory, or the tracking of the bullets.

"Yes, we do that."

"Was Dr. Peacock able to do that in this case?" asked Van Winkle.

"No, because of the condition of the body, that was extremely difficult. The body had become decomposed. There was multiple damage to his internal organs, and that sometimes is a factor in determining trajectory."

According to Dr. Bayardo, the specific internal damage to Jimmy Joste included both lungs, heart, liver, urinary bladder, intestines, spleen, aorta, ribs and his spine. "She recovered six bullets and three small fragments from the body," testified Bayardo. "One was recovered from the right lung. Another was recovered from the diaphragm inside the chest, another was recovered from the back of the eighth left rib, another from the inside of the pelvis embedded in the bone, another from the spine, another from the right chest, and then there were three small fragments that she doesn't make mention of exactly where she found them."

"Is it possible to determine whether or not a wound is a close range, distance range or medium range?" asked Van Winkle.

"Most of the time, yes," he replied.

Van Winkle was asking this question in an attempt to establish that the final six shots, and especially the shots to the groin, were delivered at close range, with Rhonda standing over Joste's body.

"How we do that," Bayardo explained, "is measure the distance based on the presence of gunpowder residue found around or inside the gunshot wound. There are three categories for this—contact, close range and undetermined distance. With the contact type, the entire residue is in the wound. The close-range wound has residue outside the wound and is characterized by powder, smoke or stippling by the gunpowder flecks. The distant or undetermined is the type when there is no gunpowder residue—that depends on the type of gun and ammunition, but usually farther than three feet you don't expect to see any gunpowder residue around the wounds."

In the specific case of Jimmy Joste, the body was so decomposed and discolored that it was impossible to make any determination on the distance from which the shots had been fired. There could be some conclusions made, however, on the position of the body relative to the position of the shooter, based on the angle of the wound and where the bullet was found.

Questioned regarding the wounds to Joste's hip and groin, Bayardo testified that the wounds were consistent with Joste lying down or almost lying down, but basically horizontal. To say with absolute precision that Joste was lying on the ground while receiving the final six shots was impossible, but Bayardo acknowledged that the wounds were consistent with that sort of body position. Bayardo felt confident enough, however, to state, "Joste was shot at least once while he was lying on the ground. There were six shell casings from six bullets near the body. Another four shell casings were found in the bedroom."

That was Bayardo's professional opinion as medical

examiner, but Bayardo was not a ballistics expert in general, nor an expert of the Glock 9mm specifically. Rhonda was using a Glock 9mm, which has certain characteristics. According to Rhonda's attorney, just because there were six casings in the hallway did not mean that his client shot the gun in the hallway. He maintained that his client, in self-defense, shot Jimmy Joste in the doorway of the bedroom.

"Once you chamber a round and squeeze the trigger," explained Rhonda's attorney Joe James Sawyer, "a semiautomatic pistol literally reloads itself. It harnesses the energy of the expanding gases from a spent cartridge, and in a millisecond the slide comes back, the expended cartridge flies out, and the gases from the expanding cartridge load the second round. It slams shut and—literally as quickly as you squeeze the trigger—you are back in business. The speed at which the Glock reloads is one of its selling points," said Sawyer. "You can empty the magazine before the first shell casing hits the floor. With enough adrenaline in your body, be it from fear or anger, you can empty that weapon into someone in less than three seconds."

The placement of the shell casings ejected from the Glock was indisputable; the reason for that placement was open to dispute. Testimony by ballistics expert Greg Karim, firearm and toolmark examiner for the Austin Police Department forensic science division, could either bolster Sawyer's contention that Rhonda Glover did not fire shots in the hall, or confirm the prosecution's allegation that Glover continued shooting Joste in the hallway, even after he was dead.

First, of course, Karim's duties and expertise were firmly established for the jury. "What we get is all the handguns seized off the street by the officers and sometimes by the surrounding counties, federal agents, such as ATF, FBI, DEA," said Karim, explaining his duties. "What we do is an extensive examination of the firearm, and we test-fire it. We put it in a national database to see if it was used in another crime somewhere else.

"When we get fired projectiles, bullets, fired casings that are submitted as well from crime scenes from patrol officers, and from detectives, we will examine them, intercompare them on a piece of equipment called the comparison microscope, where I would compare all, for example, five casings that came from a particular crime scene to determine whether or not they were fired from the same gun, and place those in the computer system and see if there is another shooting involved with that same gun."

Karim was specifically asked about the ejection characteristics of the Glock 9mm. "You would think that if you are pointing the firearm at a particular target, that the shell casings are going to eject basically in the same area," Karim testified, "but with Glocks, that isn't always so. One time it will go sixteen feet away. Next time it drops six feet. Next time it drops on top of your nose or gets stuck in your glasses."

That was exactly what Sawyer wanted to hear. Karim was essentially saying that Rhonda could fire the gun in the bedroom, and the shell casings could wind up in the hallway.

Bryan Case, however, was adamant about the "common sense" story told by the placement of the shell casings. "The shell casings from a Glock nine millimeter hit the ground pretty fast," said Bryan Case. "You pull the trigger four times in the bedroom, and it is most likely that there are going to be four shell casings in the bedroom. You pull the trigger six times in the hallway, and there are going to be six shell casings in the hallway. You don't pull the trigger ten times in one room, and have six of the shell casings land on the floor in another room. It can happen—I'm sure if they bounce off a wall or something—but I think the shell-casing placement in the Joste residence indicate exactly where she was when the shots were fired."

Another aspect of Karim's expertise was especially important in the case against Rhonda Glover. "We compare a gunshot victim's clothing and try to determine a distance of when a particular shot was fired toward the victim." The particular item of clothing submitted to Karim was Jimmy Joste's shorts.

"Specifically, one pair of white Knights of the Roundtable dress shorts, one hundred percent cotton, zipper fly, had a short strap with a button waist, size thirty-four, with apparent biohazard and soiled sections." According to Karim, there was a bullet hole in Joste's shorts. "From the top of the waist of the waistline down, it was 8.75 inches. From the hemline up, it was 9.5 inches." There was also a second bullet hole in Joste's shorts, "basically on the right-side front section by the zipper." Whether or not the holes were from the same bullet, or from separate ones, was debatable.

"The point, I believe," offered Jeff Reynolds, "was that Rhonda specifically shot Jimmy below the belt, on purpose, and after he was already on the ground. There were too many variables involved, from a scientific standpoint, to establish, with complete accuracy, exactly from where the shots were fired."

It wasn't so much "guessing" as it was arguing about where Glover was standing when she fired the shots. Some insisted that she was not standing still, but rather was moving toward Joste, shooting him as he stumbled backward down the hall.

"Rhonda Glover," asserted ADA Bryan Case, "was in the bedroom when the first four rounds were fired. There are four shell casings there. We have photos of those. We don't have to have exact measurements. There is a diagram. We know where those casings are in relation to the walls and the door."

"That opinion," countered Joe James Sawyer, Glover's trial attorney, "is not founded upon science, and that's the problem. The door to the bedroom was open—we all know that. You are surrounded by hard surfaces, and we have no exact measurements. We know that the way a Glock works, those shell casings could have gone anywhere, bounced off of the wall or whatever. Just because we know for a fact where the shell casings are doesn't tell us with any scientific precision where she was when she pulled the trigger."

Rhonda Glover's lawyer wanted hard science not guesswork when it came to placing where his client was when the shots were fired. When the prosecutor wanted Karim to pinpoint where Glover was standing when she pulled the trigger, based on photographic evidence of the bullet hole in the wall, Glover's attorney strongly objected. As it turned out, Karim's testimony was in Sawyer's favor.

"Without doing an ejection pattern analysis on that particular gun with that particular ammunition, it would be speculative," said Karim. "The shooter could be anywhere in the bedroom or, under certain circumstances, in the hallway. It depends on the angle of the gun and how it was being held."

It wasn't rocket science to figure out that she was either in the bedroom, the hallway—or both—for the simple reason that there was no other place for her to be. As for placement of the shooter, the conclusions of Dr. Bayardo, the ME, were not, he insisted, the result of guesswork. The evidence was simple and incontrovertible: Glover "fired four shots while in the bedroom, and six more shots were fired while she was in the hallway." At least one was fired from directly above Joste, and at close range.

If Rhonda Glover stood over Jimmy Joste and shot him while he was already down, even the most remote claim of self-defense became absurd. Sawyer did everything possible to cast doubt on any inference that his client did such a thing. In the final analysis it could not be stated with absolute certainty that she did so, but there was every indication that she most likely did.

Assistant District Attorney Bryan Case put together a slightly different scenario on where Rhonda Glover was standing when she shot Jimmy Joste, a scenario also plausible based on blood splatter evidence.

"Rhonda Glover wanted us to believe that she never moved from the doorway when she shot him," said Case. "He was standing right in her way, right? No. He takes the first round right at the doorway. The cast-off blood is consistent with that. A bullet goes through him somewhere, right there at the doorway, blood on the door. *Bam*, three more times. *Bam bam bam*, while he is going down the hall. But then, you know what, he falls down. You know why there is three or four shots right through one place, because it is very likely that he was already dead at that point.

"She then approaches, and we don't know how close, but some number of steps toward him, and she aims the gun down so that the cartridge will eject out of the top of the gun and come to rest at Jimmy's feet. She shoots him six times. She discharges six shells into him while he is lying there. It's a tight pattern. She did not miss. She was a good shot."

The mental image of Rhonda Glover standing over the dead body of her child's father, and intentionally shooting him in the groin, is not one to elicit sympathy for the accused. The entire concept of her doing that was incredibly off-putting to jurors and spectators. The fact that the physical evidence—although disputable—gave every indication of that taking place, it was impossible to erase from the mind of anyone who heard it.

"I heard that Rhonda shot Jimmy's balls off," said one of Glover's former Austin acquaintances. "From what the experts said at the trial, she probably did. That's not only evil, that's creepy. Bad enough that she killed him, but did she have to do that too?"

"As hotheaded and outspoken as she was, none of us ever seriously believed she would kill Jimmy," said Rocky Navarro. "Fifteen years is a long time, and that's how long they were, more or less, together. Maybe if they didn't have a child together, they would have split several years earlier. But Jimmy loved his son. So did Rhonda. That meant they would be tethered together as, I guess you could say, 'spousal equivalents' no matter what. During the trial they didn't talk about Rhonda's mental problems, or how screwed up on drugs both of them were at a certain point."

There were other things that could not be mentioned during the guilt/innocence phase of the trial. Joyce Imparato was all prepared to speak about Jimmy telling her that Rhonda and he were going off together, but when she started to testify, Rhonda's lawyer objected that it was hearsay and prejudicial. Bryan Case objected to the objection, and there was another huddle with the judge on the issue of hearsay. This happened almost every few minutes because the trial of Rhonda Glover came immediately following United States Supreme Court rulings that threw the entire system of American justice into turmoil and confusion. The two rulings were, in the words of Loyala Law School professor Laurie Levenson, "revolutionary—they turned a bit of the criminal justice system upside down."

The one causing the greatest trepidation for everyone in the Glover trial was the ruling simply known as Crawford, named after *Crawford v. Washington,* a ruling that limited, as never before, prosecution evidence of statements made outside the court.

"There were two new rulings from the United States Supreme Court," said Jeff Reynolds, "and both decisions were at least short-term victories for defendants, and both were written by Justice Scalia—who, besides being one of the most conservative justices in the court's modern history, is a stickler for enforcing the rights he finds in the Constitution."

One of these important rights is the right under

the Sixth Amendment to confront one's accusers at trial. It acts as a constitutional limit on prosecutors' use of hearsay, a secondhand account of an out-of-court statement.

Hearsay statements usually take the form of a police officer conveying the words of a witness who was unable or unwilling to testify in court. "Police have been known to not always tell the truth," said former law enforcement officer Fred Wolfson. "I have a real issue with dishonest cops."

In the Supreme Court case, jurors in Michael Crawford's assault trial heard a tape recording of a statement to police by his wife, Sylvia, that conflicted with Crawford's claim of self-defense in stabbing a man. She was prevented from testifying by Washington State's marital privilege law, which prohibits one spouse from testifying against another without the latter's consent.

State courts upheld Crawford's conviction, relying on the Supreme Court's 1980 ruling that allowed prosecutors to use hearsay evidence if the circumstances showed that the statement of the witness was trustworthy. But in a 7–2 decision on March 8, 2004, the high court overturned the 1980 ruling and said the Sixth Amendment prohibits hearsay evidence of a witness's "testimonial" statement—no matter how trustworthy—unless the defense has had a chance to cross-examine the witness.

"That's the important part," added Jeff Reynolds, "you have the right, under our Constitution, to cross-examine someone who is testifying against you. If someone can just get up there and speak for someone else who isn't there, and you can't confront them or cross-examine them, your rights as an American have been violated. Because of the Supreme Court's Crawford decision, you have to put people on the stand so they can be cross-examined. If they're unavailable, you can't use those statements."

Scalia refused to define "testimonial" hearsay but said it included, at least, testimony at a previous legal proceeding, and statements made during police interrogation. Since 1980, judges and legislatures had been relying on Supreme Court authority to allow police to tell juries what witnesses had told them.

Jimmy Joste was unavailable to be questioned about what he said to Joyce Imparato because he was dead. Joe James Sawyer invoked the Crawford decision to keep her from telling the jury what Joste said to her.

"I don't see how this is prejudicial," said Judge Lynch.

"Oh, it is way prejudicial," countered Sawyer, and Lynch asked for an explanation.

"Well," said Sawyer, "I'm sure that the state is going to, in the final argument, say that obviously Rhonda had told him that they were going away together. It raises a whole new issue."

"I think it is probative," said Case, "because it sheds light on any number of things that have already been brought up. . . . If the defendant testifies, then the jury will get one version of their relationship, but the state believes it is probative in that it explains why the victim would have expected to see Rhonda at the house, why he might have depleted his resources and not cared if they were going to go away and leave together. Our theory of the case is that Jimmy believed that, but Rhonda knew it was never going to happen."

Caught up in his own argument, Case proceeded

to validate Sawyer's objection. "Jimmy was out of money," Case said, "Jimmy was wanting Rhonda to go away with him, and the three of them would have their family—her and Jimmy and their son. Jimmy was telling her this, and I'm sure that the defendant is going to testify about whatever she thought the relationship was when she was living in that five-thousand-dollar-a-month condo in Houston, but the state's belief is that Jimmy was hoping and wanting to be back with her and their son, and she let him continue in that belief, but she knew he was running out of money, and—"

Judge Lynch interrupted him, asking, "Is all this going to come out of this witness's testimony?"

"No, no, all that won't come out. But this is why her testimony is significant as to what Jimmy was thinking, and—"

The judge ruled that Imparato could testify that Jimmy came to her house and gave her back "stuff," but she was not to say anything about why he gave it back.

"But that's not the story," complained Imparato, knowing full well that the reason she was there was to tell the jury that Jimmy believed that he and Rhonda were going away together.

"You understand the ruling," said Lynch.

"Yes," she acknowledged.

"Then obey the ruling."

Joyce told the jury about Jimmy coming over and returning the blankets, but not about Jimmy believing that Rhonda and he were leaving the country together.

"The witness was obviously upset," recalled Fred Wolfson. "She wanted people to know about the frame of mind of a man she cared about deeply, a man who was a close personal friend. But the way it turned out, the jury was not allowed to hear about Jimmy believing that Rhonda, Ronnie and he were all going to be one happy family in another country."

"They were going to Canada," said Danny Davis. "The extradition laws up there are different. He told someone he was going to France, but it was Canada. He went away, all right, but not with Rhonda, but because of her. I really can't imagine how she could claim that she shot him in self-defense."

In the state of Texas, the Texas Penal Code clearly defines self-defense as a person justified in using force against another when and to the degree he reasonably believes the force is immediately necessary to protect himself against the other's use or attempted use of unlawful force.

A law originally enacted in 1973 required Texans to attempt to retreat when criminally attacked. In 1995, the state legislature passed an exception to that law allowing the use of force without retreat when the intruder had illegally entered the victim's home. The law signed by Governor Rick Perry in 2007, after the Joste homicide, extended the 1995 exception beyond the home to vehicles and workplaces. The law allows the reasonable use of deadly force without retreat when the intruder is committing certain violent crimes, such as murder or sexual assault, or is attempting to commit such crimes; unlawfully trying to enter a protected place; or is unlawfully trying to remove a person from a protected place. The law provides both

criminal and civil immunity for persons lawfully using
deadly force in the above circumstances.

"Texas is considered to be one of the most conservative states," said Joe James Sawyer, "and we pride
ourselves on that. I am from here, and I'm proud of
it, but I want you to consider that even in our conservative state, we allow broad terms of punishment for
the crime of murder, and that is because our legislature determined that it is inappropriate to just
blindly mete out punishment.

"In 1974, we had the last major change in Texas
law," Sawyer recalled. "I was then a young practicing
lawyer. It was one of the most dramatic and sweeping
changes you can imagine. In 1974, if someone were
convicted of a crime of rape, for example, the penalty
was death. If you were convicted of burglary of a
home that night, it was an automatic life sentence.
The jury did not get to deliberate. It was an automatic punishment. Those days are gone, and they're
gone with good reason. Now the legislature has an
amazing new form of freedom to a jury. It is the freedom to slowly and carefully consider what punishment fits the crime."

The nature of the crime might depend upon the
circumstances of the crime. The circumstances under
which Rhonda Glover shot Jimmy Joste formed the
essence of the trial in Travis County.

The mental condition of Rhonda Glover at the
time of her arrest, and prior to the trial, was something her lawyer wanted brought to the jury's attention. At no time during the guilt or innocence phase
was the jury made aware that Glover suffered from a

proven medical disease or disorder of the mind. Joe James Sawyer, Glover's lawyer, believed that it was necessary for the trial jury to know that Rhonda Glover suffered from a mental illness.

"Before this trial commenced, and before I actually represented Ms. Glover," Sawyer said to Judge Lynch, "there was a judicial proceeding in this court [that was] based in part on expert testimony about a mental disease from which the defendant suffers. A jury returned a verdict finding that she was incompetent to stand trial. Finding incompetence necessarily reflects the jury's belief of the definition of incompetence, that is the inability to sufficiently understand the charges against her, coupled with an inability to effectively assist her lawyer in representing her.

"I would particularly note that she has been in custody for some many months and that it clearly was not drug related. I anticipate argument from the state that all of the behavior of 2003 and 2004 was drug driven, and not the result of her suffering from a mental disease or disorder."

Sawyer asked that the judge allow him to bring in witnesses to establish that fact so the jury would be aware of Glover's mental illness. Speaking for the prosecution, Bryan Case didn't like that idea. "The issue of competency is not relevant. It has been kept out of the trial, and the state objects to any kind of mentioning of the defendant being competent or incompetent at some point."

The judge agreed, and no one was called to testify about the extent of Glover's illness, or her previous condition of incompetency. "It was diagnosed, and Glover was on three medications during her time in jail, and was supposedly receiving her medications during her trial," commented Fred Wolfson. "Glover, however, says that she stopped taking her medications during the trial, and also says that she was overmedicated during the trial."

Sawyer asked if Judge Lynch would at least take judicial notice of Glover's mental condition, and Case objected to that also. "The problem I have with that," he explained, "is that it would be a comment on the weight of the evidence, and the evidence speaks for itself, and the state doesn't dispute that she had a mental disease."

The jury was remanded to separate truth from fiction in a case where, in order to reach the truth, one had to hear fiction. The same confession Rhonda Glover gave to Detectives Walker and Fortune was what got her declared mentally incompetent.

"The really bizarre thing," commented Jeff Reynolds, "is that the jury is hearing all this, and applying the reasoning of a sane and rational person to the information presented to them. The missing ingredient is that Rhonda, on the day she pulled the trigger, was not rational at all. Her experience of the world, her operational reality, is far removed from anything these people can imagine. The prosecution successfully argued that her demented view of what was going on around her was secondary to the fact that she shot Jimmy Joste."

"It is a difficult job," Sawyer told the jury in his opening remarks. "I think you are going to conclude quite reasonably that what happened there on July twenty-first in the afternoon was, in fact, an act of self-defense by a woman who justifiably believed that she was in danger of losing her life."

* * *

The prosecution's witness list was extensive. They built their case with sequential in-depth testimony from law enforcement, crime scene specialists and everyone who interacted with Rhonda Glover and Jimmy Joste, leading up to the shooting. Jurors heard of Glover's extensive training at both Top Gun and at Red's, and details of her movements on the day of the shooting.

Rhonda Glover's defense team was, despite presumption of innocence, on the defensive. There were no witnesses they could call to refute the truth of Glover shooting Joste. The only witness who could put forth testimony of self-defense was Rhonda Glover. Forbidden to mention Glover's mental condition and paranoid delusions, Sawyer could only hope that someone, somehow, would "open the door" by inadvertently mentioning those topics.

"The door was pretty much kicked in," recalled Jeff Reynolds, "by the time real estate agent Debbie McCall took the stand. The prosecution called her as a witness to refute the idea that Rhonda Glover was a successful businesswoman who purchased the Mission Oaks house with her own funds."

"I represented Rhonda as a buyer on the purchase of her Mission Oaks property that was being sold in 2000," testified McCall. "She asked me if she could have some of my commission, and I said, 'Well, it is illegal for me to give my commission to anyone, unless they are a licensed agent.' I did agree to give her five hundred dollars. She called me on the day before closing and she said, 'You know, you agreed to give me all of your commission,' and I said, 'No, I didn't.'"

Glover, according to McCall, became quite irritated. "She told me that she didn't have enough money to pay me my commission. She said, 'Jimmy didn't give me enough money, and I need more.' Well, I didn't take any commission on that sale." It may have been Rhonda's name on the property, but it was Jimmy's money that made the purchase possible.

"Did you ever have occasion," Bryan Case asked McCall, "to spend the night at her house?"

"Yes, I did," replied the witness. "She called me a couple times and told me that she was scared because she thought there were demons in her attic, so I told her I would come over and spend the night with her."

The word "demons" was hardly out of her mouth when hell broke loose. "I guess I don't understand the demons in the attic," said Judge Lynch to Case.

"Well, I wasn't expecting—"

"Why don't you talk to your witnesses ahead of time," asked Judge Lynch rhetorically.

"I did talk to her, Judge," said Case.

"And you told her not to talk about the demons in the attic?"

"Last time we spoke," replied Bryan Case, "I did not tell her specifically not to, Your Honor. I didn't tell her to not mention the demons. I'm sorry."

The jury was instructed to disregard the remark about the demons. "We could go down that road, with the demons in the attic," said Judge Lynch, "but I don't think any of us really want to go there."

17

Rhonda Glover freely admitted to difficulties with alcohol, and women who abuse men are frequently alcoholics. "Alcohol abuse is a common harbinger of domestic violence," asserted Donna McCooke, health care professional in the United Kingdom. "Personality disorders are also primary characteristics of women who are violent and abusive. Borderline personality disorder is a diagnosis that is found almost exclusively with women. Women are three hundred times more likely to have this particular condition. Approximately one to two percent of all women have a borderline personality disorder. At least fifty percent of all domestic abuse and violence against men is associated with women who have a borderline personality disorder. The disorder is also associated with severe mood swings, lying and sexual issues, such as lack of sexual response, or excessive sexual behavior. Abuse and violence are behaviors chosen by a woman to cause physical, sexual or emotional damage and worry or fear."

Women who abuse their husbands or boyfriend

are characterized as being promiscuous, selfish and narcissistic. "They tend to be attention whores," asserted researcher Travis Webb. "And they get addicted to the drama they stir up. It's like they live in an emotional state of 911. They lie, and use anger or actual physical violence to get what they want and to get noticed. The more crafty ones hide their true nature by being affable and polite in public."

Women who are abusive toward men usually have unrealistic expectations and make unrealistic demands of men. These women will typically experience repeated episodes of depression, anxiety, frustration and irritability, which they attribute to a lack of support or understanding by men. They blame men rather than admit their own problems, take responsibility for how they live their lives or do something about how they make themselves miserable.

"Almost all abusive women will fake injuries, and they consider themselves excellent actresses," stated Webb. "They cast themselves in the role of victim, while they are, in reality, emotional terrorists and social tyrants. Sooner or later they falsely accuse their husband or partner of a crime, and often toss in allegations of child abuse. A close look shows that claims of domestic violence accusation has become their current weapon of choice, because it is easy to fabricate. They love tearing down their husband or partner's reputation, and get some sort of weird delight in raining destruction upon their husband or partner."

"A troubled or disturbed woman," observed health care expert McCooke, "may often insist that it is the man who needs treatment, just as a violent woman will often accuse her victim of being an abuser. They blame a man for how they feel, often medicate with alcohol and/or drugs, and when men can't make them feel better, they get angry and think that the man is doing this on purpose. Quite often, if the woman has borderline personality disorder, or other forms of mental illness, this will be accompanied by delusions and paranoia. A woman such as this may also be emotionally intense and of strong will."

Whether or not you can kill someone and still receive your inheritance is one of the classic questions in American law. "It is a famous argument and a real brainteaser," commented Fred Wolfson. "Once upon a time, there was a man named Elmer Palmer who poisoned his grandfather in order to get the money 'dear old granddad' was going to leave him in his will. Palmer was found guilty of murdering his grandfather. The question was whether or not Elmer should still get the inheritance. The question was put to two judges, and the two of them did not agree.

"Judge Earl thought that Elmer, by killing his grandfather, had forfeited his right to collect the inheritance, but Judge Gray thought that the court had no right to make that decision. After all, he reasoned, the grandfather made a will. If the court refuses to honor it, then the court is making the will, not the grandfather."

If the law does not specifically state that killing a person keeps you from getting your inheritance from them, then you get that inheritance.

In Texas, if you kill someone, you can't claim your inheritance from them. Simple.

"Jimmy's will," said John Thrash, executor of the Joste estate, "was dated September 27, 2001." Five days after allegedly putting Rhonda Glover in the hospital, Jimmy Joste willed her $5,000 a month for life, and established a trust for their son. "There was no money left at the time of his death," said Thrash. "There really wasn't enough money there to pay any bills, let alone make any disbursements. Jimmy set up a trust fund for his son, but didn't set aside any funds in advance. Rhonda would get, as I mentioned, five thousand dollars a month for life, but not if she is found guilty of his murder."

Until 1982, anyone who called premeditated murder self-defense would have been laughed out of court. But in 1982, Lenore Walker won the first legal victory for her women-only theory of learned helplessness, which suggested that a woman whose husband or boyfriend batters her becomes fearful for her life and is helpless to leave him, so if she kills him, it is really self-defense—even if she has premeditated his murder. The woman is said to be a victim of battered woman syndrome. Is it possible a woman could kill, let's say, for insurance money? Lenore Walker would say no: "Women don't kill men unless they've been pushed to a point of desperation."

Ironically, feminists have often said, "There's never an excuse for violence against a woman." Now they were saying, "But there's always an excuse for violence against a man . . . if a woman does it."

"Glover's lawyer was sort of heading in that direction," commented Fred Wolfson, "but there wasn't sufficient documented evidence of violence against Glover by Joste to make it plausible, and the only evidence of any kind of assault by Jimmy Joste was the Barton Creek Country Club incident back in 2000, and he did take the fall for that."

Joe James Sawyer did not agree one bit with the state's portrayal of the incident at the Barton Creek Country Club. "We know as an absolute truth that Jimmy Joste, a man of considerable means, pleaded no contest to a charge of assault and family violence in open court on a given day back in 2000. So what? The state wants you to think that he wasn't guilty because Rhonda admitted on the stand that she tried to get him off the hook. Yes, she is the one who put up the money, or called one of her friends to bail him out that night, because she felt bad. Well," said Sawyer, "if you believe that, then you must also believe that the county attorney of Travis County is so morally bankrupt that he would continue to prosecute a man he knows to be innocent. The state says that she spoke to the county attorney, and that she submitted an affidavit. Now, do you really think someone said, 'Gee, you know this guy is not guilty, but let's go ahead and prosecute him, anyway?'

"You have to believe that a man of Mr. Joste's means, his educational background—and the lawyer he could afford—would walk into court and not contest a criminal charge when he knows he is not guilty. You have to believe his lawyer is so venal that he ignores his prime duty as an attorney, and that is—you may not plead a person guilty to a crime if you believe that person is *not* guilty!"

Sawyer then offered a compromise scenario, one in which the state of Texas, in good faith, believed that if it took Jimmy Joste to trial on a charge of violent assault, that the jury would find him guilty. "If that was indeed the situation, then it would explain why a decent, ethical lawyer would say to his client, 'You know, you can get up there on the stand and say it didn't happen that way, but there is a very real risk, given the other evidence, that the jury could find you guilty. If they do find you guilty, and get real carried away, they could give you a year in jail. So I suggest that instead of fighting this and running that risk, take advantage of the option of pleading no contest.'"

Sawyer made it clear that as far as he and the previous courts were concerned, Jimmy Joste was a proven abusive wife beater. Rhonda Glover took this one disputed incident and used it as a springboard for accusations that were completely unfounded. "The police were at my house at least once a month," insisted Rhonda Glover. "I was always calling them because of Jimmy's abuse."

"There is no evidence," insisted Bryan Case, "that any police officer went out to her place on Mission Oaks in response to a call that he was abusing her. There is none. It is all in her head. It does not exist. She said that the police were called out to the Mission Oaks house once a month because of family disturbances. Where is the evidence of that? If that were true, there would be police officers lined up to testify about how they went out there and saw her abused. Where are they? Where are the police reports? They don't exist."

The police reports that did exist were all ones where officers confronted a delusional woman who claimed there were bodies in the trash, people in her sink and demons in her walls. The times that police encountered Jimmy Joste at the residence, he was the calm, centered, cooperative gentleman

who assured police that Rhonda Glover was not a
danger to herself or others.

"Rhonda, when she's not out of her mind, is very
personable and pleasant," stated a longtime acquaintance. "She had friends, of course, but they were
party pals. And even those who seriously and honestly
cared for her discovered that she could turn on them
in a heartbeat, or, for that matter, turn toward them
in friendship. She was unpredictable, to be sure. Vivacious, sexy, and Jimmy Joste absolutely loved her
no matter what. Even if her other friends fell away, or
were scared away."

"I have friends," said Rhonda. "I have lots of
friends, but do you think my lawyer got any of them
to come speak on my behalf? No, he didn't."

"Where are the people who will say that she is
truthful?" asked Bryan Case. "Where? Can you imagine that? Not one person will come forward and say
that she is truthful, not one person will say that she is
nonviolent. You know how many people she knew.
She knew people in Houston. She knew people in
Austin. They couldn't get anybody, because everyone
who knows her knows who she is, knows that she is capable of doing exactly what she did."

None of Jimmy Joste's friends have bad things to
say about Rhonda—other than she murdered someone they loved. None of them say horrid things about
her for two reasons: they don't want her son hearing
any more bad things about his mother, and they all
are familiar with her volatile and almost predictable
unpredictability.

"I would never say anything bad about Rhonda,"
confirmed Rocky Navarro, and even Danny Davis bal-
anced criticism with compassion.

"What it boils down to," observed Fred Wolfson, "is that everyone knows, or knew, that Rhonda was afflicted with a mental illness, and that Jimmy loved her, anyway. Also, Jimmy himself changed in the last few years of his life due to a combination of drug use and emotional environment. He, too, became delusional, although not with anything near the consistency and depth of Rhonda Glover."

This speculation raised a question not posed previously, and a theory not formerly uttered. It was possible, in light of Jimmy Joste's own history of peculiar behavior in the final years of his life, that his entire plan of going off to Canada to live as a happy family was an ardent desire and longing that he envisioned transforming into reality, but had no foundation in reality.

An examination of the situation sets the stage for Joste's plan: He lost custody of his son following the Barton Creek Incident. Rhonda also lost custody of Ronnie, and took off rather than surrender the boy to her mother, Mrs. Shotwell. It is easy to understand how Jimmy Joste could conceive the plan of all three of them taking off to Canada. Once there, they could not be compelled to return.

Perhaps he believed that he could—through a combination of sincere love, charm, a $350,000 engagement ring, a significant amount of cash and the power of persuasion—convince Rhonda to go with him to Canada. Of course he had no idea that she was completely convinced that he was Satan and his eyes were on American currency, and that he was planning to kill her.

We have two people operating on two different
sets of delusions: Jimmy, convincing himself that if he
and Rhonda go to Canada and get married, everything will be all right. Rhonda, thoroughly convinced
that Jimmy is a murderer with plans to sacrifice their
child in a pagan ritual. When their delusions collide
in the Austin home, death is the result. Jimmy calls
out, asking for his son, excited at the prospect of
seeing him. Rhonda takes it as a bone-chilling threat.

Realizing that the two of them are alone, Jimmy
proposes that they make love. He craves sex with
Rhonda, as she is the woman he loves. When Jimmy
approaches, Rhonda feels in danger for her life. It
may not be a reasonable fear for a reasonable person,
but Rhonda was not reasonable. What you believe
greatly influences how you interpret what you experience. For her, her fear was real. She was psychotic
and the actions she took were what she thought was
right in her psychotic state of mind.

"I think the main message here is that for a long
time it was known that this was a woman with severe
mental-health issues. This tragedy could have been
averted. Again I must ask," said Rocky Navarro, "what
the hell motive could Rhonda have for killing Jimmy?
She sure didn't kill him just because she was tired of
him, or he ran out of money."

"The state doesn't have to prove motive," responded
Bryan Case, "and everybody wants to understand why
things happen. What you have to understand in this
case is that a correct, right-thinking person cannot
fathom the magnitude of this event. Not really, because you can't put yourself there, you can't put

yourself in that position, in her position, because it doesn't make sense until you realize that Jimmy Joste is obsessed with her.

"What is hard to understand," said Case, "is that someone would actually go through this much trouble to kill someone to get them out of their life. Rhonda Glover could not get Jimmy Joste out of her life, and Jimmy was always giving her more money, showering her with things. She couldn't say no."

Getting Jimmy Joste out of her life because he was broke or sexually unappealing wasn't Rhonda's motivation, but that didn't matter. The "why she killed him" wasn't something the prosecution had to prove. They only had to prove that it was murder, that Rhonda Glover shot him dead when doing so was not necessary to keep him from killing her.

There is an old joke that—in light of this tragedy— takes on new meaning. A psychiatrist, offering an evaluation of a patient, reported that the patient is doing well. She had progressed from "everyone is trying to control my life," to "no one cares about me."

"I have come to realize that many of my clients suffer from mental disease or serious intellectual impairment," stated New York defense attorney Scott H. Greenfield.

"One of the big problems that have come before me is bipolar disorder," Greenfield said, "leaving defendants incapable of making rational choices or controlling impulsive urges. They know right from wrong, and often appear quite normal in most regards. But there are signs [that], if you are attuned, smack you in the face."

It is his opinion that lawyers limit their interactions with, and concern for, their clients to the criminal case in front of them. "By doing so, they ignore the person in front of them, with these problems that have caused misery in their lives and, in a very real sense, led to their current problems. By ignoring this cause/effect piece, a lawyer is only doing half a job. It is quite likely, given the socioeconomic, family and educational worlds in which they functioned, that no one has ever bothered to figure out why the client is 'a little weird.'"

In the matter of Rhonda Glover, her reason for being a little weird was diagnosed and confirmed more than once. Glover suffered from a medical condition that had a most disastrous impact on her decision-making abilities, and the lives of those around her.

Dr. E. Fuller Torrey said there are three factors that predict violence in people with a psychotic disorder. The first is a previous history of violence, the second is a substance abuse problem and the third is noncompliance with medication. All three indicators were manifested in Rhonda Lee Glover.

In the holistic approach to lawyering, the attorney looks beyond the criminal case to the cause of the client's antisocial behaviors. Be it anger, frustration, inability to distinguish choices in real time sufficient to avoid bad ones, this is a chance to actually do something to really help a client.

Mental illness does not negate criminal responsibility, as the client is fully capable in a rational moment, to distinguish right from wrong or legal from illegal. "But it does," commented Fred Wolfson, "negate the malevolence of the offense, and suggests an alternative to incarceration that will truly provide help to the client instead of merely warehousing him."

The biggest stumbling block, said attorney Scott Greenfield, is that many prosecutors and judges know and understand so little about mental illness, and their appreciation is so simplistic, that they have a steep learning curve. "They must be taught that all people with mental disease or impairment are not drooling idiots. They similarly can't appreciate why, if the client suffers from mental disease or impairment, they don't fall into the legally incompetent classification."

"I don't like sending dangerous people to mental hospitals," objected an Austin resident, "because they can escape easier from a hospital than a prison. Just look at the movie *Halloween* and Michael Myers!"

It isn't only in the movies that such things happen. In September of 2009, an insane killer slipped away from the staff of a mental institution on a field trip to the Spokane County Interstate Fair. He was recaptured more than 180 miles away in south-central Washington State.

Phillip Arnold Paul, forty-seven, killed an elderly woman in 1987, then doused her body with gasoline to throw search dogs off the scent. Diagnosed as schizophrenic, he was acquitted by reason of insanity. He voluntarily gave himself up, but Spokane County sheriff Ozzie D. Knezovich said Paul had just tried to thumb a ride from an area resident who alerted authorities.

There was a lot of fear in the community, and people were locking their windows. Authorities said that they were committed to finding out how and why this happened, why there was an unacceptable two-hour delay in notifying local law enforcement of his escape, plus how potentially dangerous patients were brought to such a public venue. Shortly after the escape, there was ordered a halt to all field trips for "forensic patients"—those committed for treatment as a result of criminal proceedings—at all three of the state's mental institutions.

While this is a scary scenario, in this particular situation the "insane killer" received an injection designed to maintain his mental stability for about two weeks on the Wednesday prior to his escape. Only at the end of that period would he have needed another dose to avoid the potential for a serious deterioration of his mental condition.

Paul aroused no suspicion when he left the mental institution with a backpack loaded with clothing, food, an electric guitar and $50 from a Social Security check. "It appears that Mr. Paul had planned this for quite some time," said authorities. The field trip to the fair, which included thirty other patients, was an annual event that Paul easily could have anticipated. This example obviously fueled fears that someone crazy enough to kill can still be smart enough to get on the loose. Many people feel that the best place for an emotionally disturbed person with a proven history of homicidal violence is a prison with security far exceeding that of a mental hospital.

"Everyone thinks that I'm crazy," Rhonda Glover admitted. "And they think I'm crazy because I'm a Christian, and I hear the voice of God, and I've been given this assignment, and I've been chosen for this mission. I am on a mission from God. I have built my case against these people. Jimmy is the one. He is the ringleader."

Given the opportunity, and supplied with the appropriate audio cues, Rhonda Glover's mind magnetically returns to the realm of delusion. This is not a character defect, nor an evil of the soul, but rather a medical condition. Glover can transverse the emotional spectrum from tearful vulnerability to icelike disdain in mere moments. During the trial in Judge Mike Lynch's courtroom, everyone present witnessed the melodramatic behavior and quickly changing moods of the defendant.

On February 16, 2006, the Rhonda Glover who walked into the Travis County Courthouse bore little resemblance to the vivacious Glover of years past. She exuded none of the raw sexuality for which she was rightly famed. Conservative in dress and demeanor, with her hair pulled back, she would take the stand in her own defense, and tell why and how she shot Jimmy Joste. She was cautioned by her attorney, however, not to mention the cave, the clones, George W. Bush or the pagan sacrifices because "they were too dangerous to talk about."

The delusional or dishonest are not always delusional or dishonest. Some of Rhonda Glover's assertions about Jimmy Joste were so bizarre and absurd that her lawyer Joe James Sawyer referred to them as such. Yet, some of her statements about Joste were borne out by objective investigation and sworn witness testimony.

Glover claimed that Jimmy Joste stalked her, and repeatedly attempted to get into her Houston apartment. A review of Houston police records attested to the truth of her statement. In April of 2004, there were trespassing complaints filed against Joste, and these did not come from Rhonda Glover. They came from the manager of the property where Glover lived.

"She stated that a man named James Joste has been trying to get on the property for several days to see his ex-wife," testified Houston police officer Silvas. "She stated that she was told by Rhonda Glover that she did not want to see the suspect, and not to let him on [the] property. The manager stated that the front entrance has twenty-four hour gate attendants, and they were advised of the situation. They have had several contacts with the suspect trying to get onto the property."

The list of dates and times that Joste made contact with the gate attendants and was turned away from the property are as follows:

> *4/12/2004—5:58 P.M., 7:18 P.M., 9:29 P.M. and 10:10 P.M.*
> *4/13/2004—9:15 A.M. and 6:15 P.M.*
> *4/14/2004—3:44 P.M., 3:48 P.M. and 4:10 P.M.*

The suspect, it was noted, was driving a blue Volkswagen. He was advised each time by the gate attendants that he needed to stay away from the property. "He wouldn't leave me alone," insisted Glover. "He hounded me relentlessly. He was supposed to stay away from me."

The validation of Glover's claim was the first true

ray of credibility to her story. It was an established fact that Jimmy Joste was repeatedly turned away from Glover's Houston residence by the request of property management. These unwanted visits, plus Joste pleading no contest in the Barton Creek Incident, were about all Sawyer had to portray Jimmy Joste as a violent and abusive stalker worthy of fear.

Now, at long last, Rhonda Glover would take the witness stand and explain why she shot Jimmy Joste at least ten times with a Glock 9mm handgun. First, Glover testified about her relationship with Joste, and how the initial joy of their relationship evaporated in the heat of his heavy drinking and repeated beatings. For the next fourteen years, they lived together and apart in a host of homes in the Houston and Austin areas. They even tried to start over in California. Each time they tried to make a go of it, said Rhonda, Jimmy's violence tore them apart.

According to Glover's testimony, she entered the Austin residence she and Joste once shared to reclaim some camping gear from the attic before taking her nine-year-old son, Ronnie, on a planned cross-country excursion in a rented mobile home. Joste, however, surprised her by his sudden appearance. Glover, her voice trembling, and every movement and gesture communicating a soul-wrenching level of despair, told of the intense fear gripping her when she heard Jimmy Joste arrive.

"What did Jimmy say to you when he realized you were in the house?" asked Sawyer.

Glover didn't respond. Silence stretched between lawyer and client until Rhonda Glover said, "I think I'm going into a state of shock."

The bailiff poured her some water. Everyone

waited for Glover to regain composure. Instead, she leaned forward, buried her head in her arms, and took a brief nap on the counter in front of the witness stand.

"Ms. Glover," prompted her lawyer, "we need to continue. What did he say?"

The disheveled witness raised her head and replied, "He said, 'Rhonda, are you in the house?' and I said nothing. I just sat there in fear."

"What happened next?"

"I can't remember," said Glover. "I think I'm going to faint."

"Ms. Glover, these people want to know what happened," Sawyer said. "Tell the jury what happened."

She told of him screaming at her as he came up the stairs, first demanding his son, then calling her a bitch and saying he was going to kill her. The jury heard of them meeting at the doorway to the bedroom, and Jimmy grabbing her by the throat. "He was choking me, and I reached in and pulled my gun out and shot him. I shot him. Because I thought he was going to kill me."

"You emptied the gun into him, didn't you?" asked her attorney.

"I emptied the gun in him. Yes, I did. I am so sorry!"

Glover sobbed on the witness stand, but a moment later, when Bryan Case cross-examined her, she was suddenly a different person altogether. The tears were gone; her tone brittle. Her eyes were ice.

"Ms. Glover," asked Bryan Case, "your earlier testimony on direct was that you and he basically met at the threshold of the door?"

"Yes, and he began choking me."

"He began choking you. And you are going toward him, pointing a gun at him, right?"

"Yes." .

"Going toward him, yes?"

"Yes," Glover replied coldly.

"And is that the way they taught you in the defensive use of firearms to deal with a dangerous situation?"

"Yes."

"To go at it with a gun?"

"Yes."

"And he begins choking you, and you have shot this gun a number of times, correct?"

Glover was getting progressively irked.

"Yes."

"And if you shot it a number of times, you know how to shoot the gun, and how is it that your testimony now, I assume, is that you started pulling the trigger and just never stopped, right?"

"Yes. I shot him. It just . . . ," Glover paused, and then snapped, "I shot him. The gun just went off. It just perpetuated."

No one could fail to notice the difference between the tone of her replies to Joe James Sawyer and those to Bryan Case. "It was a remarkable and visibly stunning transformation. It was like something from a movie. Crocodile tears on direct examination," said Bryan Case. "And then . . . who was that person who testified on cross-examination? It was like a different person in the same body. Who was that person who sat there and looked at me with the coldest, hardest, meanest look imaginable?"

When Rhonda Glover looked coldly at Bryan Case and said, "Yes. I shot him," her complete lack of any emotion, other than the complete disdain for him communicated by her inflection and body language, shocked those in the courtroom.

"It was like she wasn't the same person who, minutes before, was weeping away in the witness stand," recalled Fred Wolfson. "It was, in a word, scary."

When Glover's testimony was over, and she was asked to step down, she had her own objections. "I thought I was going to get to talk about Jimmy sexually abusing our son."

There were several simultaneous gasps in the courtroom, and an equal number of laborious sighs. "It wasn't relevant to the trial. There was absolutely no evidence," said Bryan Case, "and it absolutely contradicts a conversation that Rhonda had with Christy Dillon in Houston shortly before the murder."

In her conversation with Dillon, Rhonda Glover said that she thought that one of her mother's friends was sexually abusing her son. She never said anything of this nature about Jimmy Joste until she was in the courtroom.

"This is," said Gail Van Winkle, "another example of a woman who will say anything at any time if she thinks it will help her. She is a woman who is admittedly not truthful by her friends' own accounts."

Even if Rhonda believed that Jimmy Joste was molesting his own son, that still wouldn't make shooting him an act of self-defense. "We don't live in the kind of society," Van Winkle said, "where you can shoot and kill someone that you believe has done something bad, or even if they have been convicted of a crime. That is not self-defense. That does not make killing justified."

18

There was more than one version of the shooting offered from the witness stand, and both of them allegedly from Rhonda Glover. The second version was one supposedly given by Glover to a fellow inmate in the Travis County Jail. This "alternate version" offered a different reason for the shooting that had nothing to do with self-defense.

Jackie Pierce-Ray, who also goes by the name Jackie Pierce, admitted an extensive criminal history characterized by various forms of fraud. She also had a background of working in the Texas Legislature. At the time of Rhonda Glover's residency in the Travis County Jail, Glover sought out Jackie Pierce. "She wanted to discuss legal questions," confirmed Ray. "During the course of our conversations, she talked about a pending murder charge.

"She told me that on the day of the murder, that she was going to her house to pick up camping equipment because she was going to take her son camping, and on the way to the house, she passed the post office on the left and realized that it was closed. She was going down to Red's Gun Shop and stop there. So she went there and stopped there and practiced her shooting, and then she drove back to the house.

"On the way," Ray clarified, "Rhonda stopped and made a call at the pay phone. She said that she asked Jimmy where he was—if he were in Vail or in Austin, and he said he was in Austin. She told him that she was coming by the house to pick up some camping equipment.

"When she arrived there," recounted Jackie Pierce-Ray, "she saw that the garage door was open. She knew he was home. She proceeded to go in the house, go upstairs, and she went into the upstairs area. She came out of the bathroom and emptied the gun on him."

According to this woman, later characterized by Rhonda's defense attorney as a "jailhouse snitch," Glover was upset with Jimmy Joste. In fact, she was outraged and furious. The trigger for her outrage wasn't clone sex, pagan sacrifices or homosexuals creeping into the aquifer. "She was upset about him not having bought her anything in about a year and a half."

Glover was also angered, according to Pierce-Ray, "because she had found some stuff in his vehicle that indicated that he was going to strip clubs and other places like that, and she said, 'Nobody messes around on me!'"

It was Jackie Pierce-Ray's impression, based on statements from Rhonda Glover that the reason she emptied the Glock into Jimmy Joste was because she believed he had been cheating.

"I'm just telling you what she said to me," stated

Pierce-Ray flatly. "She said that, and I'm just saying
what she said to me in the Travis County Jail."

It is possible that she was telling the truth, yet with
one simple error. She mistook "bedroom" for "bathroom." Glover could have, while entering the house
through the garage, peered into Jimmy's car and
seen something from Rocky's and Jimmy's recent get-
together that triggered insane jealousy and suspicion.
After all, Rocky and Jimmy stopped at a "strip joint"
so Rocky could have a smoke in air-conditioned com-
fort.

"She is a liar," Rhonda Glover later proclaimed,
"her testimony is not only a complete lie, but it contradicts all the physical evidence that was already presented. Her mother called the chaplain at the Del
Valle Jail and said that Jackie cut the monitor off her
leg and went on the run. The mother told the chaplain that everything Jackie Pierce-Ray said on the
stand was a lie. It is easy to see that she lied about the
physical evidence. She said I hid in the bathroom,
and then opened fire on him. Look at the floor plan.
The bathroom is in front of the door where he was
found. Jimmy's body was found facing the bedroom.
The shell casings were found in the bedroom, not in
the hallway. And he was shot in the front of him, not
in the back, and not facing the bathroom door. The
ballistics do not corroborate Jackie's story at all. My
loser lawyer didn't catch that, but I see things that
others don't see."

"Her lawyer certainly caught that," remarked Fred
Wolfson, "but if he were to mention it, he would be
accepting the prosecution's presentation of the bal-
listic evidence, and the prosecution's definition of
what that evidence proved—evidence that her lawyer

was doing his best to raise doubts about. She can't have it both ways. She can't say the prosecution's evidence is faulty, and then say it isn't just to cast doubt on that other woman's veracity."

Rhonda Glover's mother took the stand, and Joe James Sawyer asked her directly, "Was there a time in November of 2004 when you became concerned about Jimmy Joste's behavior?"

Before she could go into any detail regarding her concerns, the state objected with concerns of their own. "I object to the relevance of this concern for Jimmy Joste's behavior, and whatever it may be going next," said Bryan Case.

Sawyer and Case met up at the bench, and Sawyer explained his purpose of this line of questioning. "I am going to ask if she became concerned about his mental state and whether she undertook to call anyone to express these feelings and who she called. She called Kelly Joste, she called the guy at UBS and the guy at Prosperity Bank. The relevance is this—the state has asked at least three witnesses, by my count, if Jimmy Joste was docile, mellow, nonaggressive. This, I think, is relevant on the issue of his behavior, and I mean, how do I—how do they [have] it both ways? I am not going to ask what the behavior was."

"If this woman has testimony," said Judge Lynch, "that he was aggressive or nondocile of her own knowledge and personal knowledge, she can answer those questions."

Things did not go well with Sherlyn Shotwell on the stand, even though she had her sworn affidavit in front of her. She didn't have her glasses and repeatedly answered "no" to questions for which "yes" was reflected in her affidavit. If that wasn't enough, any mention she made of concern for Jimmy Joste's mental state or behavior was met with further objections from the prosecution. When Sawyer asked Shotwell how often she saw her daughter with bruises—the implication being that the bruises were from being beaten by Jimmy Joste—Shotwell's testimony came to an abrupt and truncated conclusion.

One interesting, yet overlooked, piece of testimony was offered by Jimmy Joste's financial advisor, Mike Cook. Sawyer's co-counsel, Ms. Darouzzet, asked Cook to detail charges made against Joste's bank account by debit card or personal check.

"Are you familiar with a company named Identigene?"

Identigene is the Houston firm to which Rhonda Glover submitted the piece of bubble gum that she believed indicated that Jimmy Joste was murdering children. There were three charges to Identigene reflected on Joste's checking account on January 19, 2004.

"Could you please tell us those amounts?"

"The top one," replied Cook, "is eight hundred seventy, the next one is six hundred, and the bottom one is for one hundred fifty dollars."

This meant that Jimmy Joste paid over $1,600 to Identigene for DNA testing on items submitted to them by Rhonda Glover. "It would certainly indicate," commented Jeff Reynolds, "that Rhonda Glover had full access to, and use of, Jimmy Joste's checking account. Here she is accusing him of being a murdering Devil worshiper, and she is using his money to conduct her so-called investigation. There were also significant charges to Joste's account for thousands of dollars in women's clothing at various Houston specialty stores. She may have thought he was a cruel killer of innocent kids, but she had no qualms about using his money for new clothes, car rentals, shoes and DNA investigations."

The total amount of funds that came out of Joste's account in the month of February 2004 was over $300,000. In one day there were several thousands of dollars spent at various women's clothing stores in Houston. The following month there were an incredible number of returns and credits, including over $10,000 from Louis Vuitton of Houston, to Joste's MasterCard.

There were cash advances on the card of over $32,000, and total MasterCard activity of $313,706.43 for a combined total $346,477.13. "That's a hell of a lot of money for a short period of time," commented Fred Wolfson. "Even taking into account Rhonda's extravagant lifestyle and Jimmy's generosity, that is still a breathtaking amount of money spent on clothes, expensive hotels and jewelry. The vast majority of it was spent in Houston, not in Austin."

When people talk about Rhonda having money because it was Jimmy's money, his bank account records, which show where and how the money was spent, certainly lend credence to that point of view.

"Take a look at the names of the stores," offered Wolfson. "The women's stores where the money was being spent are all fine stores with high-priced quality merchandise. None of this was trash."

"It's trash!" exclaimed Bryan Case. "What she said on the witness stand was trash. In order to even think of finding her not guilty, you have to believe what she says. You have to believe that trash, and that is exactly what it is, trash.

"There is no reasonable doubt," insisted Case. "There is not one specific thing you can put your finger on that offers real reasonable doubt. What she did was, in the most coldhearted way, killed Jimmy Joste."

Prosecuting attorney Gail Van Winkle passionately weighed in on the murder and its surrounding deception.

"When she took the cab back to the Barders' after shooting Jimmy," said Van Winkle, "she was in the same pink floral dress. There are absolutely no pockets in that dress, so that means she walked out from the attic in that dress pointing a loaded gun at him. Well, is it logical, then, that he would suddenly start choking her as she is standing there with a loaded gun? Is that logical, or [is it] logical that he would be surprised and start stepping back, and she would shoot him and continue down the hall shooting him?"

Under the law, and common sense, if Jimmy had indeed grabbed her, he would be legally entitled to do so because she started it by threatening him with a gun. "It is much more logical," Van Winkle said, "that she heard Jimmy, she called him. She knew he was going to come up into the bedroom, and that he was actually excited to see her. He worshiped that woman, and she surprised him with the gun and started shooting. Rhonda testified that at one point she took the gun out from her pants. She had put the gun in her pants."

This is the problem with lies, noted prosecuting attorney Van Winkle. "When you get caught in lies, you forget what lie is going to be supported by the evidence, and what is not. Giving her the benefit of the doubt, let's say she did change into those pants. If she did, it is directly contrary to her version of events that she had just left Red's, swung by the Mission Oaks house to put that gun up, because she knew she couldn't carry it on the camping trip, and just happened to run into Jimmy. If you believed that, she would have had to have changed clothes and put on those black pants before the encounter with Jimmy. Does that make sense, other than those are her shooting pants? Either way, her version of what happened is not logical and is not supported by the evidence, and is certainly not a version in which the killing is justified. It is not self-defense. It is absolutely not self-defense."

Bryan Case had his own views on the pants/dress issue. "She says that she pulled the gun out of her pants. Well, she was wearing a dress when she left Red's at about two-thirty. They even identified the dress she was wearing. She drives over to the house, and at some point she changes out of her dress into the pants she wears when she shoots. Maybe she changed into the pants in the car, I don't know. And it makes sense because, as we know, every time she shoots the gun, she does it wearing pants, not a dress. She's in the dress. She changes into pants.

"Oh, and there is the phone call to Jimmy before she gets to the house. Why did she call from a pay phone? She is not a dumb woman," said Case. "She isn't stupid. She calls from the pay phone to make sure he is at the house, and she does not want to have a record of it on her cell phone. She doesn't want anything, if she gets away, to link her to contacting Jimmy directly before the murder.

"The woman goes into the house," continued Case, "and she has changed into her pants after calling Jimmy to make sure either that he is home, or that he is on his way to meet her there. And then she lies in wait for him. Is there really any doubt in your mind that her story, which keeps changing, is ridiculous? How absurd can it get? How absurd? There are four cartridge casings in that master bedroom, four. She fired that gun four times. She says she never moved, that she kept firing the gun from the same spot. He was standing in her way. No. No way."

Case pointed to the forensic evidence, primarily referencing the bloodstain patterns. "He takes the first round right there in the doorway. The bullet goes through him right there in the doorway, and there is blood on the door from that shot. *Bam*, three more times. *Bam! Bam! Bam!* while he is going down the hall. But then you know what, he falls down. You know why maybe there are three or four shots right through one place on his body? Because he was very likely already dead on the ground at that point."

Bryan Case then painted a chilling picture. "She then approaches a number of steps toward him, aiming the gun down at his lifeless body so the cartridge will eject out the top of the gun and land at Jimmy's feet. She shoots him six times while he is lying there. You can take a look at the photos, and you can see the bullet wounds. It is a very tight pattern. She did not miss. She was a very good shot, especially when the victim is on the floor. She is standing above him, and he's not moving."

Finished shooting, Case said, Glover changed

back into the sundress before returning to the
Barder residence. "That is one way that her statement about wearing pants at the time she pulled the
trigger could be true," commented Fred Wolfson.
"But [when you] look at in context of her pattern
of changing into those pants, it certainly appears to
confirm intent to shoot. I mean, those are her shooting pants."

According to Bryan Case, if you want to make
sense of this murder, you will never succeed because
it makes no sense. "Even though the state does not
have to prove motive," said Case, "everyone wants to
understand why things happen. What you have to understand is that a correct, right-thinking, rational
person can't fathom the magnitude of this event because you can't put yourself in the position of doing
these things, because it doesn't make sense."

The murder itself was irrational, and so was
Rhonda Glover. "She killed Jimmy Joste in the most
coldhearted way, and we are never going to understand it. She is mentally disturbed, that's part of it,
but you are never really going to understand it. It is
too mean, too cold, and it is beyond comprehension,
but beyond a reasonable doubt, Rhonda Glover is
guilty of murder."

Rhonda Glover's story, or various stories, did not
make sense. "Murderers are generally not rational
people," said Gail Van Winkle. "The law is judged by
what a reasonable ordinary person would think, not
an irrational murderer."

There was absolutely no evidence, even based on
Rhonda Glover's own testimony, that she shot Jimmy

under the "required necessity" of the laws regarding self-defense. "That is what is required to acquit the defendant," Van Winkle explained, "that self-defense was immediately necessary. Rhonda Glover wanted to base self-defense on her stories about Jimmy being abusive in the past."

When Gail Van Winkle stood in front of the jury, she made her position clear: "We are here to decide what happened on July 21, 2004, and her testimony does not even rise to the level of the legitimate self-defense claim. At first, she wanted you to believe that she was unsure of what happened. She cried. She said she was in shock. She couldn't even tell her attorney how the killing happened. Suddenly, when Mr. Case got her on cross-examination, her demeanor changed one hundred percent. She was lucid. She was evasive. She was even assertive—this is a woman who knew what she was talking about. She had planned this murder, and she had planned what she was going to testify to on the witness stand.

"She's not a truthful person," concluded Van Winkle. "The evidence speaks for Jimmy Joste. The evidence speaks to what really happened. It speaks to the truth. Listen to the truth, and you will find the defendant guilty of murder beyond a reasonable doubt."

"The state wants you to believe that there was a plan at work here," said Joe James Sawyer in his closing argument, "and, frankly, I agree with them. The question is, was it a plan to murder another human being, or was it a plan finally to run away and stay away? Was it because in November of 2003 events occurred that led Rhonda Glover, after all of those years, to conclude, 'No more.' The issue is not whether Jimmy Joste gave her presents and bought her cars. You know, you have to believe, if you buy into that has been her motivator, why bother to work? I mean, if you are a millionaire and you are this much in love, and [he is] lavishing these gifts on you, why work? I mean, if you are a goldbrick, why would you work? Do you remember Mr. Case asking her, 'Well, you must have some financial records, certainly you must have something to show that you actually do work.' I chose these two years, neither the beginning nor the end but some place in the middle—1997, 1998—and you'll see she had a gross income in excess of one hundred thirty-seven thousand dollars in one year. You can't have it both ways. She can't be just a gold digger and also be responsible to [her] own business and work at it and have it succeed. I think one of the problems we see here when there is a woman saying that one of the mainstays of this relationship was the fact that 'he would periodically abuse me,' and that is an ugly thing. Invariably, a perpetrator is ashamed of it himself. I wasn't just kidding when I was asking one of those witnesses, 'Do you think the men who do that go out and talk about it, brag about it, confide in their friends about it?' 'Gee, I have a problem, you know. Periodically, I'd just beat the hell out of the old lady.' Do you question that? Wouldn't it be true that like many of us, there is a public face and there is a private face. There is the person we are in our daily lives and with our friends, and there is a person who we are when we are alone with our family. Those are two faces [that] can be strikingly dissimilar, but when you ask coworkers and friends, 'Is he a violent guy?' is it surprising that the answer is 'No, pretty passive, pretty docile.' Well, except for the incident at Barton Creek, where we know they say he wasn't *really* guilty, he just chose to plead no contest. Maybe he did that because he didn't have a good enough lawyer, or unfair prosecution, or"—Sawyer changed his tempo, making sure the next line sunk in—"that is the one time you see that you can *prove* that there was *violence* by Jimmy Joste in that relationship. Maybe that is the one time he couldn't get off the hook. Maybe that is the one time you have real evidence of him being violent and abusive.

"Again I ask you to consider," said Sawyer, "was this a plan to run or a plan to murder? I think that the most illusory thing in this case is the gun range and the gun training. Every one of you picks up the paper, looks at a television. We hear about murders every day. No one has to get trained to commit murder. It does not require a lot of training to just go get one of these guns, walk up to whomever you are going to kill and let them have it. But I honestly believe the state says, 'No, she was getting this training to commit murder.' God forbid that you might believe she was getting the training because she intended to defend herself, because fear and concern would've been perfectly legitimate reasons to learn how to use a gun, and how to learn to use it in certain situations, particularly in your own home."

When both the defense and prosecution had given their final arguments, Judge Lynch addressed the jury. "It now becomes your duty to retire to the jury room to elect a foreperson, and then to begin deliberation of your verdict." The jury did as it was instructed.

Despite her defense attorneys' best efforts, there was never any reasonable doubt about the outcome. Perhaps Joe James Sawyer's strategy in putting Rhonda Glover on the stand was to let the jury experience Rhonda Glover. If he couldn't introduce evidence or testimony of her mental illness during the guilt or innocence phase, he could dramatically demonstrate it by putting his client on the stand.

"Because of her demeanor on the stand, the over-the-top emotional display while being questioned by her attorney, followed by her hostile attitude toward Bryan Case, it was easy to see the wide range of her emotional responses, and how quickly she could change from almost one personality into another," said Fred Wolfson. "That may have been the idea behind her attorney having her take the stand in her own defense—something she didn't have to do. By seeing and hearing Rhonda Glover respond under pressure, the jury could see that she at least had emotional problems, if not full-blown mental illness."

There were no long, arduous arguments amongst the jurors. Rhonda Lee Glover was found guilty of murder after less than three hours of deliberation.

"Ladies and gentlemen of the jury, this concludes the first phase of the trial. The second phase is the punishment phase. When there is a guilty verdict, a defendant, prior to trial, makes a determination of who they would like to have do punishment, either the jury or the court. In this case the defendant has opted for the jury to do punishment. Therefore, we will start the second phase tomorrow morning."

"I have to compliment Mr. Sawyer," admitted

Bryan Case, "he did an excellent job of offering his client the best defense, and putting the best possible spin on what seemed to us to be an open-and-shut case. He is a very good lawyer who did what he was supposed to do."

The punishment phase, or, as some call it, the mitigation phase, was a battleground for Rhonda Glover's future. This is where factors that could have influenced her behavior could be brought to the jury's attention as factors they should consider when deciding appropriate punishment.

On August 17, 2005, Douglas K. O'Connell notified Joe James Sawyer, Rhonda's attorney, that the state of Texas intended to present a list of crimes, wrongs and bad acts committed by Glover for the jury's consideration during the punishment phase of the trial.

The list was impressive, if not corroborated by arrests or convictions:

3/1/1999: Use of cocaine or other controlled substance or drug

12/16/2000: Use of cocaine or other controlled substance or drug

3/3/2003: Use of cocaine or other controlled substance or drug

10/3/2003: Use of cocaine or other controlled substance or drug

11/15/2003: Use of cocaine or other controlled substance or drug

11/25/2003: Use of cocaine or other controlled substance or drug

*1/13/2004: Use of cocaine or other controlled sub-
    stance or drug
3/11/2004: Loss of parental rights by order of the
    284th Judicial Court of Montgomery County,
    Texas
7/20/2004: Use of false names and addresses
(date unknown): Physical assault on James Joste in
    Harris County, Texas. The defendant was pregnant
    at the time of the attack.*

"They were pulling out all the stops to make sure
the jury saw what a mess Glover was," said Jeff Reynolds, "and show her as a chronic and recalcitrant
drug user who also was abusive and downright nasty.
The state even brought out Kim Waters, the former
employee terrorized and threatened by Rhonda
Glover. They also let the jury know that Rhonda shot
up cocaine and allegedly abused her own son."

The punishment/mitigation phase was, however,
the one place where Joe James Sawyer could bring
forth hard-data documentation that would give jurors
a clear picture of a woman who, in her heart of
hearts, believed Jimmy Joste was Satan, a cannibal,
ringleader of pagan sacrifices, murderer, child porn-
ographer, child killer and a violent man.

"Sawyer wisely paraded all those cops," recalled Jeff
Reynolds, "who had been out to the Mission Oaks
house. They told of when she called up claiming that
Jimmy had killed her son, stashed him in the attic, or
whatever, when the truth was Jimmy had taken his son
to the movies, and she knew where they were the
whole time. She just forgot, and naturally assumed that

Jimmy had killed the kid, so she calls the police. By the time that long line of police were done testifying, the jury knew Rhonda's history of delusions, false accusations and history of being emotionally and mentally disturbed."

Having made it clear, either directly or indirectly, that Glover was emotionally or mentally disturbed, Sawyer then elicited testimony from expert Alexandra Gauthier confirming that Texas offers excellent mental-health treatment to people placed on probation, but comparatively little or no mental-health care for people sent to prison.

"I have an undergraduate political-science degree from San Diego State, and a law degree from Ohio State," testified Gauthier, a criminal defense lawyer practicing in Travis, Williamson and Hays Counties, Texas. "At the time of the Rhonda Glover case, I had been practicing law in Texas for ten years."

Gauthier, familiar with representing emotionally disturbed persons in the criminal justice system, has been consulted often by both defense and prosecuting attorneys, and she helped edit and review a handbook by the Advocacy Foundation. ("It is a nonprofit advocacy group," she explained, "for people with mental illness.")

"The purpose of the condition of probation is both rehabilitative and punitive as well," explained Gauthier. "There is a wide range. It goes from doing community service, to taking drug and alcohol inpatient treatment. They go from all sorts of things—paying restitution, paying court costs and fees, paying for whatever types of programs the district judge would impose, including prison and jail time as well.

"If the judge deemed it appropriate," she said,

"and even if the jury were to grant probation, the judge can send someone to prison for drug and alcohol treatment for up to one hundred twenty days. Probation is a fairly adaptive mechanism in Texas, as it is elsewhere. It attempts to meet the needs of the person, the defendant, and needs of society to know that this person on probation is being watched, and is also benefiting from being on probation."

The judge also has the power in Texas to add any conditions of probation that he or she deemed reasonable. "Additionally," added Gauthier, "with mentally ill people, the judge can require them to take their medication, and do an inpatient or outpatient mental-health treatment, wear an ankle monitor. There are some pretty serious things that can happen on probation. It is like going to prison without walls. There are consequences for your behavior that are pretty serious, and the probation officers report to the judge. If you don't comply, you go to prison.

"Some of the best Social Services available to people with mental illness are made available to them while on probation in the state of Texas," Gauthier said. "There is a wraparound attempt made through private and state organizations to provide quality care, housing, employment and other types of opportunities to individuals who cannot afford to pay for those things themselves. This county has special programs for people on probation and parole to receive medication and counseling, housing and other issues to meet their needs."

Asked if these same services are provided to mentally ill people inside the prison system, her answer was quick and succinct: "No. These services simply do not exist inside the Texas penal institutions."

* * *

By putting this expert on the stand, Joe James Sawyer established an excellent foundation for the jury to select probation and mental-health care as the appropriate way of handling the strange case of Rhonda Glover. The state, of course, did not agree in the least.

"This isn't a probation hearing," Gail Van Winkle reminded the jury. "This is a punishment hearing. I anticipate that the defense counsel will ask you to strongly consider probation for the defendant in this case. I want you to know that just because you are instructed on the possibility of probation, just because a defendant is legally eligible for probation, does not mean that the defendant is entitled to it. Any person convicted of a first-degree felony, including murder, who has never been convicted of a felony in this state or any other state—as you heard was true of the defendant—is legally eligible for probation. You need to ask yourselves, 'Is probation appropriate for this case? Is probation appropriate for the taking of a human life? Is probation an appropriate punishment for taking Jimmy Joste from his family and friends?' Think about that. This was a cold and calculated act."

Van Winkle said that Rhonda Glover was mean. Exceptionally mean. "You cannot rehabilitate meanness. You cannot rehabilitate a manipulative woman. Yes, she has mental illness. There are lots of people in our community who live with mental illness, and they do not take the lives of other human beings."

Van Winkle then stated that it is appropriate that Texas provide mental health resources for "those individuals out in the community with mental illness who are not violent, who live a peaceful life, and do not commit violent acts, and do not take human lives."

Van Winkle's argument clearly characterized the denial of comprehensive mental-health resources as appropriate punishment for felons. If Glover were granted probation, Van Winkle asserted, she would go back out into the community. "She would be among us. She could be your neighbor, be on the bus you take, be around your children. Putting her on probation won't control her behavior. Probation can't make sure that she takes her medication.

"Probation can do a very limited amount of things," said Van Winkle, "and it is unfortunate that we can't save every person. We can't protect every person in our community, and our first obligation is to the law-abiding citizens of Travis County, and think what is best for them, and for the rest of our community. Is it really in the interest of justice to let this woman back out on the street with just supervision through probation?"

19

The jury was previously instructed that there were two ranges of punishment from which they could select. The jury would have to agree unanimously that Rhonda Glover did not act under the "immediate influence of severe passion arising from an adequate cause" in order to sentence her to somewhere between five years and ninety-nine years in prison. If she did act under the immediate influence of severe passion arising from an adequate cause, they could select a range of up to twenty years.

"Sudden passion arising from an adequate cause," explained Gail Van Winkle, "is generally a circumstance where, for example, you come home and find your spouse in bed with another person. Now, that's a situation where the jury could see someone being so surprised and upset that they would not be thinking clearly, and murder someone.

"We had nothing close to that in this case," Van Winkle said. "What we had was a woman who planned out this murder since May of 2004, and acted out her plan.

"You remember Jackie Pierce, the convicted felon. She testified as to what Rhonda told her. And, yes," said Van Winkle, "the judge instructed the jury that if they didn't want to believe her because she was a convicted felon many times over, that was up to them. By the same token, just because she is a convicted felon does not mean that the jury has to disregard her testimony.

"I think what is significant about that testimony," Van Winkle said, referring to Jackie Pierce, "is that she came in contact with Rhonda Glover in July of 2005, and Rhonda told her that she sought out the victim. She went to the house, believing he was there. She went up the stairs and unloaded the gun into him. Then, later, Rhonda told her that she was mad at Jimmy because she thought he'd been cheating on her. He had been hanging out with strippers, and he quit buying her things. As you know, John Thrash testified that Jimmy ran out of money right before his death, and they spent quite a bit of money around the time of his death, and there was nothing really left in his accounts."

Speaking to the jury in Judge Lynch's courtroom, Van Winkle referred to Rhonda Glover as "coldhearted, manipulative and mean—the kind of person who, because of her mental state and her unwillingness to take medication, cannot be rehabilitated. I ask you to think about what number of years in prison would be appropriate, and I know it is very difficult to put a value to Jimmy's life in a number of years."

The state also expressed concern for Rhonda and Jimmy's only child. "Shouldn't the son be allowed to grow up away from Rhonda Glover and be safe? Shouldn't our community be safe? Oh, I'm sure that defense counsel is going to make some issue about her mental health, and ask you to consider that as a mitigating factor. She has had numerous opportunities to get help for her mental problems, and she has medication that she refuses to take, and even if she does take them, she mixes them with illegal drugs. This is a very dangerous woman.

"You have heard a lot about the defendant," concluded Van Winkle, "and the defendant has rights, and they have all been met. She has had her day in court. Jimmy isn't here, and I ask you that if there is anything you can do, when you go back in that jury room, please remember Jimmy and remember him the way that Kelly, his brother, would want you to."

Kelly Joste was one of the last people to take the stand during the punishment phase. "He was exactly one year younger," said Kelly of his brother, Jimmy. "We were born on the same day, exactly one year apart. I don't know how my mother did that. Both our parents are gone, and we had one other brother who was killed early in life in a motorcycle accident when he was twenty-one or twenty-two."

"Jimmy and I were very close," said Kelly Joste. "Especially in the last ten years since our mother died. I spent a few holidays with Jimmy. He had his life and I had mine. In fact, I used to get mad at Jimmy because he wanted to exchange Christmas presents. I thought that was foolish, as we were grown men. He was very generous and I could never match his gifts. I always think of him on our shared birthday of January fifteenth, and at Christmastime. I think of him every night in my prayers."

Kelly Joste was not asked his opinion of Rhonda Glover, but Joe James Sawyer had a fairly good sense of intuition on such matters. "It should be no surprise that friends and family of Jimmy Joste sit there and think, 'Dear God, punish her severely,'" Sawyer said in his final remarks to the jury. "I don't think Rhonda Glover is evil. I don't think Jimmy Joste was evil. No person deserves to be killed. Death comes to all of us, too soon in many cases. It is a tragedy for that family and close friends, and I understand their anger, but is it appropriate that you transfer their anger to you?"

Whatever emotional reward Jimmy Joste's friends and family would receive from hearing the jury sentence Rhonda Glover to ninety-nine years would be, Sawyer insisted, a "feast of ashes." In a year or two, or three or four, "what will it mean?" Sawyer asked. "It will not bring Jimmy back to life. It will not be a balm to their hearts.

"Life in the penitentiary really means what it says," he told the jury. "I want you to think back and answer the question 'What did I do for my birthday last year? Who was I surrounded by? What was Christmas like?' How much the days of our lives mean to us, and do you think that the days of Rhonda Glover's life are any less meaningful to her?"

The jury, denied any information about Glover's mental health during the guilt or innocence phase, was now informed of her condition. "Sawyer wasn't going to go overboard playing the nutcase card," recalled Fred Wolfson, "but he certainly had his way of reminding them."

"I don't want any special sympathy for her because she suffers from a mental disease," Sawyer said, "but I do want you to know that I handed over to you everything I could think of to help you make your decision—not to get a special break, it is not for special sympathy. I'm asking you to deliberate and think, 'How many birthdays? How many Christmases?' Think what it would be like to be locked up and your family members die away—you get a letter, and you can't even go when your father dies, your mother or your aunt. Some of you may think, 'Well, good.' That is appropriate. So be it. I'm only asking you to consider. The decision you'll make all the next hours will be the most important decision ever made in this woman's life. Please do it with care, and do be respectful of each other."

"This isn't the most horrendous murder," admitted Bryan Case. "If it were, Rhonda Glover would face the death penalty. Maybe this is one of the most evil. No, I shouldn't say that either," he said, searching for the proper term, "because no human being has the right to declare someone evil."

After brief reflection he found the perfect word. "She's mean. In fact, she is one of the meanest people I've ever seen. She is also dangerous. Jimmy should have taken Rhonda's father's advice, taken his checkbook and gone. But goodness gracious, this woman needs to be held fully accountable for what she did to get out of that relationship."

There was another reason why Case believed it was in everyone's best interest for Rhonda Glover to be locked up. "Think about this," he said. "Think about Danny Davis, Joyce Imparato, Kim Waters, Christy Dillon, Patti Swenson, Rocky Navarro and others. What do they all have in common? Some of them live in Austin, and some of them live in Houston. I will tell you what they all have in common. If this woman is ever on the street, their lives are in danger, and that is simply a matter of fact. If this woman is ever on the streets of Austin, Texas, their lives are in danger, and the lives of many other people are in danger. I am not speaking in hyperbole here. I am not making up some outrageous argument or exaggerating. I am stating this as an absolute fact."

This line of reasoning was not something that hadn't already crossed the minds of those whose names he mentioned. Rhonda Glover was quick to anger, and carried a grudge with the same ease with which she carried a Glock 9mm.

"She is," Case restated, "just so mean. Take a look at what she says about people who were once her friends. Look at what she has done. I think you'll agree. I don't know what you do about mean. And I don't know how she could have gone this long and made it as well being this way, except that she's smart, attractive and has an outgoing personality. But what you have heard is witness after witness testifying to literally horrible things she has done for years and years and years, and, you know, I may be mistaken, but I don't know if anybody said anything good about her, period. Did anybody say anything good? Where? Is she a good mother? No. I mean, no one even in her family would say that she is a good mother. She is not. Debbie McCall, during the penalty phase of the trial, got up on the stand and said that Rhonda Glover was physically abusive to her son."

Dwelling again on the topic of Glover's only offspring, Case raised the question of what would be best for the child. "What would it do to him to think, to realize, that after all that evidence was presented, that a jury decided for some reason that the most appropriate thing to do was to reward his mother with either probation or a light sentence? In my opinion, probation or a light sentence is just a direct reward to her.

"Face it," said Bryan Case, "she just couldn't stand the thought of being pursued by Jimmy Joste, a man obsessively in love with her, and the father of her child, for the rest of her life. She has got to deal with Jimmy, and she's able to concoct all manner of justifications and excuses for what she had planned for some time. If he is not dead, then he is following her from here to eternity, and she can't stand it. She can't stand him sexually. He is no longer attractive to her at all, and the thought of him crawling all over her in that big RV is just too much. No, there is only one thing to do—and she telegraphed it long ago to Ms. Swenson—kill Jimmy Joste. It doesn't which came first, the decision to kill him, or the bizarre justification that he was Satan. The act and the outcome are the same. She empties the gun into him. He's dead. She killed him."

Joe James Sawyer was correct in his prediction of how the state would frame their closing arguments— that they would insist that Glover planned on killing Joste as far back as when Patti Swenson and she spent that evening at Mulligan's, and that the only thing that changed was the method of murder. That concept, successful in getting a guilty verdict, was used again in the state's arguments regarding the proper punishment for Glover's crime of murder.

When the punishment phase concluded, and before Rhonda Glover was to be sentenced, Sawyer wanted to leave the courtroom. Judge Lynch was a bit taken aback.

"You want to leave your client just sitting there by herself?"

The reason Sawyer wanted to walk out was because the only thing remaining before the sentence was read was what is termed "victim allocution." That's when the victim gets to make a statement to the court. It isn't preserved in the court records, but the judge and jury hear it.

In this case, as Jimmy Joste could not speak, his brother was going to make a statement as allowed under recent "victims' rights" rulings: *Every victim must be allowed to speak at the time of sentencing. The victim, no less than the defendant, comes to the court to seek justice. When the court hears, as it may, from the defendant, his lawyer, his family and friends, his minister, and others, simple fairness dictates that the person who has borne the brunt of the defendant's crime be allowed to speak.*

Those who favor victim impact statements believe they reveal information about the harm of a crime, and that's relevant to a purpose of sentencing: making sure that the punishment fits the crime. Proper punishment, advocates believe, cannot be meted out unless judges and juries know, in full, the harm caused by the crime. Victim impact statements educate judges and juries about these important facts so that an appropriate sentence can be imposed. Not everyone agrees, and one who disagrees is Joe James

Sawyer. He is not alone in his criticism of the policy, and the use of the policy in America's courtrooms.

Critics have taken the position that victim impact statements are such powerful evidence at sentencing that they overwhelm judges and juries. Some have even gone so far as to refer to the idea of victim impact as the "pollution" of sentencing with emotion.

Professor Susan Bandes, who might be the nation's leading scholar on emotion and the law, put the claim this way: "Studies suggest that victim impact evidence, particularly when it conveys intense emotional pain, evokes sympathy and anger in jurors. Jurors perceive greater suffering after hearing such statements, and hear the emotional intensity of the statements as 'a cry for help or relief.'"

There is evidence that the anger they feel upon hearing victim impact statements translates into feelings of punitiveness. There is also evidence, more generally, that anger tends to interfere with sound judgment—it inhibits detailed information processing, increases tendencies to blame, including misattributions of blame, and exacerbates the urge to punish.

"The legitimacy of victim impact statements is open to serious question," confirmed Travis Webb. "After all, how much influence should an individual's emotions have over the outcome of a case?"

The idea of fairness is popular but frequently disconnected from reality. There is even a more troubling concern, seldom expressed, that a call for equality between victims and defendants is actually a false front hiding the real objective: an abandonment of the rights and freedoms enshrined in the Constitution of the United States of America.

Victims' rights advocates often seek to portray the unrealistic dichotomy of the "good victim" and the "bad defendant." Real life isn't that simple. A mobster who gets shot by another mobster is just as much a victim as any other victim. The man who stabs his mother with a knife, and then is shot by his brother, might be the victim, or he might be the defendant, depending on what happened to whom, when and how.

Victims' rights advocates, according to law professor Mary Margaret Giannini, believe that our nation's scales of justice have tipped in favor of defendants and to the detriment of victims, who became faceless strangers expected to behave like good Victorian children—seen and not heard. The victim, an individual with a substantial personal interest in the trial proceedings, was sidelined and excluded.

Over the last thirty years, the victims' rights movement has made great strides. The criminal justice system is far more accepting of the presence of victims in criminal proceedings and in responding to their needs and interests. One area where this is particularly evident is in victims' increased participation at sentencing. Congress's most recent piece of federal victims' rights legislation, the Crime Victims' Rights Act, highlights the victim's expanded role at sentencing in that it grants to victims the express and enforceable right to be present and "reasonably heard."

Jimmy Joste's brother was reasonably heard in Judge Lynch's courtroom. Joe James Sawyer didn't walk out, after all. "Oh, c'mon, Jim," chided his longtime acquaintance and frequent legal adversary Bryan Case.

"Okay, I'll stay," said Sawyer to Judge Lynch, "but only because my friend Mr. Case asked me to."

The jury, entrusted with deciding the punishment, came back with a forty-six-year prison sentence for Rhonda Lee Glover. "I don't know if Rhonda was surprised that she didn't go free," commented Fred Wolfson, "but there were people who knew her who thought she deserved worse."

20

"I know Rhonda very well," stated a longtime acquaintance, "and she is completely insane. She would repeatedly tell me that she was Mary, the Mother of Jesus, [and] her son was Jesus Christ. There were snipers on the roof trying to kill him. George Bush was Satan and Joste was the Antichrist. She mentioned several times that those two teamed up and murdered and raped children in aquifers under the city, and then sold their meat in grocery stores. She should have gotten the death sentence."

Rhonda Glover didn't get the death sentence, but prison was almost the death of her. "She was a mental wreck," reported a former inmate Rae, who became friends with Glover in the Mountain View Unit of the women's prison in Gatesville, Texas. "She cried much of the time, and her hair was falling out by the handful. She had bald spots in several places over her head. Her heart was breaking over not being able to raise her son. She, too, had believed in the judicial system and found out the hard way that it is a joke. She was put on the field squad for her job assignment and it just about did her in. Women our age should not be put out in the fields to work. On the field squad, no matter what your age, you are expected to keep up with the twenty-year-olds. It is not a job for an older woman. At one point she just couldn't do it anymore. She was not going to go, and she didn't care about the consequences. Which is not good, the consequences or the fact that she didn't care.

"Several of us got together and gave her a pep talk and finally got her to go. I think if she could have sat down and made her heart stop beating, she would have. There was not much left of her at that point. I talked to Rhonda a lot about putting her attention on God and not to take her eyes off Him. He was her only hope to help her get through the valley she was going through. I also encouraged her to take some classes to keep busy.

"You cannot know the feeling unless you have been there," said Rae, who chose to take Glover's version of reality at face value. "We have been taught our entire lives to respect police and the judicial system. The feelings you have when you realize that the system has betrayed your trust is like a brick wall hitting you in the face. With that realization you also realize there is nothing you can do about it. That pretty much takes all hope away and without hope, what do you have? Rhonda would sit in the dayroom and talk to us mostly about her son, some about her case and the betrayal of attorneys and witnesses. You could feel her pain when she talked to you. Most people you talk to about their case, laughing about the stupid things they did to get where they are—not Rhonda. She was so distressed over the situation, I truly felt what she told me was truth. I have never met anyone that could stay in character that long for it to be an act.

"She was living in the hell of reality that she could do nothing about. She had been given a long sentence for defending her life, and what was the point? Her body got to live longer on this earth, but her spirit was without hope, therefore, dead. Rhonda began to go to church, spend her time reading her Bible, and before I left, I thought she was going to be okay if she stayed focused. I was very excited when I began to get letters from her that actually had a little hope in them. As time went on, she began to get to a better place in her own head and began to fight back.

"Let me tell you," said Rae, "the system does not make it easy for you to fight back. To get to the law library is a major ordeal. It is such an ordeal that most people give up. There was not a law library on Sycamore Unit. Offenders had to be bused to another unit and back. Returning from another unit, you had to wait in a fenced-in area to be searched before allowed back on the unit. We are talking year-round—cold, rain, hot—it didn't matter and it took several hours of waiting in the outside area at times before an officer would come to perform the strip search to allow you back on the unit. There is no access to typewriters, copies have to be handwritten, books outdated. Work had to be done in the library one hour at a time. Each trip to the library had to be a separate request that could take up to several weeks to get. God bless, Rhonda. She kept at it, wrote letters, and just kept on until she finally got to a unit with a law library. You would think that would solve the problem, but they would send her layins to go to the law library between work and college classes and there just wasn't time to go. I haven't gotten any reports of making this as difficult in some time, so, hopefully, she kept on until she resolved the issue. I pray every day Rhonda gets another day in court."

In July 2008, the Texas Court of Criminal Appeals declined a petition to review the Travis County murder conviction and forty-six-year prison sentence of Rhonda Glover. The 3rd Court of Appeals in Austin had previously affirmed the sentence and conviction.

Glover asserted that the district court abused its discretion by refusing to submit an instruction on the lesser included offense of criminally negligent homicide. *Every case in which someone points a loaded gun at another does not require that a charge of criminally negligent homicide be given. Nor does the allegation of accidental discharge necessarily raise the issue,* stated the court. *The attendant circumstances from which the defendant's mental state can be inferred must be collectively examined in light of the definition of criminally negligent conduct. Evidence that a defendant knows a gun is loaded, that he is familiar with guns and their potential for injury, and that he points a gun at another indicates a person who is aware of a risk created by that conduct and disregards the risk, such a person is at least reckless.*

The evidence at trial established that at the time of the shooting, Glover was familiar with firearms, had practiced on multiple occasions using the specific firearm that was used in the shooting, and had received lessons in "advanced firearms training" involving "very specific scenarios." Americo Mastroianni, Glover's instructor, testified that Glover was "very efficient" at hitting targets, and Mack Farrel, the general manager of Red's Indoor Range, testified that Glover had improved her shooting technique "tremendously" from the day she purchased her gun to the day of the shooting. In light of this evidence, no rational jury could have found that Glover was unaware of the risks associated with her use of firearms or with her firearm in particular.

Furthermore, the physical evidence at the crime scene established that Joste was shot ten times, and that some of the bullet wounds and bloodstain patterns found around his body indicated that Jimmy Joste was shot while he was retreating from the shooter and after he had already fallen to the ground. This evidence, along with Rhonda Glover's own testimony, excludes criminally negligent homicide as a "valid rational alternative" to murder. There was no evidence that would permit a rational jury to acquit Glover of murder while convicting her of criminally negligent homicide, and, accordingly, the district court did not abuse its discretion in refusing the instruction.

Glover contended that the district court erred in admitting evidence seized in her Houston apartment. Specifically, Glover argued that the state failed to prove that she "freely and voluntarily consented to the search of her apartment." The basis of this complaint during trial was that on November 1, 2004, Glover had been found incompetent to stand trial, although she was later found competent to stand trial. At the competency hearing Detective Walker's videotaped interview of Glover—in which Glover consented to the search of her apartment—was admitted as evidence of Glover's incompetence. Glover contended that if the interview was evidence of her incompetence to stand trial, then it was also evidence that she was incompetent to give her consent to search the apartment. *We need not address the merits of this issue,* said the court, *because any error in admitting the evidence was harmless.*

With the high criminal court's decision to decline review in the case, the conviction and sentence stood. Rhonda Glover remained at Mountain View.

It's not really so bad here, wrote Rhonda Glover to the author. While those on death row bemoan their treatment, inmates such as Rhonda Glover don't seem as miserable as one might imagine.

It's not like I'm in a dreary cell with bars and all that stuff. I live in a dorm like I'm in college. I have a cubicle with a big window and red tiled and a red brick wall. I am not locked behind any cell block bars. God is good. I know a lot of Jimmy's people wish I were dead but they have no clue what he did to us. He had totally lost his mind. I spend a lot of time in the law library, and I had to fight for that time in the law library, I'll tell you that. I do a lot of work for the blind here, making things in Braille. I'm being useful. When are you coming to see me? Do you know that there is going to be a television show about my case? I'm being interviewed here in prison, Glover wrote.

The television show *Snapped* airs on the Oxygen Network, and has a loyal following. The 2009 season finale featured the story of Rhonda Glover and Jimmy Joste.

Lest anyone think that life at Mountain View is like a live-in junior college, here is an indication of the

types of concerns voiced by inmates in a recent petition
to the warden:

> *The inmates are unable to sleep through, because
> of permanent checks all 30 minutes throughout the
> night. During the checks, the riot door is being opened
> and slammed shut loudly; huge key rings are clang-
> ing up and down the run, lest the inmates have to be
> awakened every 30 minutes. At 4:00 a.m. they are
> waken up again for breakfast and then once again
> at 5:30 a.m. to get ready for work. The constant
> broken sleep leads to mental and physical health
> problems for the women. We understand that checks
> may be necessary, but ask to do them without inter-
> rupting the sleep.*
>
> *Those that need medication have to get out of bed
> at 3:00 a.m. in the night to take their medicine. Addi-
> tional to the early time they have to take the medica-
> tion, the huge flood lights are turned on for a mouth
> check. They have to open their mouth and stick out
> their tongue and raise their tongue to inspect whether
> or not the adult persons were able to swallow their med-
> icine. Why aren't they given the medication together
> with breakfast?*
>
> *There are daily cell-searches, often combined with hu-
> miliating strip searches. Sometimes the women are forced
> to strip off their clothes several times a day, and get
> searched. These searches are often conducted by male
> prison personnel, which is degrading and has to be re-
> fused as a violation of their female intimacy and
> human dignity. Mountain View and all US-prisons
> should join international standards in making sure
> that women are only [to] get searched by female staff.*
>
> *Since in-cell-crafting has been taken away from the*

*inmates, they are not allowed to crochet, knit, do needle-
work or any other kind of craft in their cells, which was
most of all their solace and distraction. This restriction
also cut the women off the possibility to do handicrafts
for their children's birthdays or Christmas gifts to their
relatives. The women who decided to work are allowed
for group recreation in a common room from 6 to 8
p.m. after work. They are only allowed to do crafting
during this recreation time. With the TV playing on
high volume it's hard for the women to concentrate.
The women who do not work, have no chance to do
any crafting. We ask to take off this restriction and
allow in-cell-crafting again.*

Rhonda Glover sits at Mountain View, miles north
of Gatesville, on FM 215 in Coryell County. There are
314 total employees, of which 232 are correctional officers. As for medical staff, there are 19 contract medical employees for 645 residents, and a psychiatric
staff of 5. According to the facility's online information, ambulatory medical care, dental and mental-
health services and inpatient psychiatric care are
available. The health care is managed by UTMB
HealthCare Systems, a wholly owned subsidiary of the
University of Texas Medical Branch (UTMB).

Mountain View holds all levels of custody, including a death row for women scheduled for execution.
Death row offenders are housed separately from the
rest of the prisoners in single-person cells measuring
sixty square feet (5.6 m²), with each cell having a
window. They don't have recreation individually. They
are allowed to watch television, and all have a radio.

Rhonda Glover isn't the worst inmate at Mountain

View by any stretch of the imagination. Among the better-known death row offenders at Mountain View are Brittany Holberg and Darlie Routier. Holberg, awaiting execution, robbed and murdered an eighty-year-old man in his home after asking him if he would be nice enough to let her use his telephone. The victim was struck with a hammer and stabbed nearly sixty times. The weapons used were a paring knife, a butcher knife, a grapefruit knife and a fork. A foot-long lamp pole had been shoved more than five inches down the victim's throat. No one suggests that she is innocent.

Darlie Routier, convicted of slaughtering her two young boys, has mounting widespread support for a new trial due to various legal irregularities, plus the possibility of new evidence that could vindicate her.

"I have widespread support too," Rhonda Glover has insisted, but there are no organized grassroots campaigns to get Rhonda a new trial or a pardon by the governor. The simple fact of the matter is that Rhonda Glover killed Jimmy Joste. There was absolutely nothing in her testimony, or in the physical evidence, that came even close to meeting the definition of self-defense under the law.

You can't claim self-defense based on alleged bad acts by the victim in the past. Such justification may work in the troubled mind of the person who did the killing, but not in the rational minds of twelve jurors, or in the laws of the state of Texas.

Epilogue

I can't wait for you to come see me, wrote Rhonda Glover. *I have so much to tell you.* The Texas prison system is very cooperative with the press, radio and television. If you are a newspaper, radio or television reporter seeking an interview with Rhonda Glover, there is no problem. Although I do a weekly radio show, "True Crimes," write articles for the internationally acclaimed "In Cold Blog," which are then featured in major newspapers and magazines, what you are holding in your hands is a book. The Texas Department of Criminal Justice (TDCJ) has disallowed interviews between "book authors" and inmates.

According to Suzy Spencer, veteran true crime writer, "Authors might possibly get an interview through the research department. But that involves filling out a long form that must reveal any criminal history, including DWIs, subjects us to urine tests, and orders us not to name our inmate in our books. That form must then be notarized. . . . Obviously, if other media were required to go through such scrutiny, TDCJ wouldn't have to bother setting up very many inmate interviews."

According to TDCJ public information officer Michelle Lyons, the problem is that authors cannot verify identity as journalists can with "letterhead," and that the TDCJ is too short-staffed to accommodate extended research visits: "The bottom line is that it's an issue of public safety—we do have the right to approve and deny all visitors."

This meant that my visit to Rhonda Glover would take place as a friend, not as an author of true crimes. This also meant no tape recorder, computer or writing tablet. My visits were as if I were family, or an enamored fan of a woman convicted of murder. Believe me, there are plenty of those.

Eager to meet Rhonda, I traveled to Texas on four different occasions to meet with her. Three times I returned without seeing her. The first time the Texas prison system was shut down due to an inmate somehow procuring a cell phone, and making a fortune in illegal calls. Then, next time, my visit corresponded with Glover being sent out of town for medical treatment. The time after that, it was the swine flu scare that shut down the prisons. Finally, nearing the book's deadline, I made it through security to spend two hours with Rhonda Glover.

She wasn't expecting me, and was delighted by my surprise visit. She came bounding into the visiting area, separated from me by a solid pane of glass. Her energy was as I anticipated, and her looks even better than I imagined.

By the time Rhonda and I met, I had read the psychiatric reports, medical records, police documents and trial transcripts. Yes, she has a vibrant and enthusiastic personality, and she is easier to read than *Junior Scholastic.* Her emotions—impatience, anger, frustration or happy enthusiasm—manifest themselves like neon signs in Times Square. Watch the eyes, the body language, and learn what she regrets.

She is blessed with a quick mind, creativity and intense energy. I can see why she had friends, and lost friends. If she sets her mind to something, I doubt there is little to stop her. When the conversation veers away from Rhonda Glover, it is only allowed to stray for a moment. She is the center of her known universe, and gravity pulls everything into her orbit. It is easy to see both the attraction and the aversion.

If you anger her, she knows how to manifest anger. She is still mad at her mother, despite her mother having devoted her life to caring for, protecting and rescuing her, Jimmy and their son. Beyond the tragic death of Jimmy Joste, there is the living tragedy of a mother seeing her daughter become a murderer, and a blameless child losing both his parents—one to senseless violence; the other to prison.

"My son asks me why I don't just admit that I'm crazy," Rhonda Glover shares. "Well, I won't do that. I'm not going to say I'm crazy. I've been tested here in prison, and I'm fine. I don't have mental illness at all. You can see the test results yourself. Well, obviously there was something seriously wrong with me to stay in a dysfunctional relationship," says Glover. "It was crazy for me to be involved with Jimmy Joste.

"After I went to Betty Ford in 1998, I was sent to a lady who, upon her observation, diagnosed me with bipolar. No doctor diagnosed me. I agreed to go on a litany of drugs because that is how I functioned. I was in denial that I had a relationship problem, and being on pills gave Jimmy the excuse to use when the cops came. 'Don't worry, she's just off her medication.' I was taking antipsychotics and Antabuse. I wasn't off my medications. I was on medications for a mental illness that I didn't have. Someday the truth will come out. I know it will. Then they will all know. It will be on the news. But I want to forget about all that. I just want to go home and be a mommy again."

"Rhonda," I ask her, "may I quote you in the book saying, 'I believed *at that time*' about the cave, the clones, the bodies?"

"No, you don't understand. All that is true, Burl. Listen to me. In the book, please don't say that I killed Jimmy. I didn't kill him, don't say that. I don't want my son to read that I killed his father. Okay, I shot him, and he died, but I was only protecting myself. It wasn't like I killed him, or murdered him. I have people who believe in my case, people who know how a woman must have the right to defend herself in her own home. There are so many things I didn't tell, so many things I was afraid to tell. Things that my lawyer said not to mention, that he told me to keep secret. Like the cave, for instance, that's true. They may have told you that there are only two entrances to Cave X at Regents School. There are other entrances, and all those things I said about what goes on in there is true. I just had to not mention some things because it was too dangerous, so my lawyer told me not to talk about them."

Rhonda is referring to the competency decision: she was competent to stand trial if she could keep her mouth shut and follow her lawyer's instructions on what not to talk about. If she could keep some things "secret," then she was competent. That is, admittedly, a rather mind-boggling standard of mental competence.

"Why did Jimmy believe that the three of you were going to leave the country?"

"How did you know that?" she asks as if I had just announced the location of Amelia Earhart. "How did you know that?"

"He said so, Rhonda. Jimmy told more than one person that all of you were leaving together for Canada."

Her mind races so fast you can almost smell burning rubber coming from her cerebral cortex. "He didn't tell Rocky Navarro," she says as if laying out a perfect hand of poker. "They were best friends. If Jimmy really believed that, he would have certainly told Rocky, and he didn't."

She pauses for a moment; her eye movements indicate the creative process at work.

"He was planning to leave the country after he killed me," she says, improvising with remarkable fluidity. "He had his plans, and I knew he was going to either pay to have me murdered, or do it himself. He had both in mind. He hired two men to help him kill me that day."

This version was never told to the police, nor was it presented in the courtroom. "Jimmy brought help with him to take me down. He did not expect for me to have that gun, because I have always been adamantly against them. He knew I would never resort to that. Or, at least, he thought I would not. So, if I were planning to kill him, why would I go to the gun store where we knew the owners so well? There are ways to get a weapon on the streets. I have met many of his thug friends. I was in rehab. I speak the drug language, money talks. I could have gotten a gun from the streets. Why would I do it the legal way?"

I don't mention the fact that she didn't get it the legal way. She gave false information on the ATF form, rendering the transaction illegal.

"If I were going to claim it was self-defense," she continues, "then why wouldn't I just immediately call the cops and cry rape or something?"

Good question.

"Innocent people run, that's why. My intentions were to get my son to my mom's and then tell her to help me, but she wasn't there. Then my son asked me why I was crying so hard, and I said, 'Something happened to Jimmy and I am sad.' He said, 'Mom, why are you going to let him ruin our last summer trip?' I just knew that I was coming to prison. I truly did not know he was broke and my thoughts were all about them saying I did it for money. You see where I am coming from? Plus, with those guys seeing my car and my face, I believed they knew more about me and my family and they would come after me. I did tell my first and second lawyers about them, but neither one chose to investigate it. They said unless I knew them, there was literally nothing we could do. I can pick them out of a lineup. I am certain about that."

Joe Lanza, her new attorney, has been informed about these two mystery men who came to kill her, but they hid behind Jimmy when she started firing. "They used him as a shield," insists Rhonda. Jimmy wasn't bulletproof, and two shots went right through him and into the wall.

"I told Lanza that Sawyer did not want me to tell the jury all that stuff. I was not prepped for the stand at all. I had no idea what to say and I was out of it. I

was on pills that do not go together, Burl. I refused
my pills before trial. That is an automatic ground for
reversal. I hope you get to see the truth come out and
the book takes on a whole different perspective for
you. So, you see, that the bullets that went to his
elbow were the first ones fired at him to stop him.
The next ones were where the black dude used
Jimmy as a shield. I had not intended for him to have
a fatal wound, Burl. I was firing at another attacker as
I was being attacked. There were two other men
there with him that day. He showed up and came
straight up to the guest room. I had been in the attic
looking for my camping equipment to take on the
RV. I went to hide the gun there because the gun
store told me I did not have a concealed carry license, the only way to carry it was to and from the
gun range. So I legally own that house. I was planning
on hiding it in my Christmas stocking upside down.
It would fit perfectly without detection. I carried it in
a computer case.

"If I left it out like that, then they would want to
hock my computer, right? I mean, I already knew that
strangers had been in there. Do you have any clue
how violated I felt and scared? I had been robbed
there before. There is a police report on it. Anyway,
Jimmy came in and started screaming and asking
about our son, and I said, 'You will never see him
again,' and that is when he started choking me. I pre-
tended to be passed out and he found the gun. Then
there was a knock at the door downstairs. He went
into the bathroom and fixed his shirt and put his
glasses back on and went down there. When he left
the room, I ran to the desk to call 911, but there was
no phone.

"You don't realize how connected Jimmy was," Rhonda continues. "You don't know who he was tied into. I ran away, and I thought those men would call 911 and Jimmy would live. I didn't think I mortally wounded him. I'm not that good a shot. I could tell you the names of the men who were with Jimmy that day, the day he tried to kill me to stop me from saying what I found on his computer. I was told not to say anything at my trial about it. They came to kill me, all three of them. One of them jumped me. When I was shooting Jimmy, they were hiding behind him, using him as a shield. I thought I was going to die. My lawyer told me not to mention this at the trial. You see, Jimmy was very highly connected. He wanted me killed because I knew too much. I knew what he did, especially after what I found on his computer."

"You mean child pornography?"

She makes what is known in body language as the "defensive beating gesture"—the hand goes suddenly up to the back of the neck. It is called the defensive beating gesture because the arm begins to rise as if about to beat someone, but instead goes to the back of the neck. For those who read body language, it indicates that the person making the gesture would like to beat you for what you just said, and is defensive. In short, it is my opinion that Rhonda Glover wishes she'd never said a word about the nonexistent child porn.

"No," says Rhonda. She isn't talking about child pornography; she's talking about evidence of more commonplace criminal wrongdoing. "He was cooking the books," insists Rhonda. "He was ripping people off, falsifying data, and he was in big with the Mexican drug gangs and Mexican oil swindles."

There is no proof whatsoever of her allegation

that Jimmy Joste had any connection to criminals, specifically drug gangs who tap remote pipelines, sometimes building pipelines of their own, to siphon off hundreds of millions of dollars' worth of oil each year. What Rhonda Glover appears to do is simply take anything and everything that has any linkage to any aspect of Jimmy's life and make it part of his evil empire. She never said a word about Mexican oil until it was in the newspaper. Within twenty-four hours she has Jimmy connected to Mexican drug lords and the nationalized Mexican oil industry.

"We spent a lot of time in Mexico," she says. "We went there all the time." That clinches it. When an oilman holidays in Mexico, there are nefarious dealings afoot.

Rhonda Glover has little or no patience for those who doubt her accusations against Jimmy Joste. "People don't believe he beat me, for example," Rhonda says. "Look at my face. Look closely. I'll point out all the scars inflicted on me by Jimmy."

She points to one above her eye. "See that? He hit me with a candelabra. See this one? And here above my lip? On September 11, 2001, he put me in the county hospital with broken ribs."

Rhonda, confident in her ability to persuade, offers logical "proof" that she didn't plan on killing Jimmy Joste, that it wasn't premeditated. "Think about this," she says, "I never called in advance for a sitter. My friends, the Barders, were called at six-thirty the night before and asked to watch my son. If I had plans to meet Jimmy at my house that day, I would have made arrangements for my son way in advance. Anyone with kids knows you don't plan anything without a sitter arranged in advance. Tony and Duanna

Barder will tell you I was not even in touch with them for one year prior to me asking them to watch my son that day.

"I want you to know," says Rhonda, "that the things Danny Davis said about Jimmy buying me homes and cars are lies. He did not. He once bought me a Jeep Cherokee because while I was pregnant, and went into premature labor, he told GMAC to come get my Cadillac. I'm not crazy. I'm not delusional. I know exactly what I'm talking about. I have the evidence. I found bubble gum in the house, and my son hadn't been there in months. There had been a child in that house."

"I know adults who chew bubble gum, Rhonda—"

"Nò!" She cuts me off, and her impatience and anger at my comment is obvious. "Children chew bubble gum, not adults. And this was a big, really big, wad of bubble gum."

"Adult size?" I am pushing my luck.

She rolls her eyes. She heard me. She understood me. She has chosen to ignore it.

"I told them about the bubble gum," says Rhonda. "I have that gum, and the shoe on the snow. We found that shoe, you know. You read about that, right? There was a child's shoe in the snow."

This is the Rhonda Glover I saw on the DVD of her interrogation by Austin detectives. This is the Rhonda Glover, declared incompetent to stand trial, the Rhonda Glover who told people her son was Jesus Christ and that Jimmy Joste and George Bush were murdering children in a cave.

"Oh yes, I remember that," I say, with encouraging enthusiasm, "you collected all that evidence and sent things to Identigene." The money to pay Identigene, it was revealed at her trial, came from the bank account of Jimmy Joste.

"Yes!" She's pleased that I know this. "The DNA wasn't mine, Jimmy's or our son's."

I purchase Rhonda another Coca-Cola, and our conversation continues. She speaks of her supporters, the horrors of domestic violence, and the Second Amendment Foundation. "They are big supporters," insists Glover.

"In the *Gun Week* magazine that my dear friend Alan sent me was an article about a man who shot four people, then went to play video games. He received four life sentences. The article said he would have to do twenty-three years before he saw parole. I got forty-six years for self-defense in my own home, with my own weapon, against someone who had been in jail for assaulting me and threatening my life, and I will have to do twenty-three years before I talk to the parole board if things do not get overturned in court. I learned that I had a twenty-year deal, and did not know about this until recently. Please pray for the courts to allow me a new trial. But isn't that an amazing story? I have the equivalent of four life sentences in Maryland. Aren't we all living in America, and under the same Constitution protected by our Second Amendment? Why is Texas so off-kilter in their sentencing?"

Under the same Constitution enshrining the Second Amendment, Rhonda Glover did not have the right to bear arms. She lost that right when she put false information on her application to purchase the Glock 9mm. She can't claim a right she forfeited. The Second Amendment Foundation is a big supporter of the right to self-protection and defense of liberty by all those "eligible" to own guns. Rhonda Glover was not legally eligible to own a weapon. It would be difficult for them to champion her when her possession of a handgun was a violation of federal law.

"Do you ever speak to my lawyer?" Rhonda asks. "I write him all the time, but I don't hear from him."

I assure her that Joe Lanza, her current attorney, is a knowledgeable man of excellent reputation. Yes, he gets her mail.

"You know, if you reveal too much, it could be dangerous for you too," says Rhonda, concerned for my safety.

"Hey, this is what I do, Rhonda. I investigate, I report. I search for truth. Sometimes I find it. Sometimes I find that under a layer of fake lies and half-truths are real lies and half-truths."

"Some people have stood by me, unconditionally," asserts Rhonda. "I have friends who care about me, friends who would have testified on my behalf at my trial, but they were never called."

I find myself thinking of Patti Swenson, who testified for Rhonda at the custody hearing, saying what a good mom she was, and how Rhonda and her son were only doing Bible study role play when Rhonda was Mary and Ronnie was Jesus. Rhonda isn't happy with Patti anymore. Based on previous patterns, it is possible that Rhonda could embrace Patti as her dear pal on a moment's notice. Rhonda has been mercurial with her friendships all her life. Sometimes you are on the bus; sometimes you are off the bus. Sometimes you are under the bus!!!

One friend who has stayed loyal is Stephanie Vaughn, Rhonda Glover's best friend since the fourth grade. "I believe that a true friend walks in when the rest of the world walks out," Vaughn has said. "Rhonda was there with me through every milestone I experienced in my life. My prom, my wedding, the birth of my children, and when I was diagnosed with multiple sclerosis. She was a beautiful, strong, confident, assertive and successful woman. I never witnessed the actual physical abuse, but I did witness some of the out-of-control drinking. I did see Rhonda on several occasions when she had left him due to his alleged abuse. I had no reason to doubt her. I cannot imagine the horror of what drove her to that fateful decision, but I do know her and I will tell you that she could never have done anything like this, unless she thought she had no other choice. This is indeed a tragedy and my heart grieves for my dear friend Rhonda, for her son, who now has lost his mother and father, for Rhonda's family, for Jimmy's friends and family, and for Rhonda's countless friends, who are no doubt left as perplexed and saddened as I."

If there is anything to offset Rhonda Glover's sadness with incarceration, it is her assertion: "I have found my calling through all of this—criminal justice reform. I want to be a lawyer or at least play one on TV. I will write writs of habeas corpus for those who are stuck in here without justice and are innocent. There are thousands left behind in here. I really just want to go home," she says, wherever home is. "I want to go back and be a mommy."

A corrections officer interrupts. It's time for Rhonda Glover to leave her side of the glass divider. Visiting hours are over. She will be eligible for parole in twenty-odd years. Even then, she won't be going home to be a mommy. Her son will be over thirty years old by then, and probably have a family of his own.

* * *

"I hear from Rhonda Glover all the time," says attorney Joe Lanza. "She writes me constantly."

Lanza is working on a "collateral attack" on behalf of Rhonda Glover. "This isn't an appeal, or part of the appeal process," explains Lanza. "This is different than an appeal, which is a challenge to the decision made in the same case. A collateral attack refers to when a separate and new lawsuit is filed to challenge some aspect of an earlier and separate case because an obvious injustice or unconstitutional treatment occurred in the earlier case.

"We are looking for a reversal of judgment in Rhonda's case," Lanza explains. "We are raising several issues [that] we believe could result in the case being tried all over again. This doesn't happen very often, but it does happen. You see this type of reversal of judgment in cases where there is suddenly new evidence, such as DNA, or the law has changed, or there is blatant misconduct by prosecutors, or ineffective counsel for the defense. Yes, it may be a long shot, but we are working on it."

Should success crown Lanza's efforts, Rhonda Glover would get another trial. It is all very questionable, as would be Rhonda's ability to assist rationally in her own defense. One must wonder what the ramifications would be if she was found a second time incompetent to stand trial, after spending five or ten years in prison following conviction.

She does get some mental-health treatment in prison, but nothing compared to what she would get if she was serving her sentence at Texas State Hospital or in a proposed but nonexistent program of separation from society, coupled with complete psychiatric care for the full length of her sentence.

"When in prison, your health care is limited, both physically and mentally," explains Lanza. "If you are on probation, you have access to the same health care as anyone else. In prison you get what they give you. Taxpayers are not known for wanting to pay too much for prisoner care. I get mail from prisoners all the time who are dying from some illness that could have been caught and treated, had they only had basic decent health care while in prison. They don't."

"You know, it is not that far-fetched," offers Fred Wolfson, "that Lanza gets Rhonda a reversal. It all goes back to the beginning, and what if . . . what if . . . you know, here she is in prison still talking about Cave X, bubble gum, and Devil worshipers. She is still nurturing the same delusions. The big difference is that she is in a structured environment, and is getting at least some care. It is almost as if her condition, and the denial of it, is a mirror image of the entire approach to crimes committed by the mentally ill, diseased or brain damaged. It's delusional, ignores reality and has really no use for the discoveries of modern medicine."

Texas laws are not much different than most states' laws, and most states have locked themselves into situations regarding crime, punishment and prevention that resonate more with the world of Charles Dickens than anything related to the twenty-first century. America justice calls for the imprisonment of both the irresponsible criminal and the criminally irrational, and places them together in the same facility.

That could be a new definition of insanity, and I doubt there is a defense for it.

I am glad Rhonda Glover is not walking the streets with a Glock 9mm. If she was in a paranoid delusional state, and was convinced someone was Satan, it could be fatal. There is ample evidence that the combination of Rhonda Glover, firearms and paranoid delusions are deadly. The death by gunfire of the affable Jimmy Joste is irrefutable evidence.

I also think we would all be better served if we could simply deal with what's real when it comes to crime, punishment and prevention. Under the current laws of many states in America, no one is "insane" if he or she knows killing is "wrong." Saying that someone is sane—no matter how crazy they are—simply because they know what they did was illegal makes no sense in this century of information and scientific discovery. Denying comprehensive psychiatric treatment to the mentally ill as punishment for acts committed as symptomatic of the illness might not come under the category of cruel and unusual punishment, as usually defined. However, when the mentally ill are punished by imprisonment, and a primary characteristic of that imprisonment is the denial of the same level of treatment that they would receive in a mental hospital, the punishment, in the opinion of many, is then both cruel and unusual.

In this debate over how to deal with mentally compromised felons, it is easy to forget that Jimmy Joste, a man well loved by friends and family, was shot dead and left to rot in the home at Mission Oaks. Kelly Joste rightly characterizes Jimmy as a kind, caring, compassionate and generous man who welcomed all, showed kindness to all and cared so much for the mother of his child that he was willing to endure all manner of madness. There was a picture of Jimmy Joste shown in Mike Lynch's courtroom that depicted Jimmy the way his brother remembers him—a good-looking guy with an easygoing attitude and warm, inviting smile.

"You know," said Danny Davis, "if Rhonda, bless her heart, had been okay mentally, or simply taken her medications and stayed off illegal drugs, and if Jimmy had stayed off that crap too, then they might have all really had a good life together. They were both basically good people from good backgrounds. He loved her with all his heart. They had a wonderful son together. You can see in your mind how if they had just not gone down that road, they could have had a life that was the kind other people only dream about—two physically attractive people, plenty of financial resources, the creativity to do great things, a warm, loving family with supportive friends who loved them. Yes, there was always the potential there for unlimited happiness. Instead, he's dead and she's in prison. My heart goes out to his brother, Kelly, and Jimmy's son, and everyone in both families. Having known Jimmy ever since I was a kid, it is as if I lost a member of my own family. No, let me rephrase that. Jimmy was family."

Jimmy Joste was a good friend, an excellent cook, a fun companion and, in the final analysis, a man who allowed wishes to overrule reason, and feelings to obscure established facts. He always believed that he could control Rhonda Glover. Not even Rhonda could control Rhonda.

Acknowledgments
and Clarification

This book is an interpretive version of events adapted from personal interviews, witness depositions, police reports and court records—many of which were recalled from memory. All statements, testimony and/or conversations were subject to editorial emendation for purposes of clarity, concision and readability, and are not to be taken as literal or verbatim. All effort has been made to retain factual accuracy. Any mistakes of fact are unintentional. Some names have been changed for reasons of legality or courtesy. Any and all allegations of illegal acts or moral wrongdoing made by anyone in this book against anyone else are allegations only, and/or matters of personal opinion that do not reflect the opinions or positions of either the author or the publisher.

Due to the complexity of this story, and the wide range of emotions and opinions it evokes, I summoned to the page numerous experts, psychiatrists, psychologists, judges, lawyers and a plethora of my fellow true crime authors, including Steven Long,

Ron Franscell, John Semander, Caitlin Rother and many more whose viewpoints are as divergent as those expressed by the legal and medical sources. One thing you won't find in this book is 100 percent agreement on what should be done in a homicide case such as this, and that is what makes this case so fascinating.

As with my previous book, *Mom Said Kill,* I called upon Fred Wolfson, internationally famed private detective, and Jeff Reynolds, requested alias of an outspoken investigative journalist, for insightful observations and opinionated commentary. Joining them is Travis Webb, also an accomplished researcher and journalist who assisted me in the preparation of my book *Head Shot.*

Rhonda Glover was afforded every opportunity to speak her mind, and her mind is central to the story. Glover has a well-documented medical condition that severely impacts her ability to think rationally. She suffers from relentless and recalcitrant paranoid delusions. For her, these delusions are irrevocably woven into the fabric of her personal reality. She is not, by legal definition, insane. She is capable of functioning with productive normalcy in the structured environment of the Texas correctional facility in which she is currently housed.

Gratitude is expressed to the Austin Police Department, the city of Austin and the various departments that, via Mr. Smiley, of the Office of City Attorney, made an incredibly daunting research assignment considerably easier; Danny Davis, Rocky Navarro and many others offered generously of their time and memories. Deep appreciation to Michaela Hamilton and her dedicated editorial staff at Kensington Publishing

Group's Pinnacle True Crime imprint for encouraging me to produce the best book possible under what were not the easiest of conditions.

On a very personal note, this book would not have been possible without the kind support of my son and daughter, Anea and Jordan Barer, son-in-law Isaac Cummings and the following vastly diverse individuals who made it possible for me to maintain a relative degree of sanity and stability during the writing of this book: Matt Alan, Lori Downey, Don Woldman, Michael Hirshensen, Marty Sherer, Kip Addotta, Howard Lapidas, Shadoe Stevens, Ryan Stiles, Elya Baskin, Prescott Niles, Richard Tyson, Jimmy the Printer, Robert Hayes, Johnny Cosmo, Robo and Billy Dilly, from the Big Fish in Glendale. Special gratitude is expressed to both Ms. Susan Balcuns and Dr. Ata Egrari for their kind hospitality during the completion of the final manuscript.

Resources

Rhonda Glover was initially diagnosed as suffering from bipolar disorder, and later revised to psychosis NOS. People with this diagnosis live on a mood roller coaster. When they're up, they may feel on top of the world, spend money they don't have and do reckless or even dangerous things. When they're down, they may feel so guilty and worthless that they want to die.

Bipolar disorders, or other forms of psychosis, are chronic illnesses, not character flaws. Your loved one's brain chemicals are out of balance. Medicine can help bring them back into balance. Taking the medicines as prescribed can help prevent mood swings. Without treatment they often get worse. It's also important to know what you can't do. For example, if your loved one is an adult, you can't force him or her to take prescribed medicine or go to appointments.

People with bipolar disorder or psychosis NOS are at higher than normal risk for suicide. Take all talk or threats of suicide seriously. Get help if your loved one talks or writes about death, gives away possessions, has a weapon or a plan for committing suicide. Call 911 or take your loved one to a hospital right away.

People with bipolar disorder may often say things they don't mean or do things that embarrass them later. Try to let go of hurtful actions and remarks. If they're harming your relationship, talk to a counselor. It can really help to talk to others who know what you're going through. Find a support group for families with bipolar disorder or for those who have been diagnosed with psychosis. You can call the Depression and Bipolar Support Alliance (DBSA) at 800-826-3632 to locate a support group in your area.